Fostering Academic Excellence

Other Pergamon Titles of Interest

ALBERT
Genius & Eminence: The Social Psychology of Creativity and Exceptional Achievement

MORRIS & BLATT
Special Education: Research and Trends

STEPHENS, BLACKHURST & MAGLIOCA
Teaching Mainstreamed Students 2nd Edition

WANG, REYNOLDS & WALLBERG
The Handbook of Special Education: Research and Practice 3 Volumes

Fostering Academic Excellence

JOHN McLEOD
University of Saskatchewan, Canada

and

ARTHUR CROPLEY
University of Hamburg, Federal Republic of Germany

PERGAMON PRESS

OXFORD · NEW YORK · BEIJING · FRANKFURT
SÃO PAULO · SYDNEY · TOKYO · TORONTO

U.K.	Pergamon Press plc, Headington Hill Hall, Oxford OX3 0BW, England
U.S.A.	Pergamon Press Inc., Maxwell House, Fairview Park, Elmsford, New York 10523, U.S.A.
PEOPLE'S REPUBLIC OF CHINA	Pergamon Press, Room 4037, Qianmen Hotel, Beijing, People's Republic of China
FEDERAL REPUBLIC OF GERMANY	Pergamon Press GmbH, Hammerweg 6, D-6242 Kronberg, Federal Republic of Germany
BRAZIL	Pergamon Editora Ltda, Rua Eça de Queiros, 346, CEP 04011, Paraiso, São Paulo, Brazil
AUSTRALIA	Pergamon Press Australia Pty Ltd., P.O. Box 544, Potts Point, N.S.W. 2011, Australia
JAPAN	Pergamon Press, 5th Floor, Matsuoka Central Building, 1-7-1 Nishishinjuku, Shinjuku-ku, Tokyo 160, Japan
CANADA	Pergamon Press Canada Ltd., Suite No 271, 253 College Street, Toronto, Ontario, Canada M5T 1R5

First edition 1989

Library of Congress Cataloging-in-Publication Data
McLeod, John.
Fostering academic excellence / John McLeod and Arthur Cropley
p. cm.
1. Gifted children—Education. 2. Academic achievement.
3. Creative thinking (Education) I. Cropley, A. J. II. Title.
LC 3993.M38 1988
371.95-dc19   88-19582

British Library Cataloguing in Publication Data

McLeod, John
Fostering academic excellence.
1. Gifted children. Education
I. Title II. Cropley, A. J. (Arthur John) *1935–*
371.95

ISBN 0-08-036460-8 (Hardcover)
ISBN 0-08-036459-4 (Flexicover)

Printed in Great Britain by A. Wheaton & Co. Ltd., Exeter

Contents

Foreword

Education has often been referred to as an investment in a nation's future. If this is accepted then it is reasonable to expect that investment in the proper education of exceptionally able children will pay high dividends. At the same time, recent history, at any rate in the Western democracies, has been marked by increasing respect for, and emphasis on, the rights of the individual. In education this has involved stressing the need for all children to receive an education which takes account of their special characteristics as learners. Finally, it is increasingly being recognized that many clever children, especially those from homes where there is little interest in intellectual or artistic pursuits, suffer from their giftedness. In other words, they are treated less humanely than could be the case. From the perspective of both individual and society, therefore, it can be argued that children with exceptionally high ability should receive an education which takes account of their special needs.

The question then arises of how this is to be done. The practice, when the educational policymaker has been confronted by children with special educational needs, has usually been the superficially obvious: first identify the students — whether they be blind, deaf, mentally handicapped, learning disabled, physically handicapped, unusually clever or whatever — then segregate them (or more euphemistically, "congregate" them or place them in a "self-contained" classroom or school) and provide them with an appropriate education. This approach might be thought of as "the three I's:" identify, isolate and improve.

Such an approach is logical and beyond reproach — if we are dealing with inanimate matter which has no meaningful interaction with its environment. For instance, if landscape gardeners want granite chips whose diameters are less than (or greater than) say, 1 cm, then all they have to do is pass them through a 1 cm wire mesh. This will sieve and separate the chips into those greater than and those less than 1 cm, with a fair degree of accuracy. The chips may then be despatched to the use for which they are most appropriate. But the education of children with special educational needs poses some basic additional questions,

questions which are often begged. These questions apply to educational provision for *any* child with special educational needs, although they take on a special form when applied to children whose special needs arise from their exceptionally *high* ability. Other practical questions, as will be seen later, are unique to such gifted youngsters.

The questions which take on special importance when applied to the exceptionally able are:

1. What dimensions of exceptionality are to be recognized as socially acceptable and important? Do all the exceptionalities recognized in the *Guinness Book of Records* warrant the allocation of special educational resources from the public purse? The Prime Minister of Australia, Mr Bob Hawke, is clearly an exceptionally gifted person: not only did he lead his political party to defeat the incumbent party decisively in 1983, but in his younger days he was a Rhodes Scholar at Oxford, where he established a record for drinking a "yard of ale" in the shortest time. Which, if any, of the talents that he demonstrated ought to attract special nurturing: leadership, academics, sport or drinking ability?

2. Assuming that we have agreed that we know what we are looking for, i.e., what sort(s) of giftedness we should be nurturing, can we identify them? Are the characteristics for which we are looking tangible, so that they can be measured?

3. If they can, how well do our measurements pick out truly unusually able people? That is, how reliable and valid are our identification procedures?

4. Assuming that we *have* identified a group of clever children with special educational needs, do we accelerate the children, i.e., encourage them to proceed through the regular curriculum at a faster rate? If so, what happens when they reach the end of the elementary school grades? Or what happens to them in secondary school when they get to the end of the syllabus in a particular subject, or in a group of subjects, perhaps two years before they have completed the rest of the curriculum? Alternatively, do we provide "enrichment"? That is, do we allow students to proceed through the curriculum at a standard rate, enriching their experience by treating subjects in greater depth as they go along?

5. Having made the necessary strategic decisions, how do we go about implementing them? How does one enrich the mathematics program of, say, Grade 7 students who have the ability, curiosity and zest to tackle differential calculus, if their teacher has barely survived or has not even taken Grade 12 mathematics? How does one enrich the experiences of a bright, budding political humanist if the student's home and/or teacher's cultural horizons are

limited to what the local newspaper and television have to offer?

The "obvious" solution might seem to be the best solution. That is, segregate exceptional students by placing them in homogeneous groups with their peers, whether this be through special schools for the hearing impaired, mentally handicapped, etc., or in the case of the able and talented, the selective schools for the more able, which have been traditional in Europe: the German *gymnasium*, the French *lycee* or the English grammar school. In these schools not only are the most able students congregated within a single school, but teachers who are qualified to teach able students are selected, and thus employed more efficiently than would otherwise be the case. Viewed in isolation this solution has much to commend it. However, any solution has to be seen in a total educational and community perspective. If, as has been said "only the top five percent matter," while only intellectual criteria are regarded as important, then all well and good. But if we are concerned about all pupils and all aspects of the school experience (personal and social, as well as intellectual), then one is bound to ask: "What, if any, is the psychological effect of isolating the most talented, both on themselves and on the rest of the school population?" If the results are positive, the argument for segregation of the gifted is reinforced. If they are negative, then advantages have to be weighed against disadvantages.

The present book contains a general introduction to the study of the education of academically more able students. Although it is obvious that there are other forms of exceptional ability and talent, such as are to be seen in, for instance, sports or the arts, we intend to concentrate here on unusual ability in the intellectual domain. This does not mean that we regard artistic or sporting talents as in some way second rate, but reflects merely the necessity of limiting and focusing our work in order to reduce a vast domain to handleable dimensions. The book is not designed to offer pat answers or a "paint-by-numbers" blueprint of "what to do," whether at the regional planning level or at the level of the individual classroom. Rather, it tries to provide guidelines on the basis of which those who are especially interested in fostering academic excellence can look at the factors involved and consider their significance for both identification of, and classroom provision for, the academically able.

Thus, although the book will provide a solid background of basic knowledge and a survey of research and theory which have characterized work with gifted children (e.g., definition, the nature of intelligence and creativity, and the relation between them), it will also address itself to practical issues and paradoxes. For example:

1. The desirable, administratively tidy, identification of a fixed corpus

of "gifted" students, set against the unreliability and invalidity of identification instruments and procedures.

2. The use of identification procedures which will produce the minimum number of future dropouts from programs for the exceptionally able, set against fairness or social justice.

3. The problem that provision of special educational programming for those students who are objectively identified as the best results in the selection of a preponderance of upper-middle-class whites (as well as other special groups such as Jews and south-east Asians), set against the conviction that the "true" incidence of unusual intellectual ability is constant for both sexes and across all ethnic groups.

4. The attractiveness of the prospect of developing and encouraging not only talented but also original creative thinkers, set against the extremely dubious validity of methods of assessing creative thinking ability.

5. The currently perceived social advantages of mainstreaming children with special educational needs (including the able), set against the logistical problem of availability of teachers with the necessary competencies.

6. The probable advantages to able students of being educated with their intellectual peers, set against the probable disadvantage to other children of missing out on the stimulating effect of contact with these students.

To raise such issues is not to assert that there are insuperable problems. But it does imply that providing high quality programs for children who have special educational needs, because of their superior abilities, calls for some creative thinking and originality itself. Such thinking is more likely to be achieved by people who are well briefed, and this book has been written with the intention of going some way towards providing that briefing. In particular, we hope to provide practising teachers, as well as students preparing to become teachers, with a background of theory, insights into the practical problems and guidelines for classroom practice which will help them to become facilitators of academic excellence, without losing sight of their responsibilities to all students.

1

The Case for Fostering Academic Excellence

The concept of "academic excellence"

Although discussions in this and later chapters use the conventional expression "giftedness" and associated terms such as "the gifted", these are not as clearcut in meaning as might be imagined (see in particular Chapter 2). Our interest in the present book lies in the area of successful performance of intellectual tasks requiring high levels of academic knowledge and skills. In school settings we are interested above all in rapid learning, effective storing of learned material, effortless location of stored information, skilful application of the already known, thirst for new knowledge, quick appreciation of the nature and significance of new ideas, flexible adaptation of the already learned in the light of the new and so on. Such properties manifest themselves in unusually effective participation in class discussions, high grades, outstanding scores on standardized tests, etc. Thus, in this book we will restrict the definition of giftedness to this cluster of properties, and will refer to them as defining "academic excellence." In real life, this quality manifests itself in intellectual activity and curiosity, inventiveness and productivity, and in outstanding achievement in science, engineering and mathematics, humanities, arts and letters, and the like. In general, we will mainly refer from this point on to "excellence," "outstanding ability," "the academically able," etc. Because of the predominance of the term "giftedness," this expression will continue to be used from time to time, however, generally because it is so widespread in the relevant literature.

Attitudes to special provision

On the basis of attitudes towards special educational provision for gifted and talented children, society can be divided into four groups:

1. Those who care and passionately believe that gifted children should

1

receive special educational treatment, their existence and identifiability being taken for granted.

2. Those who react with horror at the prospect of additional resources being lavished on children who, by definition, are already overendowed.

3. Those who believe that society has a responsibility to assist all individual children to realize their own unique potentials.

4. Those who are totally indifferent or who are unaware that there is an issue to be decided.

Too often, apologists for the "gifted movement" spend a great deal of time justifying the provision of help over and above what the regular class teacher can reasonably be expected to provide, in the apparent belief that most members of society fall into the second category and have to be convinced of their error. Of course, there *are* people who flatly and overtly deny the wisdom or need of special provision for the gifted. To take an extreme example of group 2 we need only to mention the keynote address of the Hamburg Minister for Education at the Sixth World Conference on Gifted and Talented Children in Hamburg in 1985, in which he drew attention to the interest of the Nazis in promoting gifts and talents. (The Minister failed to mention, however, that the Nazi government abolished special measures for promoting academic excellence in schools in a decree of 1935.)

However, it is highly likely, at least in North American/Western European societies, that the vast majority of people are to be found in the fourth category: indeed, it is even possible that some gifted programs flourish, in part at least, because of public unawareness and indifference, since this protects them from intensive, informed scrutiny. In the more articulate academically charged environment of university, college, school administrative offices and staff rooms, where people are regularly exposed to and/or involved in advocacy for the gifted, it is difficult to accept that for many people the education of gifted students is not a burning issue. That is not to say that it is unimportant. Indeed, it is arguable that if special education for the more able is intrinsically good, then there is an extra obligation on the part of politicians and educational administrators to do what is right and proper and to implement measures whose importance might not be apparent to the general mass of the population.

At the same time it must be conceded that many of those who are to be found in the first category listed above, the advocates of special programming for the gifted, are not there out of pure philosophical persuasion, but at least in part from emotional involvement. Either as parents with high aspirations for their children or as teachers who have had experience of students who were clearly far out in front of the pack, they *know* that there is a special breed of student who needs and demands different educational treatment. Furthermore, it is personally gratifying, especially for parents of clever youngsters, to be an advocate of the gifted.

This means, among other things, that it is simplistic, or even intellectually dishonest, to bracket special educational provision for the gifted and talented with other forms of special provision, for instance with special provision for intellectually and physically disabled children. As Martinson (1975) put it with lucid understatement:

> This population (of gifted) is unlike the handicapped in the fact that very few parents resist the notion that their offspring have high abilities. (p. 4)

Not only do parents seldom resist the notion that their children are gifted, if anything, the opposite is the case: some people tend to "go overboard" for giftedness. Having a child in the gifted program can even be a sign of social superiority, with the result that intense pressure is exerted on school authorities by some parents both to adopt programs for the gifted and also to admit their children to such programs. A related danger is that of "forcing:" children who seem to be clever offer a pathway to prestige for school and parents, with the result that they are prematurely labeled as "gifted" and pushed ahead with scant attention to their needs or wishes. The danger is, on the one hand, that clever children will become the victims of adults' striving and be labeled, isolated and forced (for the ego gratification of others) or, on the other, that those who do not measure up to expectations will learn to label themselves as failures, because they could not fulfil exaggerated expectations.

To those in the third category, among whose number the present authors count themselves, the question of special provision for more able students has to be looked at in a wider context. The goal of any educational jurisdiction was well expressed in Clause 8 of the English Education Act of 1944 which stated that:

> the schools available for an area shall not be deemed to be sufficient unless they are sufficient in number, character, and equipment to afford for all pupils opportunities for education offering such variety of instruction and training as may be desirable in view of their different ages, abilities and aptitudes. (Clause 8 (1) (b), p. 5)

The Constitution of the Federal Republic of Germany (Article 2, Paragraph 1) lays down the society's obligation to try to make it possible for all people to develop their personalities in accordance with their own patterns of abilities, interests, etc. Nathan (1979, p. 259), writing in a North American context, emphasized the importance of equality of educational opportunity commensurate with *all* children's skills and abilities, and this is enshrined in legislation such as Public Law 91-230.

If one accepts that it is the duty of society, through the public school system, to provide educational opportunity for all children appropriate to their individual abilities and aptitudes, and if one further accepts that some children are exceptional (i.e., they differ from the average to such a degree that the regular class teacher cannot meet their needs without extra assistance), then the issue is settled. If a child is so mentally handicapped, learning disabled, hearing impaired, physically handicapped – or of such high ability – that extra help is required over and above what it is reasonable to expect from the regular teacher, then there is an obligation to provide it. For children to receive specialized educational treatment in such circumstances is not for them to get more than their fair share; they are simply receiving what, in their individual circumstances, is appropriate. Of course, the interpretation of what it is "reasonable to expect" from the regular teacher will have implications for the question of how many students (not only the gifted) should be designated as exceptional and for the form their "special" education should take, but these are matters to be addressed later.

For the present we wish to echo Cruickshank's (1986) conclusion that special support for the academically able is a necessary element in any society which accepts its responsibility to provide educational experiences consistent with the abilities, motives and interests of all children. It is necessary to recognize that there is a difference between the urgency of a society's obligation to make a special effort in the case of the physically or mentally handicapped, the poor, social outcasts and the like, and the impulse to foster the psychological development of unusually able youngsters. Nonetheless, both evolve from the same humanistic principle, stated for instance by Pindar (518–442 BC) that everyone should be helped as far as possible to "be what they are" (see Bongartz, Kaißer and Kluge, 1985). Despite the possibility of vanity, a grasping desire to push children ahead, overweening ambition and the like — factors which may well play a role in many people's interest in the promotion of gifts and talents — it is vital to recognize that the call for special provision for the unusually able derives its legitimacy from this humanistic impulse. Such provision should be designed and carried out in this spirit. It is nothing more nor less than recognition by a society of its obligation to do the best it can to meet the special needs of all children.

Why special provision has not made headway

Despite the existence of various groups with a strong interest in promoting the cause of gifted children, albeit for differing reasons, Gifted Education (special provision for the gifted) has made only modest headway, and is even vehemently opposed by some theorists and practitioners, both inside and outside professional education. As will be seen from following sections, this opposition stems largely from misconceptions and prejudices. Among the more frequently encountered arguments are the following.

"The gifted can take care of themselves"

Being intellectually more able is, as has already been pointed out, generally regarded as a good thing. It is thought likely to lead to success by itself, and thus to confer on the gifted person a clear advantage in life. As Rader (1976, p. 36) put it, "Cream always rises to the top." It is thus argued, by some people, that special support for the gifted involves providing help where none is needed, which is at the very least unfair. Even worse, such provision for the gifted tends to siphon off resources which could be put to better use with more deserving groups, whom nature has placed at a disadvantage. Some particularly virulent opponents of Gifted Education see it as involving a deliberate intention to favor the "haves" at the expense of the "have nots," even arguing that this is a reflection of the political/economic forces they believe are at work in contemporary capitalist societies.

Superficially, the view that more able children (and adults) are more likely to be able to take care of themselves is an eminently reasonable one: it seems almost tautological to assert that the more able are more able to cope. Certainly, children of high ability will learn some things in spite of, rather than because of, being taught. For example, many children "pick up" the ability to read before they begin school, often in the absence of any formal teaching. However, these children usually come from highly literate homes where education is valued, and have usually had ready access to books. In other words, encouragement through environmental attitudes and suitable materials has presented them with an opportunity to use their abilities. However, even with these children, progress toward the limit of their capacity is impossible unless the *opportunity* to learn is available. Mozart might have had an extraordinary aptitude for music, but this could hardly have been realized unless his parents possessed a piano. It is at best inefficient to rely on nature or chance to develop talents, while for potentially gifted children in homes with limited cultural horizons it borders on neglect.

Recent research in the area has also shown that although the zest for learning is strong enough in some gifted children to survive and grow unsupported, in others giftedness produces insecurity and anxiety, which makes it a handicap rather than a blessing (Urban, 1983). The not infrequent occurrence of underachievement in pupils of high ability was documented in several countries in a number of studies two or three decades ago (e.g., Armstrong, 1967; Gowan, 1955; Green, 1962), while more recent studies have confirmed that they sometimes suffer psychological disturbances including poor concentration, exaggerated conformity, excessively inhibited behavior, anxiety, social isolation and aggressiveness, or its opposite, extreme passivity (e.g., Prat, 1979; Schmidt, 1977; Whitmore, 1980; Zillmann, 1981). Thus, the evidence does not support the view that the gifted are invariably able to take care of their own needs unassisted. Special problem groups are constituted by the extraordinarily highly gifted (for instance with IQs of 180 and higher) and the underachieving gifted (Horowitz and O'Brien, 1986).

Giftedness is not a popular cause

By definition, gifted children constitute a minority group. Yet they do not evoke the feelings of pity or compassion which have been important and influential factors in promoting the special educational claims of the socially, physically and mentally handicapped. The history of special education has been characterized by a pattern of development where an interested group (e.g., parents) has pioneered special educational provision on a self-help basis. Modest beginnings have grown into comprehensive provision through voluntary organizations, whose activities have ultimately been taken over by the state, prompted partly by effective lobbying and partly by a sense of charity. Because of an unspoken feeling that the gifted are well equipped to help themselves, there can be no question of compassion on the part of society, while advocacy by articulate, often upper-middle-class, prosperous parents, who have in any case probably felt inhibited in pushing the claims of their children, has not always made for the most effective lobby. As Sisk (cited in Nathan, 1979, p. 260) put it:

> One of the problems in stimulating support for education of the gifted is the inherent feeling of parents that it is not quite appropriate to demand programs for their children. If those same parents had children with defects, they would be willing to seek every bit of professional and educational help for their children.

If teachers or educational administrators are not confident about the justification for programs for the gifted, it is natural to assign a higher priority to other projects, where there is more likelihood of success, especially if the alternatives are more popular and less potentially contentious. It is also probable that some educators have become apprehensive of some of the impedimenta which have become part of the established gifted scenario: the emphasis on "divergent productive thinking" with implicit, if not explicit, disdain for "convergent thinking;" on "creativity," with corresponding disdain for "intelligence;" on "right brain" learning, with associated disdain for "left brain" learning (which is what teachers are said to foist upon their students). To take one example, it is salutary to compare the simplistic statements of some educators (see Clark, below) on right and left brain learning with the cautious expressions of neurologists (e.g., Bryden, 1982). For example, Clark (1979, p. 358) stated that

> Schools have concentrated their forces on the cognitive, left brain type of learning while devaluing and, in some cases, actually suppressing any use of the more holistic right brain function.

By contrast, Bryden (1982, p. 107) concluded that

> There is little reason to believe that each hemisphere acts in a unitary fashion and that one can ultimately discern that a particular hemisphere is analytic, linguistic, or integrative, or what have you.

Egalitarianism

The *Oxford English Dictionary* defines an egalitarian as "one who asserts the equality of mankind;" this is the noble sentiment that was enshrined in the United States Declaration of Independence, which held that "all men are created equal." Conant (1946) succinctly described the dilemma for educational policy in a democracy, where there are

> two partially contradictory commands; first, that of discovering and giving opportunity to the gifted student and, second, that of raising the level of the average student. (p. 27)

He maintained that

> writers on education have not uncommonly erred with the fault (of seeing one goal and not the other), setting either a standard of culture which coolly neglects the great mass or indulging in a flat and colourless egalitarianism. (p. 35)

Conant distinguished between two forces, the one valuing opportunity as the "nurse of excellence", the other as the "guard of equality" (p. 34), referring to the former as the "Jeffersonian," the latter as the "Jacksonian." What Conant refers to as "Jeffersonianism" relates to equality of opportunity; "Jacksonianism" relates to equality of provision. Proponents of special programming for the gifted, indeed proponents of special programming for all children with special educational needs, would clearly emphasize equality of opportunity rather than equality of provision. There is nothing incompatible between (Jeffersonian) democracy and special educational provision for gifted students, as long as we remember that there has to be *equality of opportunity for all*, and not a built-in bias which restricts that opportunity to a section of the population.

Not only has egalitarianism come to mean *un*equal opportunity, or even availability of special privileges only for those deemed to be more deserving, for instance because they have been unfairly treated in the past either by nature or by society, but it has also come to have a strong flavor of homogeneity. Many egalitarians seem to yearn for a world in which all are identical: as a result, they see special educational treatment as something which should be employed only to eliminate differences between special outgroups and the great, homogeneous mass constituted by the average or everyday.

Fears of elitism

If "egalitarianism" is an emotionally loaded term which proponents of special provision for the gifted sometimes level at those who argue against special provision, "elitism" is the counter charge which is hurled back. Although there are undoubtedly parents who fit Sisk's description referred to earlier (i.e., who are reluctant to exert pressure on behalf of their talented children) there are also parents for whom it is intensely gratifying to have their child labelled "gifted." Weiler (1978), a teacher and mother of two gifted children, claims that elitism is generated by some programs, and suggests that parents are no better equipped than their children to handle the consequences of giftedness. Sisk herself drew attention to the elitist nature of some advocacy groups, observing (1978, p. 267) that

> By and large, active parents (in organizations supporting special programs for the gifted) tend to be affluent, well-educated, articulate and white . . . Such an organization is an easy target for accusations of elitism and classism. And there is some justification in the charge, since little attention is given to the problems of gifted students coming from less fortunate backgrounds.

Luria (1963), a specialist from the Soviet Union, went so far as to argue that the selection of more able students for an advanced form of education is a capitalist ploy to keep the proletariat in its place. This approach would be more convincing if children's educational progress in Eastern socialist countries were not so fiercely competitive: As Gittings (1978) observed

> children [in a "Peking middle school for bright secondary-age kids"] are certainly climbing a steep pathway to receive the best education in China at a school which they have entered by competitive exams and where progress is measured solely by marks.

He further mused that "it was quite uncanny to discover the 11-plus exam and the grammar school system alive and well in the capital of socialist China."

The 1985 Sixth World Conference on Gifted and Talented Children attracted participants from Bulgaria, Czechoslovakia, East Germany, Hungary, Poland and the People's Republic of China, while the Seventh World Conference in Salt Lake City in 1987 was also attended by delegates from the Soviet Union — scarcely countries noted for the capitalist leanings of their governments. Hilgendorf (1984) presented an overview of the system of gifted education in the German Democratic Republic, as did Klein (1986). According to Kolmogorov, Valilov and Tropin (1985), every republic of the Soviet Union has at least one special school for the gifted and talented. The People's Republic of China has an extensive system of special subject schools (see Heinze, 1982, for a detailed discussion): these cover the regular curriculum, but extend it by offering intensive training in the special subject in question (e.g., mathematics, modern languages, natural sciences, music, etc.), and are thus similar in many respects to "magnet" schools in the USA. Special provision for the gifted can hardly be seen as a capitalist ploy.

Nonetheless, great care should be taken to ensure that methods of identification (see Chapter 6) of more able students do not lead to blatant elitism. This would be a violation of the principle that *all* children need to be offered the best possible opportunities.

Underrepresentation of certain groups

When giftedness is identified by standardized tests according to conventional criteria (see following chapters), and it is assumed that there is some more or less fixed proportion of the population that can be described as gifted, a number of disquieting consequences follow. These were already apparent more than 30 years ago: Miles (1954) drew attention to the fact that children with high IQs come overwhelmingly from high socioeconomic status sectors of societal majority groups. The incidence of *identified* giftedness, usually in the form of a high IQ, in upper-middle-class schools reaches 12 percent or so, the average IQ of children in such schools often being as high as 115. On the other hand, the number of youngsters identified in some rural schools, or in inner-city schools serving socially deprived children, may well be under one percent, the average IQ in such schools being as low as perhaps 90. Humphreys (1985) discusses such IQ differences between schools in detail. Janos and Robinson (1985) go into the home background factors which contribute to their emergence. The result of this state of affairs is that if the same criterion of giftedness is applied in both schools — for instance an IQ of 130 or more — possibly one student in eight from the middle-class school qualifies for special educational help, whereas only a single student, or not even one, from the other school is regarded as gifted. This occurs because the cut-off point in the middle-class school is only 15 IQ points above the school's average, whereas in the other school it is 40 points above average.

Such differences between schools take on a special social significance when the second school serves a predominantly minority group population, or draws its pupils from a socioeconomically deprived area. The fact of the matter is that, as Chapter 7 shows, certain societal groups are vastly underrepresented in special programs for the gifted and talented. (Of course, other groups are overrepresented, but this causes little dismay, since the prime motive is not to prevent children from participating in special procedures, but to facilitate such participation!) Baldwin (1985) discusses the implications of this state of affairs with special regard to minority groups. Other ''problem'' groups include the poor, the physically handicapped, even girls (see Horowitz and O'Brien, 1986 for a summary). The basic problem in this domain lies not in the fact that children from such groups are never gifted and talented, but in the equating of gifts and talents with school successes, on the one hand, and in the choice of indicators of the presence of gifts and talents, on the other. What is needed are new perspectives on the nature of gifted behavior, and development of appropriate identification procedures (Baldwin, 1985; Gallagher, 1986a).

Teachers are inadequately equipped

Experts whose opinions were solicited by Martinson (1972) were very definitely of the opinion that teachers are generally inadequately prepared for the teaching of gifted students. Indeed, teachers may be forgiven for perceiving themselves as inadequately qualified to teach gifted students. Many books on the education of gifted students are replete with thumbnail biographies of such giants as Einstein, Mozart, Michelangelo, John Stuart Mill, Picasso, etc., any of whom would be sufficient to make the most competent Grade 4 teacher feel inadequate. Descriptions of such geniuses tend to convey the impression that ''gifted children'' are some species of hyperintelligent, all-knowing computers, whom most teachers would never see. It is as well, therefore, to remind ourselves that there are likely to be one or two gifted students in a typical class of 30. In other words, despite the traditional absence of preparation for teaching the gifted, teachers are actually likely to have frequent contact with them, even if unknowingly.

The importance of teachers in the emergence of gifts and talents has been documented by Bloom (1985). In a retrospective study of people who had succeeded in achieving public acclaim as gifted, he showed how a single key person, who provided the initial impetus at just the right time, was frequently decisive in their development. Furthermore, this person was frequently someone in a "humble" role; for instance an otherwise unsung elementary school teacher who provided recognition and encouragement at a crucial point in a particular person's psychological development, awakening interest, encouraging ambition and crystallizing an emerging self-concept, quite possibly without being particularly aware of the decisiveness of his or her contribution.

This raises the question of what kind of teacher is most helpful to the emergence of gifts and talents. Martinson's respondents perceived the successful teacher of the gifted as one who is interested in learning and possesses a rich academic background, although specialized preparation and frequent contact with other teachers of the gifted were seen as more important than advanced degrees. Martinson cites research which has indicated that teachers with the "highest ability and accompanying performance" tend to accept and understand the gifted best, while those with lower ability are the most likely to feel threatened by and hostile toward the gifted. Cropley and McLeod (1986) discuss in detail the personal properties, knowledge and special skills of the ideal teacher of the gifted, and look at different models of teacher education.

Martinson's research also showed the importance of teacher training. Teachers with no special background tended to be disinterested or even hostile toward the gifted, whereas those who had worked in special programs (probably from a positive predisposition) tended to be enthusiastic. Inservice preparation produced more favorable attitudes towards both gifted children and special programs. It seems that, in this context at any rate, familiarity breeds respect and confidence. Inservice or other appropriate exposure to issues in the domain of giftedness would not only help convince teachers that gifted students are, in the main, enthusiastic, pleasant, fast learning children with a zest for knowledge. It might also enhance their own self-concept and perceived self-competence to a point where they would feel sufficiently confident to become actively engaged in promoting gifts and talents.

Why gifted students ought to have special programs

Gifted children are a resource

Some writers base their argument for special education for the gifted primarily on the needs of society. Marx, for instance, observed that gifts and talents are a gift of nature, and should be cherished and fostered accordingly. Havighurst (1958), a pioneer in the modern era, recommended that the most promising 20 percent of children should be given special encouragement because of their promise of outstanding performance. More recently, Newland (1976) estimated that 5 percent of the population must be prepared "for work at a high conceptualization level" in order for technologically complex society, as we understand it, to continue to function. An important factor which emphasizes the role of gifted people as a resource is the rapid process of change, and especially of technological change, which has gripped our world in recent years. The systems which shape even day-to-day life are becoming so complex that the presence of highly able thinkers, capable of dealing comfortably both with modern technology and also with breathtakingly complex interactions between natural and manmade systems is rapidly becoming a prerequisite for the maintenance of a way of life which is fit for human beings. Some aspects of this confrontation of human beings with technology are discussed further in Chapter 10. The consequences of high technology require more than a purely technological response. If society is not only to survive but to continue to enjoy a high quality of life, vast resources of giftedness need to be mobilized in the arts, in social sciences, in philosophy, etc.

In the social domain, the issue of leadership is one which is receiving increased emphasis in recent discussions. As Broomand (1986) pointed out, leaders emerge from among those with appropriate gifts whenever the social and political climate is ripe, with or without special efforts on the part of educators. However, the contribution of leaders to human affairs is often destructive. What is needed is special provision for the leaders of the future, aimed at encouraging them to accept responsibility (Landau, 1986, showed that many potential leaders among children in Israel regarded responsibility as a heavy burden which they would rather leave to other people), and to exercise authority and power in ways designed to promote the well-being of the society, not for purposes of self-glorification. The gifted are also seen as capable of making an enormous contribution to the continued vitality of minority groups, to the modernizing of less highly developed societies, to achieving world peace, and so on (see Cropley, 1988, for a summary of such discussions).

The gifted deserve special treatment corresponding to that received by the handicapped

The argument that if extra money can be found for programs for the educationally handicapped then it ought to be found for programs for the gifted is often linked, at least implicitly, with the contention that an investment in the education of the gifted is likely to yield at least as high a return as investment in the handicapped (see previous section). If this argument is made in a "me too!" spirit, then it is unworthy and probably an unprofitable red herring, because it is only too easy for advocates for the handicapped and for the gifted to become locked in controversy as to whether the amount saved by helping to prevent a mentally retarded person from being institutionalized for the rest of her/

his life is greater than the amount which will be injected into the economy by having a gifted person exercising her/his talents to the full. Such arguments can cause energy from both sets of advocates to be dissipated on each other, when they ought to be more productively working together on influencing educational policy decision makers! This fundamental similarity of interest between the handicapped and the gifted was noted very early in relevant thinking by Hollingworth (1926). She referred to both mentally retarded and unusually able children as "deviates:" the only difference according to her, is that clever youngsters are "fortunate" deviates, whereas the mentally retarded are "unfortunate." The unhappy tendency for interest in helping social outgroups to result in a backlash against provision for the gifted was vividly described by Passow (1977). Put simply, however, the position seems clear to us: it reduces to a corollary of the earlier proposition stated by Nathan (1979): "all children, *including the gifted*, must be provided with an education appropriate to their abilities" (our italics).

Gifted children need adequate stimulation

It is important at this point to distinguish between stimulation for its own sake and stimulation as a result of contact with intellectual peers. The latter raises a number of interesting issues. There is reasonably convincing evidence that association in school with other students of high ability raises an individual's level of performance. About 30 years ago Vernon (1957), in a study involving 865 secondary-school boys in England, showed that the mean IQ of those (top 25 percent) who had attended selective schools (grammar schools) was higher than would have been predicted from their IQs at the time of the entry exam (the 11 plus), while the mean IQ of those who had been allocated to the less demanding secondary-modern schools was lower than that predicted from their 11 plus results. More recently, an analysis of data for British schools (Jorm, 1983) showed that the overall intellectual level within a group had an effect on the development of the level of individuals within the group — contact with clever people tended to raise the level of ability of the less clever. In one of the few well designed studies on the relative merits of segregation versus integration of mentally handicapped students, Goldstein, Moss and Jordan (1965) found that, down to an IQ of about 65, mentally retarded students taught with normal peers achieved better than those who were taught in self-contained classes. In a less experimentally rigorous, but comprehensive, study on mixed ability teaching carried out in the UK by national inspectors (Her Majesty's Inspectors, or HMIs), by contrast, it was concluded (HMI, 1977) that students of *high* ability were penalized academically by being taught with students of lesser ability (the other side of the finding about less capable pupils just cited).

It seems, therefore, that if the top five percent or so are creamed off and provided with a particularly stimulating self-contained environment, their achievement will be better than it would have been if they had been left with the rest of their age peers. Nonetheless it is important to remember that the rest of the children achieve less well than they would have done if they had not been denied association with those in the top flight. If we are concerned with the education of *all* children, and not solely with the gifted, this is a consideration that has to be weighed when deciding policy. Some writers conclude that the detrimental effects on average and below average youngsters of being denied contact with unusually clever agemates is a decisive argument against special provision for the gifted and talented. However, this argument assumes that such provision automatically involves segregation, and that this must occur for all or most of the time; in fact, many models exist in which this does not occur — see Chapters 11 and 12. Indeed, we go further in this book, and argue for the development of practices and materials that can be applied in the everyday classroom with *all* children (see Chapters 8 and 9). In general, it is our contention that much of what is good for able children is good for all. Cruickshank (1986) has also made an important point in this regard. Refusing to make special provision for the unusually able, on the grounds that they are necessary for the optimal development of the other children, means that adults shrug off the task of promoting the development of less gifted youngsters onto the shoulders of clever children. Naturally, educators should be looking at the needs of the less gifted, but not at the expense of the gifted and talented.

Special provision for the gifted will prevent dropouts, underachievement and delinquency

It is logical to reason that if gifted children are held back in a lockstep curriculum, becoming bored with having to spend a good deal of time practising exercises on things that they already understand, some of them will be "turned off" by school, achieve at a level far below that of which they are capable, and drop out of school. Indeed, there are grounds for believing that many school dropouts are actually gifted. At worst, "turned off" gifted students may become involved with drugs or other forms of delinquency. Although there is evidence supporting this line of reasoning, other evidence makes the situation ambiguous. In absolute terms, the number of gifted delinquents cannot be very high: After all, if gifted students are defined as the top two percent, or even the top five percent, then this is the maximum number of children who can be gifted *and* delinquent while, as Horowitz and O'Brien (1986) pointed out, the vast majority of gifted children are far from delinquent. Nonetheless, as studies over the past quarter century in North America, Great Britain and the Federal Republic of Germany (Hauck, 1972; 1962; Pringle, 1970; Simmons, 1962; Whitmore, 1980; Zillmann, 1981) show, some do fail or even become delinquent.

As has already been mentioned, many students of high ability work below capacity. Some able students receive a shock when they move on to university. The leisurely study habits which had ensured reasonable grades in the mixed ability classes in secondary schools prove to be inadequate for the more intellectually demanding environment of the university. Of course, most gifted students survive the transition, but some suffer greatly in their first university year, and there are too many students of high ability who wastefully drop out. This was documented by Willings (1985), who reported on a number of case studies.

Caution must be exercised when reading studies of "underachievement" which are based on a definition of underachievement as a discrepancy between measured intelligence and achievement level since, when underachievement is defined in this way, it is a mathematical inevitability that the highest incidence of "underachievement" will occur among students with the highest IQs, and that the incidence will *always* steadily decline as we go down the IQ range. Nonetheless, it is very probable that many gifted children "learn to be average" or deliberately hold themselves back in order to have a quiet life in school: this is the phenomenon of "faking bad" (see also Chapter 7). Such students may have been embarrassed or suffered some ridicule in the past when they questioned some of the things that the teacher said, or displayed unwelcome originality, with the result that they have decided that it is better to be average than reveal their true ability.

Difficulties in school on the part of unusually able youngsters are by no means a purely North American phenomenon. Cropley (1982a) described the case of a Swedish boy with an IQ of 170 who longed to be allowed to start school, only to turn to complaints of stomach ache and the like in order to get out of going, or even to outright refusal, after only a few weeks. One of the preliminary findings of a recently established counselling center for the gifted and talented in Hamburg (see Feger and Prado, 1986), the first of its kind in the Federal Republic of Germany, is that many clever children who come to the center are terribly disappointed by their experiences in elementary school. The frequent passive or even active rejection by teachers of their desire to learn more sometimes leads to lack of concentration, to withdrawal, even to aggressiveness. These, in turn, inhibit the learning process, so that the children enter a "spiral of disappointment." At the time of puberty some begin to display marked underachievement and lack of motivation. Interacting with the typical problems of relating to adult authority which are seen at this age level, these achievement problems contribute to the emergence of deep mistrust of authority or serious states of self-doubt and insecurity. These cannot be eliminated in one or two counselling sessions, but require a more profound psychological treatment.

The possibility that understimulation can have deleterious effects which are difficult to eliminate is not confined to the emotional domain. Models of cognitive development also emphasize the importance of contact with a challenging external world for intellectual growth. As Piaget pointed out, the individual matches new experiences with existing internal structures (he calls this "assimilation"). Where there is a discrepancy between the existing internal model of what is "out there," and the internal representation of the world, the internal structures are altered to take account of the new experience (Piaget calls this "accommodation"). Where there is no mismatch, no accommodation occurs. In other words, the development of an ever more differentiated, detailed, organized internal grasp of how the external world hangs together (what we might well call "intelligence") depends upon exposure to an environment containing novelty; otherwise no cognitive growth occurs. At the very least, failure to be exposed to a challenging environment slows down cognitive growth. However, there are probably "critical periods" during which certain developments must take place or they will never occur with maximum effectiveness. Furthermore, motivation, attitudes to learning, trust in oneself and the like, also require exposure to situations where learning is necessary. It thus becomes apparent that deliberately hindering the development of able children, or even passively hindering it through neglect, may have deleterious effects which are difficult to eliminate later.

The pendulum effect

Previous sections have reviewed arguments supporting the provision of special programming for gifted students, but have also drawn attention to some of the forces tending to retard or oppose the development of appropriate services. The interplay of advocacy and reaction has resulted in an ebb and flow, or pendulum effect, in interest and visible action. Tannenbaum (1979) traces this effect in a broader context, ranging over the 1950s to the late 1970s. In 1957, the USSR launched *Sputnik 1*, the first earth satellite. There was an immediate reaction in the United States, characterized by much self-criticism (especially criticism of the educational system) and a resolve to do something about it; President Kennedy vowed that the United States would be first on the moon, and the massive NASA (National

Aeronautics and Space Administration) program was launched. Congress passed the National *Defense* Education Act (our italics), no doubt spurred on by reports such as that which appeared in *Newsweek* on 29 October 1956, that the USSR could expect twice as many graduates in science, engineering and technology between 1957 and 1961 as the USA.

Thus, in the late 1950s and early 1960s the United States launched massive programs designed to foster excellence and talent. Flanagan et al. (1962) in the first of a series of reports of "Project TALENT," reported that "in 1957, the United States was jolted by the challenge of totalitarian technological advances," and that "above all, public opinion recognized the increasing national need for scientific methods in improving education, *creativity*, and *productivity*" (p. 5, our italics). Project TALENT, itself, whose advisory panel contained some of the most widely known and eminent social scientists in the United States, was described by Flanagan as "a large scale educational research project to determine the best methods for the identification, development and utilization of human talents" (p. 1).

As the 1960s progressed, emphasis shifted more and more towards a concern with the rights of the individual, especially the underprivileged individual. By 1969, the need for active advocacy on behalf of the gifted had diminished. After all, a law requiring support for children with special gifts (PL-91-230) had been passed. The forces pressing for action for the advancement of gifted education thus tended to run out of steam in the 1970s, being "counterposed," as Tannenbaum (1979) termed the process, by a concern for the less fortunate — this shift was marked in 1975 by the passage of Public Law 94-142, the "Education for All the Handicapped Act."

A somewhat more sophisticated, or at any rate original interpretation of national educational activity and priorities than a simple "pendulum" effect was offered some years ago by Lowndes (1938). Lowndes' thesis was that successful wars tend to be followed by educational legislation which is designed to benefit the lot of the masses, a sort of belated thank offering to the private soldier and the social class from which most of them come. An unsuccessful war on the other hand, says Lowndes, leads to educational reform aimed at improving the officer class, i.e., directed to postprimary education. Finally, Lowndes suggests that failure in an economic war (or, in modern euphemistic jargon, "faring badly in relation to one's trading partners") leads to strengthening of the nation's technical and technological education services. Lowndes provides examples from 19th and early 20th century history: for example, the great English Education Act of 1918 was designed to benefit the children of "Tommy Atkins" who had won "the war to end wars." (If Lowndes had been writing later, he could have cited the even more significant 1944 Education Act, passed during the Second World War.)

Lowndes accommodated several European educational developments of the 19th and early 20th century within his theory. Can it be applied to recent developments in the United States? Has it any validity for other countries, or are they destined to follow in the wake of the United States, with the result that their policies towards the gifted simply replicate those found there? Certainly, advocacy on behalf of gifted students in the UK has tended to develop along lines that are familiar to the North American, following upon the relative demise of the 11 plus and selective secondary schools since the late 1950s. In any event, the historical analyses just outlined suggest that interest in giftedness is cyclical: it may well be that a further period of interest is currently emerging.

Closing remarks

Educational change cannot be left to the whim of chance trends, even if these trends reflect the workings of profound social forces. It is not the job of educational theorists and practitioners to adopt every new movement when it becomes fashionable, perhaps to drop it again when the fashion changes. On the other hand, the emergence of a surge of interest for a particular topic is not in itself a bad thing — obviously pendulum effects are essential for the appearance of creativity in a system; otherwise, thinking would be perpetually dominated by prevailing opinions and points of focus. The important thing is to seize the opportunity for renewal offered by such effects.

Crucial for this constructive use of emerging trends are three steps: crystallization of the real issues; careful examination of knowledge and theory in the area, in order to winnow out the grain from the chaff; specification in concrete terms of practical recommendations based on the results of the first two steps. We have shown in this chapter that there are a number of red herrings in the literature (for instance the notion of overrewarding people already preprogrammed for success, or of competition between unusually able children and handicapped youngsters), but also that some of the motivation to support special educational measures for the gifted and talented may be self-serving, or even not in the best interests of the children themselves. What we hope to do in the balance of this book is to adopt a critical attitude to many issues in the area, sort out the main ideas which are well established, and finally make suggestions for appropriate changes in classroom practice. We will do this by looking at four questions:

1. How should giftedness be defined?

2. How can gifted children be identified?
3. Ought such children receive special educational treatment?
4. How can they best be educated?

Question 3 has already been decided affirmatively in the present chapter, because if it is answered with "No" the other questions become purely academic. They will be addressed in later chapters.

2

Defining Academic Excellence

In a recent review Krapp (1986) concluded that the term "giftedness" is used in a number of ways, some of which are internally contradictory. It is:

1. General but also specific (giftedness is regarded as a general intellectual dimension, but is also seen as manifesting itself in particular gifts);
2. A cause but also a result (particular achievements are seen as the result of giftedness, but are also themselves grounds for labeling someone gifted);
3. Both quantitative and qualitative (we speak of the *level* of giftedness, but also of the *kind* of gifts a person possesses).

It is thus apparent that there is a considerable degree of uncertainty about the term. This is especially true if a range of associated expressions (e.g., "genius," "prodigy," "precocious child," etc.) are left undefined. It is our intention in this chapter to specify the aspects of giftedness in which we are interested in this book — as the title indicates, we call this "academic excellence."

The Definition of Giftedness

Terms associated with the concept

The earliest modern research on people of exceptional ability was Galton's (1869) study of "genius." He took "eminence" as the criterion of excellence: eminent people were those who had risen to become a judge, a bishop or a general. This study, one of the very earliest systematic research projects in modern social sciences, thus employed a pragmatic definition of excellence, based on achievement in real life rather than on academic potential. Galton also believed that eminence is general and essentially quantitative (see the three dimensions listed above).

Later writers (e.g., Hollingworth, 1926) frequently used the terms "gifted" and "talented," although with a high degree of imprecision. As Hagen (1980) observed, the words arc nowadays used synonymously by many authors, while some restrict "gifted" to people with high academic abilities and use "talented" for those with superior abilities in art, music and drama (as did Hollingworth). Clark (1979, p. 7), for instance, defined giftedness as "the highly developed thinking function". A few authors use "gifted" to refer to those with outstanding general intellectual abilities, and "talented" for exceptionality in one specific area, e.g., mathematics. The Schools Council in the UK defined the term "gifted" as indicating "any child who is outstanding in either a general or specific ability, in a relatively broad or narrow field of endeavor (2-6%)." An Australian Task Force defined "talented" students as "an atypical group possessing exceptional abilities and capable of outstanding performance." Finally, a few writers use the term to differentiate between extreme and merely moderate outstandingness, reserving "gifted" for the top 0.1 percent and "talented" for the next 1.9 percent; alternatively, the top two percent are "gifted" and the next five percent "talented." Hollingworth (1926) also used "talent" quantitatively to refer to a level of ability somewhat below the very peak (which she called "genius"). A group of experts studied by Martinson (1972) identified the gifted as being in either the top five or the top two percent of the population; however, they considered that between 11 and 15 percent of children might be "talented." Hagen (1980) concluded that, since there is no universally accepted definition of giftedness, it is probably not useful to try to differentiate between "gifted" and "talented."

Three other terms which are encountered in the literature on giftednes, although less frequently than those introduced in the preceding paragraphs, are "genius," "prodigy" and "precocious." These terms are used less technically than "giftedness," "talent," "intelligence," etc., and so are less likely to generate contentiousness. "Genius" has reverted back to its traditional usage as a way of referring to a person with extraordinary powers or abilities, which are demonstrated by brilliant accomplishment, although Hollingworth (1926), for instance, orginally used it to designate an IQ greater than 180. "Prodigy", according to Feldman (1979), has come to refer to a child who is "precocious," and "precocious" has become inextricably linked with the concept of intelligence, "with the effect that precociousness of a certain sort was already measured by virtue of the measurement of IQ." The *Oxford English Dictionary* definition of "precocious" refers to premature development, so that it is understandable that, in the context of cognitive growth, a child who reaches a given "mental age" at a lower chronological age — i.e., who has a high IQ — would qualify to be considered precocious. A prodigy, on the other hand, is generally thought of as a person — usually a young person — who achieves remarkable skill in a comparatively specific field; for example, mathematics, chess or playing a musical instrument.

The nature of gifts and talents

Establishing agreement on the kinds of activity which define, as it were, the *contents* of giftedness and talentedness, has proved difficult. Two early NSSE *Yearbooks* (Whipple, 1924; Henry, 1958) struggled with the question of whether an IQ score alone (and thus certain kinds of abilities) defines giftedness, or other properties such as outstanding personality characteristics, leadership or aesthetic appreciation are also part of giftedness. A related problem is that of whether intellectual and aesthetic gifts alone define giftedness, or whether, as Witty (1951) argued, a multidimensional definion is needed. Vernon (1971) suggested that giftedness occurs in four areas, which he called "intellectual," "artistic," "social" and "other." Piechowski (1979) argued for recognition of gifts in the following areas: psychomotor, sensual, intellectual, imaginal and emotional. More recently, Bongartz, Kaiβer and Kluge (1985) stressed the importance in the modern world of social gifts such as compassion, empathy or altruism, while George and George (1986) and Broomand (1986) emphasized leadership as a crucial gift for social development and world peace.

Probably the most quoted "official" definition is that of the United States Office of Education (USOE). This definition is enshrined in a federal law (Public Law 91–230, Section 806):

> Gifted and talented children are those identified by professionally qualified persons who, by virtue of outstanding abilities, are capable of high performance. These are children who require differentiated educational programs and/or services beyond those normally provided by the regular school program in order to realize their contribution to self and society.

Children capable of high performance include those with demonstrated achievement and/or potential ability in any of the following areas, singly or in combination:

1. General intellectual ability;
2. Specific academic aptitude;
3. Creative or productive thinking;
4. Leadership ability;
5. Visual and performing arts;

6. Psychomotor ability.*

Section 806 goes on to observe that evidence of ability may be determined "by a multiplicity of ways" and to give examples of what "professionally qualified persons" means.

As a definition, that of PL 91-230 is a catchall, with all the hallmarks of having been drawn up by a committee which was subjected to lobbying from everyone from the Juilliard School of Music to the National Hockey League. Its *defining* component is confined to the first sentence (assuming that it is the children and not the professionally qualified persons who must be capable of high performance). The second sentence is a comment on educational programming and is not uniquely applicable to more able students, while the six areas listed are, at most, guidelines. Note that the wording used is that "children capable of high performance *include* those with . . . ability in the following areas . . .," not "children capable of high performance *are* those with . . . ability in the following areas . . ." Hallahan and Kauffman (1978, p. 493) point out that a multidimensional definition of giftedness as in PL 91-230 can include children who are not truly gifted, for example those who achieve an isolated "plus" in one category. The definition can also exclude some children who should perhaps be rated as gifted, for example those who just miss the criterion in a number of categories.

In the UK, the school inspectorate (HMI, 1977) also developed a definition of "the gifted child." As the inspectors were interested in investigating a practical problem — the situation of unusually able youngsters in British schools — they adopted a practical, working definition. Gifted children are those:

> who are generally recognized by their schools as being of superior all-round intellectual ability, confirmed where possible by a reliable individual intelligence test giving an IQ of 130 or more;
> or
> who exhibit a markedly superior developmental level of performance and achievement which has been reasonably consistent from earlier years;
> or
> of whom fairly confident predictions are being made as to continual rapid progress towards outstanding achievement, either in academic areas or in music, sport, dance or art; and
> whose abilities are not primarily attributable to purely physical development.
> (pp. 4–5)

As can be seen, this definition is also multifaceted in that it includes both intellectual and nonintellectual domains. The IQ is seen as

---

*This category was later dropped from the USOE definition.

merely a helpful piece of supporting information, not a defining characteristic, even in the case of academic ability. The definition also places great emphasis on actual "performance and achievement," thus skirting the issue of unrealized potential, while also at best implying that personal properties such as determination or trust in oneself are to be taken into account. No indication is given of the nature of intellectual ability in the academically gifted (for instance, is creativity important?), although the term "all-round" was probably meant to indicate that something more is needed than simple rote learning, good memory, etc. To be fair to the inspectors, they were not trying to offer a "scientific" definition, but to develop a line of approach which would help in the analysis of existing practices and the formulation of concrete suggestions for improvement. They also pointed out themselves that issues such as maladjustment in clever youngsters or the need for special schools would be neglected by their approach.

Despite the broader approaches which have just been outlined, we focus in the present book on *academic excellence* (see for instance p. 1). This means that, although there is no doubt in our minds of the importance and value of the other areas of giftedness which have just been discussed, we will deal only with excellent thinking and learning skills and outstanding intellectual performance. This should not be interpreted as indicating a lack of respect for other gifts, or a lack of concern about their development. Indeed we believe that much of the practical advice we offer would promote artistic, social or other gifts. However, the topic of academic excellence is in itself quite sufficient for a single book!

The psychological components of academic excellence

We turn our attention now to the psychological elements which combine to produce academic excellence. As will be seen, these are both intellectual and nonintellectual in nature: in other words, although academic excellence manifests itself in the form of essentially intellectual achievements, it is itself dependent upon a cluster of various psychological components.

High IQ

The dominant approach to defining academic excellence derives largely from Terman's work (e.g., Terman 1925, 1954). His crucial contribution to the emergence of a definition was the focus on intelligence, and its concretization in the form of an IQ score. In a longitudinal study he showed the practical significance of possession of a high IQ: educational success, high occupational status, good health, enduring marriage, etc. (see later sections for a more detailed discussion of the trailblazing Terman study). Hollingworth (1938) also defined academic excellence in terms of high IQ. Cox (1926) went further, and demonstrated the relevance of IQ to excellence by restrospectively estimating the IQs of famous historical figures such as Galton. She arrived at a mean score of 155!

However, a number of criticisms of IQ, even as an indicator of *intellectual* giftedness, have been heard in recent years (despite the fact that, as will be shown in Chapter 6, IQ scores continue to be the dominant criterion for selecting children for special programs for the gifted). Gardner (1983) propounded the theory of "multiple intelligences," arguing that there are seven distinct kinds of intelligence (for instance linguistic, musical and logical-mathematical intelligence), and that an IQ score is too undifferentiated to serve as an accurate indicator of giftedness. Weinert and Waldmann (1986) also warned against the reduction of intellectual giftedness to possession of a high IQ, since IQ scores tell little about the ability to think in complex systems, or about characteristics such as thoroughness or flexibility. A major recent North American critic of the conventional IQ as a satisfactory indicator of intelligence is Sternberg (1985). He pointed out that for effective intelligent behavior a combination of factors is necessary: information gathering ability, skill in socially valued activities and the capacity to organize and weigh the value of one's own problem solving tactics. (See Chapter 3 for a detailed discussion of such extensions of the IQ approach.)

Creativity

The academically excellent, in our sense, are not adequately differentiated from the less distinguished simply by higher IQs, a fact which has been known for a considerable time — Gibson and Light (1967), for instance, showed that many successful scientists at Cambridge University had IQs under 130, the traditional cutoff point for denoting outstanding ability. In a more recent study, Facaoaru (1985, p. 209) investigated the factors in a group of engineers which were associated with "the successful carrying out of a demanding practical activity." She showed that conventional IQ scores alone did not adequately distinguish between those with high performance levels and those whose performance was not above average; exceptional achievement depended upon a combination of conventional abilities (good memory, logical thinking, knowledge of facts, accuracy, etc.) and abilities of a different kind (generating ideas, recognizing alternative possibilities, seeing unexpected combinations, etc.). This latter ability to branch out from the known, see new possibilities, etc., is frequently referred to as "creativity:" oversimplified, this is the "ability to express novel and useful ideas" (Hallahan and Kauffman, 1978).

That high IQ scores are by no means invariably associated with high creativity (however this latter trait is defined) is well known (see for instance Gruber, 1982). This fact became obvious very early in modern creativity research, classical studies such as that of Getzels and Jackson (1962) even concentrating on children who were high in the one area and low in the other. Cropley (1969) conceptualized conventional thinking of the kind predominating in intelligence tests and the newly emphasized trait of "creativity" as "styles" for applying mental power in dealing with practical problems, not as separate kinds of ability at all. Relating this kind of conceptualization to the area of giftedness, Wallace (1985) spoke of a general dimension of "extraordinariness" (p. 362); giftedness in the sense of precocious ability or talent is one aspect of being extraordinary, creativity in the sense of capacity for originality, novelty, etc., another. Precocious children may or may not develop into creative adults. Horowitz and O'Brien (1986) saw creativity as an aspect of giftedness which comes into play only in certain circumstances among highly talented individuals and leads, when it does, to exceptional performance. Gardner (1983) strengthened this view: for him, creativity is the highest form of *application* of intellect, not an ability in the conventional sense at all.

The important point for the present discussion is that the psychological prerequisites for excellence as outlined on p. 1 (rapid learning, effective storing of learned material, effortless relocation of stored information, etc.) include not only the kinds of skills referred to as encompassing "intelligence," but also those involving "creativity" (see Chapters 4 and 5 for a definition of what is meant by this term). In particular, creativity is seen by many authors as necessary for outstanding *performance*.

Noncognitive factors

Analyses of the sort found in the previous section are important, but remain, by and large, within the cognitive tradition — excellence is seen as a combination of knowledge and skills associated with knowledge getting, problem solving, and the like. Facaoaru related this issue directly to academic excellence by pointing out that, apart from a combination of intelligence and creativity, her most successful engineers also differed from the less successful on a number of noncognitive characteristics. These included motivation, task commitment, stamina, self-confidence, etc. These are discussed in more detail later in this chapter (pp. 36–37) in terms of motivation and self-image. Janos and Robinson (1985, p. 166) summarized results of studies indicating a relationship between giftedness and many noncognitive factors: "energy," "enthusiasm," "vigor," "vitality," "willpower," "perseverance," "persistence," "striving," "sacrificing for goals," "ambition," "competitiveness," "high aspirations," "curiosity," "exploration" and "risk taking!" As Klein (1986) put it, although he was writing about "giftedness," academic excellence is *an expression of the total personality of an individual* (our italics), and derives not merely from intellect, but also from a psychological constellation of interests, motives, diligence, self-confidence and similar personal properties.

Perhaps the most "radical" rejection of a purely abilities oriented approach to defining giftedness is that of Gruber (1982) in his proposal of the "evolving systems" model of giftedness. According to this approach, human beings are characterized by the way in which they organize three psychological systems: knowledge, affect and purpose. As people develop, the nature and effectiveness of these organizations "evolve," not only within systems, but also between them. Unusually able individuals are those in whom an unusual level of within and between system organization has developed: knowledge is available, well organized capable of being called upon, flexibly filed and indexed, etc. Purposes are clearly defined and acceptable to the individual, and motives, emotions, feelings and the like brought into balance. This permits "intelligent" and "creative" behavior, and is the prerequisite for the motivational and emotional states listed in the previous paragraph. The evolution of systems towards this state is the process of developing giftedness.

The "three ring" model

Renzulli (1977) proposed a "three-ring" definition of exceptional ability, which goes some way towards integrating the ideas just outlined, by stating them in practical terms capable of immediate application to the task of fostering excellence. He concluded that gifted children should be defined as those who have demonstrated:

1. High ability (including high intelligence).
2. High creativity (i.e., the ability to formulate novel ideas and apply them to the solution of problems).
3. High task commitment (i.e., a high level of motivation, the willingness to see a project through to its conclusion, etc.).

This model is frequently presented in diagram form as in Figure 2.1.

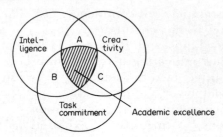

FIG. 2.1. The "three ring" model of excellence (slightly adapted by the present authors)

Hallahan and Kauffman (1978, p. 440) quantified this definition by requiring that, in order to be considered gifted, a child should be better than 85 percent of peers on all three of these criteria and better than 98 percent of them on at least one. In practice, the number of children actually identified by this definition will depend on the interrelationships between measured ability, creativity and task commitment. Hallahan and Kauffman estimate that at least two percent, but certainly less than five percent, of school-aged children could be considered gifted. In fact, fewer children are identified than had been predicted by Hallahan and Kauffman. Nonetheless, the three ring model approach represents a step in the right direction, since it offers a tangible, potentially practicable, multidimensional definition, which can serve as a jumping-off point for defining academic excellence.

Excellence as personal characteristics

There are many reports on the characteristics of gifted children (see Martinson, 1972; Laycock, 1979, etc.): these can be summed up in Renzulli's (1980) comment of "American Pie," i.e., on almost all desirable intellectual, cognitive, personality or physical traits such children tend to be superior to the average. The closer the relationship between the trait and the criterion of giftedness, the greater will be the superiority; the looser the relationship, the less will be the superiority. Thus, a group of children identified as academically superior will be far above average in reading and study skills; physically, their height and weight may be significantly greater than average if the sample is large enough, but any measured difference in stature is of only marginal practical significance. One thing is certain: the stereotype of the academically able child as a puny, undersized, eccentric oddity, or the proverb of "early ripe, early rot" has no basis in fact. Horowitz and O'Brien (1986) concluded that the stereotype of the typical able child as maladjusted is also false. Newland's (1976, p. 85) observation that "correlation, not compensation, is the law of nature" is much nearer the truth.

When working with individual children who have been identified as gifted, however, one should be cautious before assuming all-round brilliance. As Hagen (1980, p.2) has pointed out, "rarely does one find a person who is an exceptionally high achiever in all areas of human endeavor". One of the present authors recalls testing Colin, a six-year-old boy from a remote town in northern Canada, who was reading at the level of an average 15-year-old, and whose Verbal IQ on the WISC-R was above the test's ceiling. His parents, perhaps out of understandable desperation, had vainly sought to absorb some of his excess and voracious zest for learning by buying him a 2000-piece jigsaw of an abstract design. Strikingly, however, the boy's Performance IQ on the WISC-R was only 108 — deviating markedly from his remarkable verbal ability. Thus Colin illustrates the validity of Hagen's observation that one should not assume all-round brilliance.

In this context, it is appropriate to remember that perceptual skills and tasks which depend on rote learning and practice rather than insight or reason need not necessarily be highly developed in unusually able children. It is inadvisable to assume that all exceptionally clever children will automatically "pick up" without specific teaching such skills as spelling, handwriting and basic numeracy. Although these tasks should cause neither difficulty nor boredom to such a child if presented properly, it should no more be taken for granted that very able children will learn to spell or compute by some incidental process than that quality grass seed will, without any attention, automatically produce a lush lawn.

The general position with regard to the unusually able has been well summed up by Hoyle and Wilks (1974, p. 15), despite the fact that they were writing about giftedness. They concluded succinctly when they wrote:

> There is no such thing as a typical gifted child . . . Gifted children . . . fall . . . into an infinite variety of patterns. One can find individual examples of almost every personality defect, social maladjustment, behaviour problem and physical handicap: the only difference is that among gifted children, the incidence of these deviations is . . . lower than the general population.

The Terman studies

The most comprehensive study of the characteristics of highly able children was that of Lewis Terman: to a considerable degree, this study laid the foundation for modern understanding of giftedness, and drew attention to a number of problems and special issues in the area. For this reason, various aspects of his work will be presented in some detail here.

BIAS IN IDENTIFICATION PROCEDURES

The first report (Terman, 1925) described selection of the sample, and drew attention to a number of problems which have continued to be important. Goleman (1980) pointed out that "Latin American, Italian and Portugese groups were underrepresented, and there were only two black children, two Armenians, and one American Indian child, [while] Jewish children were overrepresented." Further, "there was also a social class bias. Close to one out of three children were from professional families, although professionals made up only 3 percent of the general population. Only a smattering were children of unskilled laborers, compared with 15 percent in the general population" (p. 31). The group identified by Terman contained "a significant but not overwhelming preponderance of boys" (116:100 ratio of boys to girls at the elementary level, 160:100 at the high school level). Vernon (1979) also criticized Terman's sampling procedure because emotionally maladjusted and underachieving students were probably overlooked. It is instructive to examine present-day methods of identifying children for gifted programs (e.g., Yarborough and Johnson, 1983), and to compare the current pattern of ethnic and social class representation with that of Terman's group. One suspects that things have changed little (see Baldwin, 1985; Mistry and Rogoff, 1985).

ERRORS OF IDENTIFICATION

Initially, Terman's teachers were asked to nominate the children in their classes whom they considered to be the brightest; the name of the youngest child in each class was also recorded. Terman later reported that "one of the most astonishing facts brought out of this investigation is that one's best chance of identifying the brightest child in a schoolroom is to examine the birth records and select the youngest rather than to take the one rated as brightest by the teacher" (Terman, 1925, cited in Jenkins and Paterson, 1961. p. 231). Nominated children from elementary schools were then screened by the use of group intelligence tests, and final selection was based on an individually administered Stanford–Binet test. Selection of high school gifted students was made on the basis of performance on the Terman Group Test, a derivative of the Stanford–Binet. Terman's own evaluation of the methods of "sifting" which he employed was that "possibly 10 or 15 percent of the total number who could have qualified according to the criterion (a Stanford–Binet IQ of 140 or higher) were missed" (Burks, Jensen and Terman, 1930).

PSYCHOLOGICAL WELL-BEING IN UNUSUALLY ABLE YOUNGSTERS

Terman's subjects had greater than usual interest in science, history, biography, travel and informational fiction, but less in adventure or mystery fiction. They were not characterized by "all work and no play," the "play information quotient" of the gifted group being 136. The group was, as a whole, also superior on tests of honesty, trustworthiness and similar moral traits. Many of the members had been accelerated in school, i.e., had skipped grades, and this practice was not found to have been harmful (Terman, 1954).

The majority of the gifted children had shown early evidence of superiority, the most commonly reported indications being intellectual curiosity, possession of a wealth of miscellaneous information and a desire to learn to read. In school, their favorite subjects were those which unselected children found to be the most difficult, and in the quantity and quality of their reading they far surpassed the unselected children. However, the more highly gifted (IQ 170 +) had experienced more problems of adjustment than had the more typically gifted. The divorce and death rates of the gifted group were below normal, while the marriage rate was normal (Terman and Oden, 1947). Health statistics were superior; five percent of the group admitted to having had mental health problems, but recovery rate was good. Politically, the group tended to be liberal-progressive.

SUCCESS IN LIFE

As would be expected, the gifted group attained higher than average occupational status. Nearly half were graduates and scarcely seven percent became blue collar workers (Terman and Oden, 1959). An interesting feature of the 1959 report was the comparison which was made between the 150 members of the gifted group who had been adjudged to have been most successful (the A group) with the 150 judged to have been least successful (the C group). Parental encouragement had been significantly higher for the A group; 96.5 percent of them having received parental encouragement to attend college, compared with 62.3 percent of the C group; 15.1 percent of the A group's parents had "demanded high marks," three times the number of C group parents. The number of C group gifted who had reported that they were making satisfactory adjustment had steadily declined over the years. In 1922, 82 percent had replied positively to this question, but by 1960 the percentage had declined to 46 (compared with 81 for the A group). Whereas only 16 percent of the A group who had been married were divorced by 1960, 41.5 percent of the C group had suffered broken marriages.

Which children need special provision?

Children of extraordinarily high ability (IQ > 180) seem to constitute a special group with special problems (Horowitz and O'Brien, 1986). Our interest in the present book lies not in such one-in-a-million children, but in the much larger group of those who are not adequately drawn out, challenged and spurred on by the conventional learning and teaching opportunities offered in the everyday classroom. One cause of this is that teachers must of necessity (and quite rightly, we would add) attune the content, methods and level of their instruction to the norm established by the majority of students in the classroom. This means that it is impossible to lay down a fixed cutoff point, defined by a score of some kind, for identifying the children in question. The decision on whether or not a child should receive special treatment is based on the practical situation of a particular individual whose needs are not being met in the classroom. This does not mean, however, that this need may not be identified at least partly with the help of tests or similar procedures, but rather that actual decisions should be based on the particular situation, not on some predetermined norm.

There is, therefore, much to be said for taking an individual child's school as the reference unit, rather than a complete, heterogeneous, school district. The school is certainly a preferable basis to the nationwide standardization samples on which the WISC-R or Revised Stanford–Binet were normed. To define students as unusually able relative to their immediate school peers is compatible with the notion of unusually able youngsters as ''exceptional;'' they require special educational help over and above what it is reasonable to expect from the unaided regular teacher. In a school where the average level of ability is low, it is arguable that students with average ability have just as great a need for assistance to realize their potentials as does a student of high ability in a school where most children are quite clever. By basing the definition of unusually able on within school criteria, the problem of underrepresentation of socially deprived and minority group children will be considerably eased — without having to resort to practices which appear to involve ''social engineering'' (Birch, 1984). Individual school referenced programming and identification procedures are also more likely to foster local innovations and flexibility in identification and programming practices (Renzulli, 1984).

Excellence as exceptional performance

Achievement vs potential

Some writers such as Geuβ and Urban (1982) have concluded that prodigious achievement is the only true criterion of exceptional ability. This view can be contrasted with that of, for instance, Lucito (1964), that gifted individuals are those who have the *potential* for exceptional achievement. When we think of academic excellence, it is extremely useful, or even necessary, to think of it as a potential. Otherwise, all those children who have not yet displayed unusual accomplishments would be deemed to be lacking in noteworthy ability, even those whose environment had made it difficult or virtually impossible for them to have done so (see later sections, especially Chapter 7). It is nonetheless true that academic excellence is of limited interest to the classroom teacher if it exists only as a potential, since the concern of practical educators is fostering what Renzulli (1984, p. 104) called "gifted behaviors." The decisive question which thus arises is that of how potential for academic excellence can be brought to fruition.

Outstanding achievers in real life

Although our emphasis in this book is not on the relatively small group of people who have achieved fame in life, it is useful to consider some of their characteristics, since these have obvious relevance for the study of children in school (our real focus of interest). Examination of biographical data on eminent figures of history — Albert Einstein, Isaac Newton, John Stuart Mill, Ludwig van Beethoven, Winston Churchill, Karl Marx, Peter Ustinov, Eve Curie, Paul Robeson, Mohammed Ali. Gordie Howe, etc. — suggests that there are probably several ingredients necessary for recognized eminence:

1. Ability (not necessarily *intellectual* ability);
2. Opportunity;
3. Motivation and other personal properties (such as flexibility or toughness).

However, what causes people such as those listed above to be hailed as exceptional is a fourth element — *achievement*. As Feldman (1979, p. 340) pointed out, what he calls "early prodigious achievement" results from a combination of these factors. Early prodigious achievement should be seen as "the occurrence in time and space of a remarkably preorganized human being, born during perhaps the optimal period and educated in the precise manner most likely to enable the individual to interact optimally with [a special environment]'' (p. 342).

ABILITY

The question of what *kinds* of ability constitute academic excellence is of great importance, as earlier sections of this chapter have shown. For the present discussion, however, the key question is whether ability, however it is understood, depends upon a special environment, or whether it is intrinsic and more or less preprogrammed to manifest itself. The extent to which abilities are intrinsic or are determined by the environment is one of psychology's oldest controversial issues. In the present discussion, ''intrinsic'' implies that an infant's genes place limits on intellectual potential which no environment, no matter how stimulating, can exceed. It also implies that gifts and talents will manifest themselves as long as they are not actively blocked. Such a view has been disputed at least since Helvetius' aphorism that ''l'éducation peut tout'' and in behavioral psychology since Watson's (1930) claim that, by conditioning, he could ''take any [healthy infant] at random and train him to beome any type of specialist . . . — doctor, lawyer, artist, merchant-chief and, yes, even beggar-man and thief, regardless of his talents, tendencies, abilities, vocation, and race of his ancestors'' (pp. 83–88). Optimists, who believe that mental development is truly plastic (Ferguson, 1979), and that ''we can only imagine what some of the possibilities for optimal growth might be'' include Binet (in Kirk and Kirk, 1975, p. 41), Clark (1979), Doman (1964) and Engelmann and Engelmann (1966). Those ''pessimists'' who are not so sanguine about the limitless possibilities of environmental stimulation include Vernon (1979), Eysenck (1973, 1986) and Jensen (1981), as well as such influential figures from the past as Terman, Gesell and Goddard, in the USA, and Burt in the UK.

OPPORTUNITY

''Opportunity'' is a concept that may be interpreted in different ways. Most commonly, perhaps, it is thought of as akin to encouragement by parents and/or exposure to a stimulating, challenging educational program. Many of the eminent gifted people from the past were born into affluent and/or highly intellectually stimulating homes, while a battle cry for educational reformers throughout the growth of popular education during the last century had been ''Equal opportunity for all!'' But examination of the biographies of many persons whose demonstrated qualities have clearly marked them as gifted often reveals little evidence of their having been born with silver spoons in their mouths, for example in the case of political leaders in emergent nations. On the other hand, some gifted people have achieved in spite of, rather than because of, a positively encouraging environment. In demonstrating leadership qualities, they have often *reacted* to their situation rather than having been sympathetically nourished/nursed by it. In other examples of outstanding academic achievement, the zest for learning has been such that the person is virtually *driven* to study and achieve. In both the academic and the political environments, however, there has to be an *opportunity* to realize the potential that is there. The Polish trade unionist Lech Walesa could hardly have realized his outstanding leadership potential in the middle of Siberia, as would probably have been demonstrated if the USSR had still been ruled by Stalin, nor could the latent talents of a potentially outstanding mathematician become manifest without access to "a highly evolved and . . . communicable domain of knowledge" (Feldman, 1979).

In a recent survey, Gallagher (1986b) has emphasized the importance of what we call here "opportunity." A child who has the good fortune to come from a home where certain skills (abstract language skills, concentration, expressing one's view) are modeled, special "tools" (books, musical instruments, perhaps computers or scientific instruments) are available, where interest or actual achievement in culturally valued areas is greeted with enthusiasm and support, and where the image of oneself as capable of "making it" is fostered and supported, has the optimal opportunity to distinguish him- or herself. Where the home does not offer adequate opportunity, other institutions assume a major role. Naturally, the peer group and other elements of the social environment are capable of providing opportunities; indeed, there are examples in real life of people who eventually became eminent being spurred on by people outside the family (see Goertzel, Goertzel and Goertzel, 1978; Bloom, 1985). However, the major outside-the-family influence is the school. Experience indicates (see Baldwin, 1985, or Humphreys, 1985, for summaries from somewhat different viewpoints) that certain groups of children are systematically denied access to the kind of home background which is favorable to the development of abilities, motives, attitudes and values, self-image, and the like, which favor the emergence of academic excellence, or that the forms of excellence developed by some groups go unrecognized by the majority of society. The existence of such children is living evidence of the inadequacy of the efforts at development of academic excellence which society is presently making: the practical issues will be discussed in greater detail in Chapter 7.

MOTIVATION

Motivation to a degree which amounts to dedication is an identifying characteristic of the highly gifted. As Edison, a person eminently qualified to comment, once observed, "Genius is one percent inspiration, 99 percent perspiration." Roe (1952), in a widely quoted study of eminent scientists, reported such statements as: "My work is my life," or "There's nothing I'd rather do," while Feldman (1979, p. 351) in the context of a research study of early prodigious achievement more than a quarter century later, observed that:

> perhaps the most striking quality in the children in our study as well as other cases is the *passion* with which excellence is pursued. Commitment and tenacity and joy in achievement are perhaps the best signs that a coincidence has occurred among child, field, and moment in evolutionary time.

More recently, Stanley (1984, p. 178) employed a striking metaphor when he spoke of outstanding achievers' "academic hunger."

This drive, commitment or hunger goes beyond what is normally called "motivation." It is marked by fascination for a particular subject area or special kind of activity, accompanied by the conviction that mastery of this material or skill is possible, or even that it is almost inevitable; what Rathje and Dahme (1985) called "expectation of mastery." Such commitment and conviction cannot occur without trust in oneself, a positive self-image. The urge to pursue an activity beyond the usual limits requires not only endurance, but also the willingness to expose oneself to risks, for instance the risk of being thought mad or of becoming impoverished. "Motivation" is thus used here as a label for a range of personal and affective characteristics which have frequently been displayed by people who eventually became famous as exceptional achievers. Goertzel, Goertzel and Goertzel (1978) have presented a number of case studies of historical figures which demonstrate the importance of such characteristics.

Combinations of factors in realizing potential

Looking at academic excellence in terms of the four factors just outlined (ability, motivation, opportunity and achievement) raises the interesting question of what combinations of factors, other than the happy constellation of all four together, could occur, what consequences various combinations could have and what implications this would have for educational provision aimed at fostering academic excellence. The theoretically possible combinations are shown in Figure 2.2.

Possible combinations

	1	2	3	4	5	6	7	8	9	10	11	12	13	14	15	16
High ability	+	+	+	+	.	.	.	.	+	+	+	+	.	.	.	.
High motivation	+	.	.	+	.	+	.	+	.	.	+	+	+	+	.	.
Appropriate opportunity	+	.	+	.	.	.	+	+	.	+	+	.	+	.	+	.
Exceptional achievement	+	+	+	+	+	+	+	+	.	.	.	.	.	.	.	.

Academi- cally excellent children	Over achievers	Under achievers	Non-gifted youngsters

FIG. 2.2. Theoretically possible combinations of the four factors involved in academic excellence

Children in the group, designated "underachievers" in Figure 2.2 (high ability but low achievement) might well be regarded as *potentially* excellent students who have failed to manifest their ability in the form of achievement, because of lack of opportunity or motivation, or a combination of both; these children are particularly in need of special remedial help. On the other hand, some of the children in the group designated "academically excellent children" are also likely to benefit from special treatment since, despite their high achievement, many of them have only limited opportunity fully to realize their potentials (column 4), are not fully motivated (column 3), or have shortcomings in both areas (column 2). The group of "overachievers" contains the puzzling children who do better than ability or aptitude test scores suggest they will, while the final group consists of children who are not outstanding either in ability or achievement. It is instructive to ask which combinations actually occur, which are cause for concern, which should receive priority treatment, etc.

Closing remarks

The concept of "giftedness" has a variety of meanings, especially when closely related terms are taken into account. In the present book we are interested in those aspects of giftedness related to unusual ability in thinking, reasoning, learning and the like, and to associated outstanding achievements; in real life, high achievements in science, literature, engineering, philosophy and so on; at the school level, exceptional classroom achievement in traditional areas. We call this "academic excellence." At least as important as actual achievement, however, is the potential for it; we are concerned above all in this book, not with the driving on to even greater heights of already successful youngsters, but with ways of providing the cognitive, personal, emotional and social factors which are favorable to the realization of academic excellence, even in cases where it has not yet manifested itself. In particular, we are interested in the underlying ability which is a part of academic excellence and a prerequisite for exceptional achievement, the personal and motivational factors which are needed for the realization of such ability and are also part of academic excellence, and the environmental support (called in this chapter "opportunity") which encourages excellence to manifest itself. Ultimately (especially in later chapters) we will examine organizational, administrative and instructional procedures in schools which take adequate account of these factors.

3

Intelligence and Intelligence Tests

Academic ability is usually, although not exclusively, discussed in conjunction with intelligence. Indeed, Humphreys (1985) emphasized that the concept of intelligence is central to the whole idea of gifts and talents. Intelligence itself is usually linked in practical settings with IQ scores, which purport to indicate the level of a person's intellectual ability. Intelligence and IQ scores are thus key issues in the present context, since they are at the heart of discussions of academic excellence — the IQ score is still the single most important factor in identifying children for gifted programs. In a survey in the USA, Yarborough and Johnson (1983) found that IQ scores were used in about 80 percent of programs. This finding was confirmed by Passow (1985). A Canadian survey by McLeod and Kluckmann (1985), to which over 80 percent of all school boards replied, revealed a similar picture. This is also the case in a number of other countries: see, for instance, Braggett's (1985) study of identification in the various Australian states.

The importance of intelligence is now so widely accepted that it is difficult to appreciate that the use of the term to refer to a measurable continuous variable, which different people are thought to exhibit to different degrees, is of relatively recent origin. Burt (1975) pointed out that in his own school days neither teachers nor parents described children and their behavior as "intelligent," but that they were more likely to use the word "clever." The writings of authors who reached maturity before the beginning of the 20th century support the validity of Burt's contention. For example, Whitehead (1861-1947) in his classic, *The Aims of Education* (1946), observed that "uneducated *clever* women, who have seen much of the world, are in middle life so much the most cultured part of the community," while Winston Churchill claimed that, "having been in the lowest form (at Harrow School), I gained an immense advantage over the *cleverer* boys."

The structure of intelligence

During the last decade of the 19th century and the first decade of the 20th, significant events were taking place in educational provision and

39

in the psychology of "the higher mental processes." Following the introduction of universal compulsory education in many countries, it became clear that some children were slow learners, and special educational provision was beginning to be made for the "mentally defective." In psychology, the study of individual differences, enhanced by Galton's statistical methods, had expanded considerably during the late 19th century, and culminated at the beginning of the 20th century in the measurement of human intellectual ability. Intelligence came to be perceived, not as a unitary human faculty, but as a *dimension*, which could be assessed by *scales*, or "tests," as we generally call them. Since about the turn of the present century, various analyses in both Europe and North America have yielded models of the nature and organization of this dimension. Answers to questions about the diagnosis of intellectual ability, the identification of those who would benefit from special treatment, decisions about what should be fostered, how this should be done, and by means of what processes and activities, are all dependent upon what is understood by intelligence. For this reason, an understanding of this concept is a necessary first step in considering how to foster academic excellence.

The general intelligence approach

Events moved quickly during the first decade of the 20th century. In 1904 Spearman published a paper on *"General intelligence, objectively determined and measured,"* in which he showed that measures of different mental abilities correlated positively with each other, and that the correlations could be explained by positing the existence of a factor which was *general* to all the tests, and a further factor which was specific to each test. He called the general factor "g," and it came to be thought of as "intelligence." In addition to "g," Spearman assumed that there must be a large number of specific abilities ("s") which combine with general intelligence to produce a particular level of performance on a specific task. Each task presumably requires a certain amount of general ability plus its own "s." Two different tasks yield similar scores (correlate with each other) to the extent that both require general ability, dissimilar scores to the extent that they depend upon their own specific abilities: thus, tasks heavily dependent upon "g" would correlate highly with each other, those heavily dependent upon "s" would show low correlations.

In the course of the years, the general intelligence approach was developed and expanded considerably. Patterns of correlations among scores on abilities tests indicated that a simple general ability plus task specific abilities did not correspond with reality. Accordingly, Vernon (e.g., 1971) concluded that there must be "group factors" of an

TABLE 3.1. *The structure of intellect model*

Content →	*Operation* →	*Product*
Auditory	Cognition	Units
Visual	Memory	Classes
Symbolic	Convergent production	Relations
Semantic	Divergent production	Systems
Behavioral	Evaluation	Transformation
		Implications

intermediate degree of generality: these abilities do not enter into all intellectual tasks (as does "g"), but are common to a number of tasks, so that they are more complex than "s." Out of this approach arises the hierarchical intelligence model, which sees intellectual ability as a system of abilities arranged, schematically, in layers or levels characterized by extreme specificity at the bottom of the hierarchy, general ability at the pinnacle. Intermediate levels would be characterized by increasing generality, moving from the bottom of the hierarchy to the top.

Over the years, however, the nature of intelligence has been subjected to considerable analysis. A number of alternative approaches will be outlined here.

Primary Mental Abilities

Thurstone (1938) administered a battery of 56 psychological tests to college student volunteers, and isolated seven mathematically determined factors which enabled him to account for correlations among the test scores. In order to interpret these mathematical factors in a psychologically meaningful way, Thurstone examined the tests which were most prominent in the case of each factor. He concluded that the factors represented seven dimensions of intelligence which he called "Primary Mental Abilities" (PMA). These seven PMA are "Number," "Word Fluency," "Verbal Comprehension," "Associative Memory," "Induction," "Spatial Relations" and "Perceptual Speed." He and his wife, Thelma Gwinn Thurstone, subsequently developed special tests to measure each of the abilities in as "pure" a form as possible.

The Structure of Intellect (SI) model

Guilford (1977) defined intelligence as "a systematic collection of abilities or functions for processing different kinds of information in different ways" (p. 33). He analyzed the different kinds of information, the different processes and the different products which result, arriving at a "Structure of Intellect" model, usually abbreviated to "SI" by Guilford, and to "SOI" by others (see Table 3.1). This structure of intellect is based on the "three faces of intelligence" whereby 150 factors are postulated. The three faces are: *operations* (cognition, memory, convergent production, divergent production and evaluation); *content* (visual, auditory, symbolic, semantic, behavioral); and *products* (units, classes, relations, systems, transformations, implications).

As new elements have been revealed, the number of factors in Guilford's model has progressively expanded. For example, by the late 1970s, the *figural* content had been subdivided into *visual* and *auditory*, so tha the 120 factors of the then existing model increased to 150, which is still the number currently being reported (Guilford, 1977). Guilford's SI model is usually depicted as a cube, where the "three faces" represent Content, Operations and Products, respectively. To students whose preferred mode of thought is "successive" rather than "simultaneous," the SI model is illustrated in an alternative form in Table 3.1, which suggests a relationship with familiar models of communication and mediational stimulus response models of behavioral psychology.

An important distinction for present purposes is that between "divergent" and "convergent" operations. *Divergent production* involves "a broad search of the memory store, scanning it for alternative items of information all of which could possibly satisfy the same need," while *convergent production* requires "a focused search for a particular item of information that satisfies well-defined specifications." The admonition that there has to be a "search" of one's memory store is an important detail of Guilford's description of both convergent and divergent production, but one which is often overlooked by zealous educators anxious to foster children's spontaneous creativity.

Eysenck (1967, p. 82) commented on the SI model by pointing out that:

> There is a possibility of infinite subdivision inherent in the statistical method employed [by Guilford], and evidence is lacking that further and further subfactors add anything either to the experimental analysis of intellectual functioning or the practical aim of forecasting success and failure in intellectual pursuits.

Vernon (1964a) too was critical of the "enormous" number of independent factors — 60 at that time — which Guilford had claimed to have isolated, but whose existence had not been generally confirmed by psychometrists other than Guilford's own followers. Vernon (1964a) observed that:

> it is always possible to break down broader group factors into additional narrower ones, by developing more and more detailed tests; but this does not prove that the additional factors correspond to important mental faculties.

It thus seems that, although a single global measure of intelligence is inadequate as an educational diagnostic tool, one can commit an equally great error by going too far in attempting to fractionate human ability into too many narrow segments. Favero et al. (1975) described a study in which a committee of teachers, teacher aides and psychologists constructed 76 tests, each designed to measure one factor of the SI model, and found that the average correlation coefficient between categories *within* a single dimension (i.e., content, operations or products) did not differ appreciably from the average correlation *between* categories from different dimensions, thus rendering the validity of those dimensions somewhat suspect. The authors concluded from their data that there was "the suggestion of a factor of general intellectual function."

In a comprehensive critical evaluation of SI theory, Undheim and Horn (1977) concluded that the theory is lacking in several notable respects and that "at best the research intended to support the theory must be considered exploratory." However, they expressed the opinion that the SI model has provided a useful scheme for test construction and is also valuable for suggesting interesting hypotheses about qualities of intellect. The model, as illustrated in Table 3.1, can therefore provide a useful guide for the design of innovative activities, by exploring the possible combinations of content, operation and product. Guilford (1977) himself has recognized the affinity between cognitive styles of learning and features of the Structure of Intellect.

The process of intelligence

A major characteristic of the models outlined to date is that they are essentially descriptions of a theoretical *structure* of intelligence: the essential question is that of how intelligence is *organized*. The domination of investigations of the nature of intelligence by this approach has led to a tendency to neglect the question (of vital importance for the question of how to foster academic excellence) of the properties of intelligence as a *process*. By assuming that, let us say, a high score on a test requiring the solving of arithmetic problems defines an ability called "number skill" or something similar, or that reaching the desired answer for a verbal puzzle indicates the existence of a "verbal reasoning" ability, the tendency has been to neglect the question of what happens in a person's mind during the solving of the problem or puzzle. By concentrating on *processes of intelligence*, however, one might even conclude in some cases that certain solutions were actually highly intelligent even though they had not led to a "correct" answer.

One relatively early attempt to define intellectual ability in terms of processes rather than abilities inferred from correct test solutions was that of Meili (e.g., 1964, although Meili had already published papers on this topic in the 1930s). On the basis of Gestalt psychology he theorized that intelligence must have four main properties: "complexity," "plasticity," "totality" and "fluency." Complexity involves bringing the elements of a set of information into relationship with each other, plasticity refers to the changing of existing cognitive structures, totality is seen in the relating of new material to existing mental structures, while fluency consists in moving from one idea to another. Other theorists from German speaking countries (Meili worked in Switzerland) have identified processes such as concentrating or processing information (Jäger, 1967), making combinations and imagining (Amthauer, 1973) and recognizing laws (Horn, 1962). Jäger also gave considerable emphasis not only to cognitive processes but also to motivation and personality traits, such as determination or trust in oneself, in the emergence of intelligent behavior. It is also worth noting that most of these writers saw changing mental structures or using imagination as integral parts of intelligent thinking, whereas the pragmatic North American approach had come to be dominated by convergent thinking.

More recently, Weinert and Waldmann (1986) concluded that intelligence, as defined by scores on intelligence tests, neglects important characteristics of thinking such as thoroughness or flexibility, as well as crucial processes such as thinking in complex systems — test scores permit, at best, a rough estimate of such characteristics. Klix and van der Meer (1986) emphasized the importance in intelligent behavior of reduction of complexity. A high level of complexity in a situation leads to uncertainty and ensuing discomfort; highly intelligent individuals, however, are able to organize information in ways which reduce uncertainty, but do not lose sight of the essence of the problem. Intelligence involves reduction of complexity through processes such as selection, sorting and structuring of information; highly intelligent individuals are those who can do this quickly and efficiently.

In North America, Case (1978) developed a model of intelligence which largely derives from Piaget's developmental psychology. He discerned three levels of thinking strategies which he called "schemata." At the lowest level are "figural schemata," next come "operational schemata," and at the highest level are "executive schemata." Figural schemata are involved in the accurate internal representation of a situation, for instance a problem of some kind. Operational schemata make it possible to discern the more abstract, general aspects of each individual element of the situation, and the executive schemata consist of principles for the transforming of information or existing concepts. The level of intelligence is determined by the accuracy of the figural schemata, the breadth of the operational schemata and the flexibility, complexity and differentiation of the executive schemata. These characteristics develop as a result of interaction with a challenging environment. Rabinowitz and Glaser (1985) conceptualize intelligence as the capacity for effective problem solving. Their model is highly reminiscent of Bruner's developmental psychology: they emphasize the importance of encoding and decoding of information (building of associations, comparing of new information with existing cognitive structures, "calling up" of stored information, etc.). Their research has shown the existence of a number of differences in these areas between skilled problem solvers and beginners.

The approach which has made the greatest impression in recent years is that of Sternberg (1985). In going "beyond the IQ" to his "triarchic" model of intelligence he emphasized three elements of intelligent behavior: the internal, "mental mechanisms," through which behavior is regulated, the societal norms, which determine what behaviors are regarded as intelligent, and the degree of experience an individual has had with such societally approved activities. Of particular interest here are the internal mechanisms, and especially three components which Sternberg has discerned: the information reception component (selection of the crucial elements of a situation, relating these to existing knowledge, etc.), the action component (application of appropriate solution strategies), and the metacognitive component (the aspects of intelligence through which people reflect upon their own cognitions — selection of problems deemed to be worth pursuing, setting of criteria for deciding whether or not a solution is acceptable, judging the adequacy of solutions, sorting among alternative new strategies after an approach has been abandoned, etc.). An academically gifted individual is in the position to grasp the essence of a problem rapidly and accurately, to sort out relevant from irrelevant information effectively, to distinguish promising from valueless approaches, to become aware that a blind alley has been entered and see other possibilities, to recognize a solution when it has been reached, etc.

Although they have played only a minor part in the approaches to defining intelligence most widely known among practitioners, and have as yet had only minor influence on the measurement of intelligence, the kinds of approach which we have called "process" oriented are of great importance for the understanding of how to foster academic excellence. Specifying what happens, as it were, "inside the head" of a student during the course of the activities we call "thinking," "reasoning," etc., would make it possible to select special activities aimed specifically at fostering certain tactics, processes, skills and the like. Furthermore, clearer specification of the nature of intelligent thinking makes it possible to examine the developmental processes involved in its emergence — approaches such as those of Case or Rabinowitz and Glaser just outlined are particularly valuable, since they link up the study of intellectual giftedness with existing models in developmental psychology. This means that our understanding of the origins and growth of outstanding intellectual ability, and of the kinds of experiences which hinder or facilitate it, moves forward with a sudden leap. For these reasons, the kinds of approach sketched out in the last few paragraphs are of great importance in the study of academic excellence.

Intelligence tests

In France, Binet and Simon had been appointed in 1904 by the Minister of Public Instruction to study the problem of retardation among children in the public schools of Paris, and they published the first scale for measuring intelligence in 1905, introducing the concept of "Mental Age." Items are grouped according to the age at which about half of all children can solve them correctly — items defining a Mental Age of, for instance, six years, would all be solved correctly by about half of all six-year-olds, so to speak by the "average" six-year-old. To provide a stable index of a child's level of ability, which would permit comparisons between children of different chronological ages, Stern — of Breslau and later Hamburg — suggested calculating the "Intelligence Ratio" by dividing Mental Age by chronological age.

The Stanford–Binet tests

The Binet test, an individual test, was translated into English by Burt, in the UK, and by Terman, by Goddard and by Kuhlmann, in the USA. Terman converted the Intelligence Ratio into an "Intelligence Quotient" (IQ) by multiplying the ratio by 100. He believed that the IQ was fairly constant, and that it was thus possible to predict the IQ of an adult in childhood. The Terman version of the Binet scale has become the definitive test of intelligence, and is known as the "Stanford–Binet" scale. It was first published in 1916, and appeared in revised versions in 1937, 1960, 1968 and 1985. Its items are arranged in blocks of six, covering the age levels two years to 14 years, with additional tests for "average" and "superior" adult levels. As Terman and Merrill (1937) wrote, "it is not merely an intelligence test, it is a method of standardized interview which is highly interesting to the subject and calls forth his natural responses to an extraordinary variety of situations." The items are certainly diverse in nature: they define tests of vocabulary, comprehension, absurdities (both verbal and pictorial), memory for words and for digits presented auditorily, memory for visual patterns, similarities, differences, analogies, numerical problems, etc.

Verbal and nonverbal ability

It soon became clear that whatever it was that the new tests were measuring, it was not the whole story. The first reservations came as a result of the massive group testing of US Army recruits in 1918. For example, the original "Army Alpha" tests were essentially verbal in nature. When used with recruits who could not read, for example because of inadequate schooling or because they were recent non-English-speaking immigrants, the tests underestimated intelligence, and so had to be augmented by nonverbal tests — the "Army Beta" tests. Two major subcategories were thus implicitly recognized, and this was the beginning of further analysis of overall human ability. This analysis proceeded both clinically and mathematically. On the clinical front, it was found that although there was often fairly close agreement between a person's "verbal intelligence" and "nonverbal intelligence", in some cases there was a marked discrepancy. Deficiencies in particular abilities were noted in studies of brain injured veterans from both World Wars (Mairie and Foix, 1917; Luria, 1966), verbal deficiencies being more common in the case of those with damage to the left cerebral hemisphere. It thus became increasingly obvious that a global IQ was inadequate as a sensitive diagnostic tool, and so the concept of *general intelligence* was subjected to analytic examination in an effort to identify its constituent elements. Clinicians such as Wechsler relied on empirically validated tests, i.e., from among the proliferation of tests that were appearing they selected those which were found to work best, and grouped these into verbal and nonverbal batteries.

The Wechsler tests

In the early 1940s, Wechsler, then chief psychologist at the Bellevue Psychiatric Hospital in New York, produced the "Wechsler–Bellevue Scale for Adults and Adolescents." There were two forms of the test, and subsequently Form I was modified to create the Wechsler Adult Intelligence Scale (WAIS) and Form II was "extended downwards" to make up the Wechsler Intelligence Scale for Children (WISC). The WISC rivalled the Revised Stanford–Binet as the individual intelligence test to use with school-aged children, but provided norms down to only five years. Subsequently, the Wechsler Preschool and Primary Scale of Intelligence (WPPSI) was developed for younger children, and the WISC was revised for children aged six years and up, the new test being named the WISC-R.

The most immediately obvious difference between the WISC and the Binet scale is that the items in the WISC are presented as a series of subtests with homogeneous content, whereas in the Stanford–Binet scale they are grouped, not by content, but according to age. In other words, in the WISC all children are tested (at least initially) on the same material, whereas in the case of the Stanford–Binet scale children of different ages work on different material. In a normal administration of the WISC-R there are five "Verbal" subtests (Information, Similarities, Arithmetic, Vocabulary, Comprehension) and five "Performance" subtests (Picture Completion, Picture Arrangement, Block Design, Object Assembly, Coding). These yield a Verbal IQ, a Performance IQ and a Full Scale IQ.

The Wechsler scales also incorporated a number of technical improvements over the Revised Stanford–Binet scale. One (which was subsequently incorporated into later revisions of the Stanford–Binet scale) was the replacement of the Ratio IQ by a "Deviation IQ." A child of 10 who achieves a Ratio IQ of 120 has solved items regarded as typical for 10-year-olds, but has also answered at least a few items typical of 11-year-olds, 12-year-olds, and probably 13-year-olds, even 14-year-olds. However, a child with an IQ of 80 may not even attempt the 10-year-old level, with the result that the bright and dull children would work on completely separate items.

In the calculation of a Deviation IQ, by contrast, all children attempt the same set of tasks (although it is true that the more able go further than the less capable, as testing with this latter group in a particular area such as Arithmetic ceases after several items in a row have been failed). The IQ is calculated by expressing the degree to which a particular child's score deviates from the average score achieved by his or her age group. A Deviation IQ of 120 thus means that the child in question has done better on the same set of tasks than about 90 percent of children of the same age (the scores are scaled to achieve a normal distribution with a mean of 100 and a standard deviation of 15). Despite scoring better than 90 percent of agemates, such a child would not necessarily have solved any problems "typical" for older children. A child with an IQ of 80 would have solved fewer of the same set of items than the brighter youngster. The Ratio IQ is based on the assumption that increasing age means that more and more difficult items can be solved (although this is not true in all areas after the age of about 16), whereas the Deviation IQ simply assumes that people in a given age group will distribute themselves over a range of scores.

Practical issues in using intelligence tests

Reliability and validity

A test is reliable if it gives the same results for the same children on different occasions, the degree of reliability being indicated by an index ranging from 0.00 to 1.00. If one accepts Binet's modest claim that an intelligence test provides an index of the *present* level of mental functioning, then intelligence tests have an excellent record for reliability. The reliability of the WISC-R is reported to be 0.96 for Full Scale IQ (Wechsler, 1974), 0.94 for Verbal IQ and 0.90 for Performance IQ. The manual to the 1960 revision of the Stanford–Binet does not provide direct evidence of the test's reliability, but reports that items were included in the present revision if they correlated satisfactorily with total score on the 1937 test. The reliability of the 1937 Revised Stanford–Binet had been estimated, not only for the overall range of ability (median value 0.91), but for specified subranges of ability where the test would be likely to be used as an aid in making crucial decisions. For instance, the reliability for the 140–149 IQ range was found to be 0.95 for the 14–18 year age range, 0.91 for ages between 6 and 13, and 0.83 between $2\frac{1}{2}$ and $5\frac{1}{2}$ (Terman and Merrill, 1960). Test reliabilities generally tend to be lower for younger children than for older. Other individual intelligence tests have comparable reliability coefficients; Jensen (1981, p. 272) listed the reliabilities of 33 standardized tests of intelligence, and these ranged from 0.60 to 0.97, with a median reliability of over 0.90.

To expect high reliability, i.e., consistency, of IQ scores over longer periods of time, is to presuppose that the thing that the tests measure, (i.e., "intelligence") develops at a constant rate for each individual. There is abundant evidence (e.g., Bayley, 1949) that the longer the period between testings and the lower the age of children being studied, the lower is the test–retest reliability. Hunt (1961, pp. 21–22) provides a consolidated picture from a number of scores, which suggests that an immediate test–retest reliability for teenagers of 0.89 drops to 0.70 when the period between test and retest is five years, while for younger groups the stability drops even further.

A second important practical question is that of whether or not tests really do measure what they claim to — in the present case intelligence. This is the issue of *validity*. The most obvious and convenient way to assess the validity of a new intelligence test would be to find out how well its scores correlate with those derived from the Stanford–Binet or WISC-R, which involves, of course, assuming that the Stanford–Binet or WISC-R really do measure intelligence, and therefore implies a certain circularity of argument. Indeed, the accuracy of this assumption has already been questioned in this chapter, and will also be questioned again in later chapters, for instance in the framework of a discussion of "creativity."

However, if success in intellectual pursuits rather than test scores is taken as criterion, favorable evidence of concurrent and predictive validity of intelligence tests has accumulated over the years. From the

TABLE 3.2. *IQ and success in secondary school examinations*

IQ range	Percentage of students passing in		
	4 key subjects	3 key subjects	2 key subjects
135 +	63	82	100
130–134	45	79	100
125–129	32	63	83
120–124	30	54	75
115–119	12	31	52
110–114	7	10	39
105–109	0	0	6
100–104	0	0	0
Threshold IQ (i.e., for 50% chance of achieving criterion)	133	123	115

beginning Binet and Simon (1905), as well as Terman (1916), noted agreement between test performance, teachers' estimates of intelligence and academic achievement. Low IQ was found to be the single most prevalent characteristic of children who were retarded by one or two years in school (Terman, 1916; Burt, 1937) while, at the upper extreme of the achievement continuum, Terman's longitudinal study has provided monumental positive evidence of generally satisfactory predictive validity. In the comprehensive Scottish surveys, IQ was the single most effective predictor of high school achievement (McClelland, 1949) while Stanley (1984) maintains that a well administered Stanford–Binet test is probably the best single instrument for identifying a gifted child. In a follow-up correlational study of 766 children (average IQ 128) admitted to selective secondary schools in Yorkshire, Emmett (1942) found that the best *single* predictor of later performance was the intelligence test, which was markedly superior to examinations in English or arithmetic. McLeod (1959), adopting a somewhat different approach from the conventional correlational analysis, examined data on 1597 children admitted to secondary schools in three English local education authorities, and calculated the "threshold IQ" at which a student had a 50 percent chance of passing in key subjects in school leaving examinations (G C E "O" level). Key subjects were defined as English language; mathematics; any second language, alive or dead; and any science. The results are summarised in Table 3.2.

There *have*, nonetheless, been instances where IQ has failed conspicuously to predict future achievement accurately, especially when testing was carried out in infancy (e.g., Skeels and Dye, 1939). For a definitive, scholarly discussion of the evidence for and against the hypothesis of fixed intelligence, i.e., IQ constancy, the reader is referred to Hunt's *Intelligence and Experience* (1961), especially Chapter 2.

Problems in the use of intelligence tests

Apart from the technical issues of reliability and validity which have just been outlined, a major problem in the use of scores on intelligence tests as a definition of exceptional ability — normally this means IQs — derives from the question of whether such scores truly indicate level of intellectual ability, or whether they actually reflect the influence of fators such as parental income, ethnic group membership, even sex. Although such factors may be highly relevant to the nature and speed of intellectual development (see Chapter 12), they are not in themselves aspects of intellectual ability.

There is, for example, an enormous mass of evidence that IQ scores are substantially influenced by socioeconomic status (SES). Indeed, the relationship between scores on intelligence tests and social class is one of the earliest findings in this area: Binet (1912) concluded that "family circumstances" explained differences between his norms (obtained with French working-class children) and those obtained with Belgian children from middle-class families. Stern (1918) found that middle-class German children obtained on average higher IQs than their working class compatriots, and Burt (1937) reported similar differences for English children. Such findings have been repeated over the years, not only in Europe, but also in the United States; see Humphreys (1985) for a recent summary, including comprehensive information obtained with more than 44,000 Ninth Grade boys in the framework of Operation Talent. He concluded that the correlation of IQ with SES in this group was 0.40, a statistically significant figure which indicates that there is a substantial connection between socioeconomic background and scores on intelligence tests.

Humphreys (1985) related such IQ differences between socioeconomic groups directly to outstanding academic ability by pointing out that although the *relative* incidence of children with high IQs is greater in high SES families, the *absolute number* of high IQ youngsters in the lowest four categories of a nine point SES classification system was equal to 70 percent of the number in the uppermost four categories. The largest single number came from the middle category. This results from a combination of the larger number of families in the middle SES categories plus a tendency for lower SES families to have more children. Thus, it is quite incorrect to assert that gifted children (defined by a high IQ) come exclusively from privileged home backgrounds. In addition, as Humphreys points out, well-meaning but ill-informed attempts to compensate for SES disadvantages by using criteria other than measured ability or achievement (he cites the example of allocation of college places via a lottery) can easily produce a situation in which middle-class youngsters of moderate ability are unwittingly favored over able lower SES children. This is because such people are more motivated to make use of all available channels, have more positive attitudes to educational institutions and programs, are more skilled in informal use of the language of the educational system, and the like (see also later discussions as well as Chapter 7).

There is also strong evidence of significant differences between racial groups within societies (in the USA this means, for instance, between Blacks and Whites) and between dominant and minority groups (see Baldwin, 1985; Mistry and Rogoff, 1985, for recent summaries). Findings of this kind have been reported from almost the beginning of widespread intelligence testing, and in countries such as the UK, Canada, Australia and the Federal Republic of Germany, to mention a few examples apart from the USA (see Chapter 7 for a more detailed discussion). Finally, although the construction of intelligence tests was undertaken in such a way as to eliminate sex differences, by balancing the representation of items and tasks on which one or the other of the two sex groups tends to do better, there are still substantial differences in the patterns of scores of boys and girls, and in the representation of the two sexes in programs for promoting academic excellence (see Eccles, 1985, for a recent summary, as well as Chapter 7).

The crucial question now is that of whether such differences reflect innate differences between groups, or whether they reflect the working of other mechanisms, in a situation where the "true" incidence of intellectual ability across groups is equal. Hebb (1949) made a helpful distinction in this regard. He differentiated between what he termed "Intelligence A" — intrinsic, innate ability which cannot be observed directly — and "Intelligence B," which comprises the abilities developed out of A as a result of contact with the conditions of everyday life. Vernon (1955) extended this paradigm to encompass "Intelligence C," i.e., intelligence as measured by an intelligence test. The Hebb–Vernon model provides a useful conceptual basis for analysing what the identification of exceptionally able children entails, and how differences of the kind just listed can occur.

Deutsch (1964) showed how children of lower SES suffer a "cumulative linguistic deficit" as they develop. Cropley and Ahlers (1975) showed something of the dynamics of this cumulative deficit in a study of first-born and only children. Such children typically obtain higher IQ scores than later-born youngsters, and this finding was repeated in the Cropley-Ahlers study. At lower age levels (e.g., at 6–7 years of age), first-born and only children of low SES actually surpassed high SES later-borns. However, as a group, by age 11–12 they had dropped back to average levels, although still surpassing low SES children with large numbers of siblings, and had fallen well behind high SES only children. Cropley and Ahlers attributed this phenomenon to the lack of verbal stimulation provided by low SES parents. At first the intellectual potential (Intelligence A) of capable children of low SES appears to be sufficient by itself for them to obtain high test scores (i.e., "the cream rises to the top"), but with increasing age, potential alone no longer suffices, and the "advantages" offered by the higher SES home background begin to make themselves felt in the development of Intelligence B. These advantages have been outlined by Horowitz and O'Brien (1986) and include not only the modeling of school relevant skills by parents (reading, language as the principle way of dealing with the world), but also encouragement of exploratory behavior, willingness to discuss school work with children etc., (once again, see Chapter 7 for a more detailed discussion).

What this means is that able youngsters from low SES home backgrounds are particularly in need of special help. As former Labour Prime Minister Callaghan of Britain pointed out in a speech made at Ruskin College, Oxford, in 1976, a failure to provide special facilities for gifted youngsters on the grounds of democracy, equality and the like, strikes at precisely the groups which social reformers usually want to help. Whereas well-to-do gifted children enjoy a wide variety of environmental stimulation simply as a result of their fortunate material circumstances, disadvantaged youngsters *need* provision outside the home.

In the case of children from ethnic or other minority groups, the situation is to a certain degree similar, especially when it is borne in mind that there is a tendency for SES to correlate with race and minority group status. However, it is apparent that there are further issues in this case. In particular, as Baldwin (1985) emphasized, intelligence tests, and even concepts of giftedness, concentrate on only some of the ways in which ability can manifest itself in the form of behavior (these are, it must be admitted, ways which are of proven value for success in the school system). In other words, Intelligence C (behaviors leading to high test scores) does not even correspond with Intelligence B, let alone Intelligence A. Furthermore, getting high test scores is greatly facilitated by willingness to work fast, willingness to be tested at all, a positive attitude to test situations, a positive self-image, expectations of success and the like (i.e., by factors other than ability). As will be shown in Chapter 7, there are large differences on such factors between racial and ethnic groups, SES groups, even between boys and girls. What this all means is that intelligence test scores alone are inadequate as an indicator of intellectual potential. This theme is developed further in

Chapters 4 and 7.

Can intelligence be taught?

If one subscribes to the view that intelligence is innate, uninfluenced by teaching, training or motivation, then clearly it cannot be taught, and there is no point in trying to change the unchangeable. On the other hand, if one subscribes to a conception of intelligence similar to that espoused by Hunt (1961), it should be quite possible to achieve the goal of improving intelligence through training. Indeed Engelmann and Engelmann (1966), who were probably influenced by Hunt at Illinois, provide specific guidelines on how to "give your child a superior mind" through a structured, stimulating environment during the years of infancy. To Engelmann, "[a child's] intelligence, capacity and range of skills reflect his environment — his teachers" (p. 70). He had no doubts about the power of an environment such as that experienced by John Stuart Mill, whose IQ has been estimated as 190–200 (Cox, 1926).

> This is an environment that will succeed with *any* healthy infant. Yes, if we could play a little game with history and switch the real John Stuart Mill with some unfortunate from the slums of London, the history books wouldn't change very much. The unfortunate would become a Mill. (p. 36)

In a similar optimistic vein, although apparently not in the opinion of Engelmann and Engelmann (1966, p. 11), Doman (1964) has been telling parents "how to teach your baby to read" since 1964, and according to *Time* Magazine (15 August 1983) a California-based franchise organization claiming that "learning to read begins at birth," was providing educational play for some 10,000 US infants by the early 1980s.

Binet himself believed that intelligence could be cultivated, deploring as "brutal pessimism" the opinion that an individual's intelligence is fixed (Hunt, 1961, p. 54). Spearman considered a person's "g" factor ability to be inborn, but appears to have considered specific abilities to be capable of improvement through training. Thurstone (1948) is on record as unequivocally answering the question of whether his primary mental abilities can be trained: "the answer is in the affirmative," although according to Kirk (1960), whom Thurstone taught, he did not originally subscribe to this view.

Guilford (1981) warned American supervisors of Headstart programs that "the Japanese sometimes start their 'intelligence education' at the age of two, and are even instructing mothers how to apply it."Torrance (1980a) returned from a visit to Japan apparently convinced that the whole Japanese nation is gifted. The reason why Japanese children consistently score higher in international comparative studies than children from other countries, especially in science and mathematics (Fiske, 1983), is probably more prosaic. The evidence seems to be that Japanese students begin formal education earlier, work harder, for longer hours and at a faster pace, during a longer school year, respect their (highly paid) teachers who emphasize factual knowledge in preparation for external examinations rather than fostering creativity, and are imbued with the idea that success in academic life is "the measure of an individual and reflects the honoring of mutual moral obligations" (McGrath, 1983). One suspects that, for the foreseeable future, attempts to transplant such values to North America would be as illfated as were attempts to impose American reforms on Japanese education during the postwar occupation.

Tests as diagnostic instruments

During the 1960s, test data began to be regarded more as a starting point for therapeutic treatment than as a prophetic index of the inevitable. In Britain, Bernstein (1961) argued that the "restricted code" of the home language of lower socioeconomic status children fell short of the "elaborated code" necessary for successful academic achievement, and in the USA, Deutsch (1964) spoke of adverse effects of the "cumulative language deficit" suffered by the slum child. Bereiter and Engelmann (1966) devised an efficient, compressed, language-based preschool program aimed at offsetting this deficiency.

A test which had a profound influence about this time, particularly in the diagnosis and treatment of learning disabilities, was the Illinois Test of Psycholinguistic Abilities (ITPA) (Kirk and McCarthy, 1961; Kirk, McCarthy and Kirk, 1968). Children's overall performance on this test showed close correlation with IQ (Paraskevopoulos and Kirk, 1969) but, whereas the subtests of instruments such as the WISC or Thurstone's Primary Mental Abilities Test had been selected on an *ad hoc* basis or according to some theory of the structure of human ability, the ITPA's subtests were constructed according to a more dynamic model of human communication. Children were not tested to find out "how much" of some ability such as Comprehension or Inductive Reasoning they possessed, but rather "how well" they were able to receive meaningful messages via visual material, or how well they were able to express themselves verbally, etc. In other words, a subtest score on the ITPA provided an indication of the developmental stage from which remediation should be initiated. Kirk had thus come full circle, (intentionally) echoing the philosophy of Alfred Binet that having "discovered the evil (mental retardation), our next step was to cure it" (quoted by Kirk and Kirk, 1975, p. 41).

In the mid-1960s, graduate students working with preschoolers in a

Headstart program in New York found the children to be particularly deficient on certain subtests of the ITPA, and carried out remedial training with the children in these deficient areas, *using the test format as the model of remediation*. The children showed commendable improvement on ITPA retest, but this did not extend beyond the particular format of the tests; i.e., the children were able to score more highly on a test of Auditory Decoding, by being able to answer questions of the type: "Do bananas telephone?," "Do carpenters kneel?," but did not show general improvement in their ability to derive meaning from spoken language. In experiments designed to improve intelligence, or for that matter creativity, convergent thinking, divergent thinking, etc., it is always necessary to examine the criterion against which the effectiveness of training is being judged. In particular, it is necessary to ensure that children are not simply being trained to perform better on a specific test which *purports* to measure a more general trait or quality.

Guilford's associates have no doubt about the trainability of the abilities of the SI model. In 1977, the International Society for Intelligence Education (ISIE) was set up, with an Executive consisting of persons from the USA and Japan (Meeker, 1978). Meeker states that "children [who are] not prepared for learning must have training in an additional basic . . . a basic called *intelligence*" (original author's emphasis). Cunningham, Thompson and Alston (1978) concluded that the Structure of Intellect Learning Abilities Test (SOI-LA) *does* provide useful identification information. By means of regression equations designed to predict teachers' judgements as to whether a student in a gifted program was a high achiever, very creative or belonged in a gifted program, the authors found that weighted combinations of some of the abilities assessed by the SOI-LA had a predictive validity beyond the 0.05 level of statistical significance. O'Tuel, Ward and Rawl (1983) investigated the relationship between Meeker's Structure of Intellect Learning Abilities Test Gifted Screening Form [SOI-LA(GSF)] and grades, achievement, IQ and performance in the gifted program for seventh and fourth graders. The authors concluded that the SOI-LA(GSF) did not show a strong relationship to success in the gifted program and that its correlations with academic variables may not be large enough to warrant its use as an identification tool. By contrast, traditional IQ scores obtained in Grade 7 were able to predict satisfactorily academic performance at Grade 10.

Closing Remarks

In the Hebb–Vernon analysis of "intelligence" it thus appears impossible to improve "Intelligence A," and self-deceptive, although possible in the short term, to increase "Intelligence C." But what of

"Intelligence B?" The evidence suggests that children can learn to cope with certain *kinds* of tasks more effectively than they did before training, even if their potential is not raised in any biological sense. The obvious implication for the promotion of excellence is that it is possible to foster special ways of operating, such as analyzing and formulating problems, thinking abstractly, searching for evidence, working independently, using special learning resources, carrying out self-evaluation or planning learning programs, all of which are of clear importance in the fostering of academic excellence.

The concept of intelligence and its quantification in IQ scores is undoubtedly a useful, even vital, beginning for the understanding of exceptional ability. However, it is extremely important to bear in mind that scores on intelligence tests: (a) reflect only certain aspects of cognitive functioning; (b) sample only certain behavioral manifestations of this functioning; (c) also depend upon noncognitive factors. Since there are large differences between racial groups, socioeconomic status groups and minority and majority groups in society, IQ scores tend to reflect not only innate ability, but also the effects of the conditions under which this Intelligence A has developed into Intelligence B, and the specific ways of dealing with the world which are modeled, valued and rewarded in the particular environment in which a child has grown up. as well as the complex set of attitudes, values, motives and self-image which are acquired there. The result is that, since the tests emphasize only certain skills and assume that the childhood environment has taken a particular form, substantial numbers of children are inaccurately assessed, at least in the sense of potential. This means that other, supplementary, indicators of intellectual ability need to be taken into account in identifying children who are thought to be gifted. The following two chapters are directly concerned with the extension of the intelligence concept and with other ways of spotting exceptional ability over and above intelligence tests.

4

Creativity, Intelligence and Academic Excellence

Extension of the concept of intelligence

In his 1950 Presidential Address to the American Psychological Association, Guilford (1950) delivered a systematic and influential criticism of the narrowness of thinking about the mental processes involved in intelligent behavior. He demonstrated that the current conceptualization of intelligence was limited to what he called "convergent thinking," and that this restriction had been built into intelligence tests, and hence into thinking about the nature of intellectual functioning. Subsequently, other writers such as Getzels and Jackson extended Guilford's arguments by showing that a similar narrowness of view permeates ideas, not only about intelligence tests, but also about what kinds of processes constitute efficient and worthwhile thinking in school children. By contrast, Guilford called for more "divergent thinking." Within a few years of Guilford's address the USA's collective self-concept was delivered a stunning blow by the successful launching by the Sovet Union of *Sputnik1*, the first earth satellite. The US education system was seen by many as having let the country down. In particular, it was argued that innovative and original (creative) thinkers are the key to progress, not just large numbers of graduates. The leap to the adoption of a position where divergent thinking was equated with creativity, and convergent thinking with mere routine conformist thinking, followed quickly.

In an influential study, which appeared at exactly the opportune historical moment, Getzels and Jackson (1962) established the source of what has become current terminology, by contrasting "creativity" on the one hand, and "intelligence" on the other, apparently seeing the two as more or less opposites. They compared 26 highly "creative" secondary school students (the highest scorers in their age group on creativity tests,* but not among the highest scorers on conventional intelligence) with 26 highly "intelligent" students (very high on

*A detailed discussion of divergent thinking tests is to be found in Chapter 5.

intelligence, but not on divergent thinking). Despite large IQ differences, the "creative" students did as well on tests of academic achievement as did the merely "intelligent" students. The "high intelligence" group, however, scored higher on measures of socially desirable personality traits.

The Getzels and Jackson study was criticized on a number of grounds (Burt, 1962; Cropley, 1967a; Vernon, 1964b). For instance, the students came from a highly selective school and, despite being low on measures of intelligence relative to the "intelligent" group, had a mean IQ of 127 (compared with 150 for the "intelligent" group). There were a number of technical problems, too, such as the small size of the samples and the fact that IQs were based on several different tests that had been administered much earlier than the creativity tests. There were also relatively high correlations between IQs and creativity scores; no account was taken of children who scored high on both measures; there was no real-life evidence that "creativity" tests really did measure creativity in any sense other than divergent thinking. Nonetheless, the Getzels and Jackson study provided the impetus which set in motion a huge "bandwagon" (Vernon, 1979). As a result, the early 1960s saw an enormous increase in the number of publications on creativity in psychological journals (Tannenbaum, 1979), as well as the emergence of many programs aimed at fostering creativity in children.

Why should creativity be fostered?

There is nothing wrong with respect for logic or knowledge of facts; on the contrary, there are many situations where these are greatly preferable to free association, speculation or a search for novelty. One obvious example would be the desirable behavior of a brain surgeon during an operation, or of a pilot flying a commercial airliner across the Atlantic. In such situations convergent forms of thinking are obviously extremely valuable. However this fact should not be allowed to blind us to the value of being able, in many situations, to seek novelty, see new ways of doing things, or suggest alternative possibilities.

Although a major impetus for the increased emphasis on creativity in the 1950s and 1960s was undoubtedly the competitive thinking of the cold war period, there are important educational/psychological reasons for emphasizing it. Our interest in the present book in the fostering of academic excellence does not derive from the desire to identify the cleverest and to spur them on to ever greater deeds, but from the humanistic/humanitarian goal of making it possible for all children to develop their potentials to the full, even in the intellectual domain. Emphasis on academic excellence might be regarded as a self-evident goal of the school as an institution. However, this is by no means always the case — Gross (1986), for instance, outlines the determined opposition to special provision for able children in Australia from, among other groups, teachers' unions. Sternberg and Davidson (1986) draw attention to the curious anomaly that interest in promoting giftedness in the USA is much stronger in the general public than among scholars and professionals in education.

Despite this lack of interest in some countries, Cropley (1978, 1982a) advanced a number of arguments of an essentially humanistic nature for the promotion of creativity. It is important because it:

1. Makes school learning more effective — cognitive processes and personal and motivational characteristics, such as those which will be outlined shortly, greatly enhance, among other things, "learning to learn."
2. Increases the ability of people to cope with the social and scientific changes which the next 50 years will bring — flexibility, originality, readiness to try something new, etc., are becoming, and will become even more, important.
3. Promotes the spiritual well-being of people — the ability and readiness to deal in an open and flexible way with life situations is vital to mental health.
4. Protects our human dignity — in the age of the computer it is not routine, programmable thinking which will confirm our unique position as human beings, but creative processes and products.
5. Offers new perspectives for making equality of opportunity a reality — an expanding concept of excellence which takes account of hitherto neglected areas and also emphasizes the importance of noncognitive aspects opens up new possibilities.

Definition of creativity

Although novelty, flexibility, surprisingness and the like have been referred to here as aspects of creativity, the term should not be reduced simply to these. Unfortunately it is often used loosely, and has even come to mean, to some, little more than "doing your own thing." For others, creativity means mere unconventionality, so that simply being different is regarded as synonymous with being creative. It is also true that some of the skills which facilitate divergent thinking are often mistaken for creativity itself. Approaches emphasizing unconventionality and the like are not absurd: as Brown (1977) pointed out, every real creative breakthrough in science involves an irrational jump. Creativity is also connected to "pointers to creativity" (Kneller, 1965, p. 2) such as quickwittedness or highly developed verbal fluency. However, reduction of creativity merely to such qualities is dangerous. Not only may teachers be seduced into tolerating or even encouraging disruptive behavior, but an erroneous notion of creativity may also be harmful for children falsely labeled "creative," by leading them to think that they are being creative when they are doing nothing more than indulging in trivial activities.

Fox (1981) suggested that much of the uncertainty stems from confusion over whether creativity is a personality trait, a specific cognitive ability or a type of problem solving strategy that might be learned. Fox's evaluation is similar to that in a review by Barron and Harrington (1981), who observed that creativity is usually defined in terms of achievement (creativity as product), as a personal disposition (creativity defined in terms of the person involved) or as a special kind of ability. A further problem centers on the question of whether it is really possible to speak of "creativity" as a unitary phenomenon. Burt (1962) and Vernon (1964b) for instance, distinguished between "aesthetic/ professional" creativity and "artistic" creativity. Necka (1986) went further, listing "aesthetic," "artistic," "professional" and "scientific" creativity. Wallach (1985) argued that creativity is difficult to define except in terms of a specific domain. Barron (1969) even suggested that creativity need not involve being creative oneself, but includes the ability to foster it in others, while Renzulli (1984) pointed out that a child may show creativity in different areas at different times. Nonetheless, Altshuller (1984) concluded that it is possible to develop a general theory of creativity, which would encompass artistic, technical, scientific and practical domains. He also rejects the idea of creativity as something which results from mystical inspiration and can never be understood, emphasizing that the achievement of a creative breakthrough is usually the pinnacle of long effort, and stressing the need for possession of many ideas before creativity can occur. He came to the important conclusion that everybody can be trained to become more creative.

Clarification of the characteristics of creativity — or at least the reduction of confusion about what is meant by the term — is a central task if the idea of creativity is to be incorporated into a definition of excellence, and is of vital importance for those who seek to foster or train creativity. Heinelt (1974) has made an important distinction in this regard, drawing attention to differences between genuine creativity, "pseudocreativity" and "quasicreativity." Pseudocreativity is to be seen in pointless nonconformity, undisciplined behavior, wild disregard of rules and conventions, or blind impulse expression. Quasicreativity involves high levels of fantasy (in principle highly desirable) but with no connection to reality. An example is to be seen in the "inventions" we make in the course of daydreaming. The difference between the fantasy of genuine creativity and that of quasicreativity is that the first kind of fantasy is reality oriented, what Goethe called "exact fantasy."

Taylor (1975) has made a similar point, although in a somewhat different way, by referring to "levels" of creativity. At the lowest level is what he called "expressive spontaneity," to be found for instance in the uninhibited production of ideas often seen in children. Originality is unimportant at this level, as is the quality of the product (i.e., its usefulness or degree of adaptation to the demands of the real world is irrelevant). Higher levels of creativity include "technical" creativity, characterized by unusual skill or proficiency; "inventive" creativity in which the already known is utilized in novel ways; "innovative" creativity, which requires that existing principles be taken a step further; and finally "emergent" creativity, where new abstract principles are recognized and stated.

An important point in the present discussion is that creative thinking should lead to worthwhile results, if it is to make a contribution to academic excellence. This distinguishes it from blind unconventionality or simple expressive spontaneity. The products of processes labeled "creative" should, to use the words of Sappington and Farrar (1982, p. 68), "conform to reality constraints." Furthermore, they should involve some genuine "transformations" (Besemer and Treffinger, 1981) and not simply a slick use of the well known. Not infrequently, these products have a compelling quality about them which causes a perceptible shock of recognition in the observer, perhaps the thought: "Now why didn't I think of that?" This is the property which Bruner (1967) referred to as "effective surprise." Finally, most writers agree that such products should be socially desirable before they can be labeled "creative;" otherwise, as Cropley (1982a) has pointed out, it would be necessary to speak of the creativity of a burglar or a terrorist — something which most people would be unwilling to accept. Although Vernon (1979, p. 51) focused on creativity as an ability, he too stressed the importance of "social, spiritual, aesthetic, scientific or technological values."

Uncertainty about the kinds of behavior which constitute creativity opens up a number of pitfalls for those who wish to foster creative behavior in children. Heinelt (1974) has summarized these in the form of a series of "don'ts" for teachers. His list of admonitions includes the following:

1. Creativity must not degenerate into mere innovation hysteria;
2. Creativity should not be hailed as the new cure all for human problems;
3. Creativity must not become a magic formula which can be applied to everything;
4. Creativity should not become a justification for any and all behavior, regardless of its merit;

5. Creativity should not become an alibi for weak students or an excuse for abandoning all standards;
6. Creativity should not be used as a pretext for legitimizing any and all changes in the education system.

Excellence — A combination of creativity and intelligence

The point has already been made in Chapter 2 that studies such as those of Gibson and Light (1967) or, more recently, Facaoaru (1985) have shown that excellent performance cannot be explained adequately by a unidimensional IQ approach — a high IQ alone does not distinguish sufficiently sharply between outstanding achievers, as we have defined the term in this book (see, for instance, p. 1) and "normal" achievers (although there is no doubt that IQ is the best *single* predictor of achievement over the whole range of ability as Humphreys, 1985, pointed out). Apart from technical issues such as restriction of range (see, p. 87), this has often been interpreted as indicating that what we call "excellence" in this book depends upon more than simply high intelligence in the IQ sense. However, as Wallach (1985) emphasized, simply arguing that there is a further kind of ability called "creativity," and that it is the highly creative person who is "truly" excellent, does not conform with more recent research findings. As a result, other conceptualizations of the role of creativity in academic excellence have been sought.

The idea that creativity represents the highest form of *application of intelligence* (e.g., Gardner, 1983) rather than a "new" ability, has already been mentioned in Chapter 2. Cropley (1969) argued that creativity is not an ability at all, but a *style* for applying ability. Horowitz and O'Brien (1985) took this view further and speculated that creativity is not a quantitative phenomenon at all, but represents *a qualitative reorganisation* of a specific content domain, which is only possible once certain "levels of competence" (p. 446) in that domain have been reached. In our terms, this would mean that after a sufficient mastery of the contents of an area had been achieved (presumably through the application of convergent thinking), certain basic creativity facilitating skills mastered (in the area of academic excellence this would mean, among other things, divergent thinking), and certain personal properties (such as fascination for an area, willingness to depart from the conventional and the like) developed, a certain chain reaction may occur. This leads to what we call "creativity," and manifests itself in "creative" products (although as will be shown later in this chapter, these may sometimes be labeled "crazy," "meaningless" or even "criminal"). According to Horowitz and O'Brien (1985), this does not always occur. Where it does not, the result is mere workmanlike technical competence (whose value should not be underestimated). Some people may never achieve the creative reorganization, or be afraid to make its results public, or not recognize that a product is creative and abandon it, with the result that the peak of performance in Gardner's sense (and ours too) never occurs, or is suppressed. Others may often or even regularly achieve creative breakthroughs, recognize their worth at once and not hesitate to communicate them to others, with most people in the group of the highly competent probably lying somewhere in between.

As it has just been interpreted, creativity blends easily into a more comprehensive concept of outstanding ability, instead of appearing to be a competing approach. Academic excellence cannot be understood as simply the reproduction of what is already known, nor as the blind production of the novel. Knowledge and novelty are both important, and the aim of teachers will be to help the emergence of both. Facaoaru (1985) called this a "two track" approach: excellent work on demanding tasks requires a combination of conventional knowledge, logic, etc., (high competence) and novel thinking, idea getting and the like. Facaoaru also found that personal properties, such as stamina or the ability to tolerate uncertainty or disappointment, and high motivation play an important role in outstanding achievements, thus emphasizing the importance of noncognitive factors in successful work in real life settings (see later sections).

Nature of the creativity–intelligence interaction

The threshold model

One question which now arises is that of the dynamics of the combination of creativity and intelligence to produce academic excellence. An early approach was that of MacKinnon (1962), who proposed the threshold theory. In essence, this argues that a certain minimum level of intelligence is necessary before creativity is possible. Stated in a technical way, the argument is that the possibility of being creative rises as the IQ level approaches the threshold value, so that creativity and IQ correlate positively with each other at lower IQ levels. However, once the minimum IQ has been reached (the threshold surpassed) they become more or less independent of each other. Bringing out a different aspect of the same idea, McNemar (1964, p. 879) pointed out that high IQ is no guarantee of creativity, but a low IQ means that it is impossible.

Unfortunately, the kinds of correlation just outlined would occur even if the correlation between IQs and creativity were high, as a result of the restriction of range resulting from concentrating on those with

IQs over 120. For example, Torrance (1966) reported that the correlation of creativity scores with IQ was 0.50 for children with IQ scores below 120, but only 0.20 for children with IQs above 120. If correlations across the whole ability range were in reality 0.80, Torrance's figures would almost exactly follow from the effects of restriction of range. Nevertheless, the fact that such high correlations have not generally been observed suggests that this technical issue is not the whole story.

Information search

Guilford and Christensen (1973) take a somewhat different position from the threshold theory, suggesting that there is a "one way relationship" between creative potential and intelligence, i.e., an IQ test provides an indicator of the upper limit for performance, but does not indicate the likelihood of creativity. Their interpretation is based on the argument that the IQ indicates the extent to which an individual possesses relevant information and can call it out of storage upon demand. If a person does not have access to information, there is nothing to be retrieved and divergently processed. Altshuller (1984) also emphasized the importance of possessing a large amount of information.

Channel capacity

Guilford and Christensen's model of the interrelationship between intelligence and creativity is basically a static one. A more dynamic interpretation along essentially the same lines might regard the individual as a communication channel. This approach has proved useful in other contexts (e.g., Rimland, 1964). Channel capacity, in the sense of an upper limit on the number of "bits" of information that can be assimilated, is intuitively compatible with the concept of intelligence, while the versatility and extent to which an individual can manipulate, reorganize and recombine those "bits" is compatible with the notion of orginality, creativity or divergent productive thinking. According to such "one way" interpretations of the relation of intelligence to creativity, highly creative thinkers would be found more frequently — but not inevitably — among the highly intelligent. Also, it would become progressively more difficult to predict individuals' creativity at higher intelligence levels, i.e., the correlation between IQ and creativity would be expected to decrease as IQ increased. Both of these predictions are in line with what appear to be the empirical facts — even though those facts are veiled and obscured in a mass of less than clearcut data.

Breaking barriers

Cropley (1982a) has described the relationship between creativity and conventional intelligence in a similar, if somewhat more picturesque way. The achieving of academic excellence involves breaking the barriers of what is known and accepted, and bursting through into new territory. Torrance and Hall (1980) also wrote of the need to"transcend the boundaries" in order to think creatively. However, in order to do this it is first necessary to know where the barriers or boundaries are. It is also extremely helpful to know what attempts have already been made to break through, and where and why they were successful or unsuccessful. Thus, it is necessary to be well supplied with facts, and to acquire facts requires convergent thinking activities. To take a concrete example, it is a fine thing to be able to turn a creative or witty phrase in a foreign language — to find the *"bon mot"* — but it is first necessary to learn thousands of words in that language, and the only way to do this is to learn them by heart — probably by old-fashioned rote learning, uncreative though that may be.

More recently, Altshuller (1984) distinguished between creativity as the finding of new applications of the already known and creativity as a breakthrough into the previously unknown. He also investigated the question of whether such breakthroughs can result from trial and error, and came to the conclusion that it is theoretically possible for creativity to result from a sustained running through of all possibilities until a "new" solution — which is therefore "creative" — emerges. However, he drew attention to the inefficiency of such an approach, because of the large number of unsuccessful attempts (what he called "empty" trials) which would be required for each creative solution. Consequently, he argued for a model of the process of reaching creative solutions encompassing not only the finding of alternative ideas, but also the application of criterion oriented decision making strategies which would reject most empty trials and focus effort on promising approaches.

Creativity and the person

Discussions to this point have concentrated on creativity itself. We turn our attention now to the properties of the individual person which promote the development of creativity and the emergence of creative behavior.

Cognitive processes

The initial impulse in modern times in this area came, as has already been mentioned, from the work of Guilford. Essentially, he argued that thinking about intellectual ability tends to concentrate on processes such as reapplying the already known in order to find a single, best, "correct" answer. What is needed above all is a fund of knowledge of the facts, and the ability to search among these and find the right one. He called this "convergent thinking," since there is a closing in on the best answer. Neglected, by contrast, are thinking strategies which involve breaking away from the facts, seeing their unexpected implications, using them as a springboard for the development of new ideas: this property he called "divergent thinking." Guilford developed test procedures on the basis of this analysis of human "mental power;" these have played an important role in the development of current thinking about creativity, and will be discussed in detail in Chapter 5. For our purposes here, the important point is that divergent thinking was initially equated with creativity. As Necka (1986) and Facaoaru (1985) pointed out, effective creative behavior requires more than divergent thinking — motivation, self-confidence and similar personal and affective factors are certainly very important. Even in the cognitive domain, it is questionable whether a simple divergent thinking model is sufficient.

The relatively undifferentiated approach just described (intelligence = convergent thinking, creativity = divergent thinking) has been expanded by a number of authors. Torrance and Hall (1980), for instance, concluded that creativity involves:

1. Uniting disparate ideas by putting them into a common context;
2. Being able to imagine, at least as a theoretical possibility, almost anything;
3. Enriching one's own thinking through the application of fantasy;
4. Adding spice to one's thinking through the use of humor.

Sternberg (1985) emphasized the importance of "metacognitive" processes in creativity. These are the processes through which people reflect upon their own thinking, evaluate it, choose new tactics, decide between blind allies and promising approaches, etc. Among the metacognitive processes which are important for creativity are:

1. Recognising the nature of the problem;
2. Representing the problem internally;
3. Determining which solution strategies are relevant and promising;
4. Choosing and organizing cognitive resources;
5. Combining thinking strategies;
6. Evaluating progress towards the solution of a problem;
7. Identifying new lines of attack when old ones fail.

Necka's (1986) "triad" model of creativity goes beyond a purely cognitive position. Nonetheless, the cognitive elements are of great importance: they involve original, inventive, effective thinking strategies, which are a prerequisite for actual creative behavior in real life settings, although not by themselves sufficient. These are essential tactics for processing information, and include:

1. Forming associations;
2. Recognizing similarities;
3. Constructing metaphors;
4. Carrying out transformations;
5. Selectively directing the focus of attention;
6. Seeing the abstract aspects of the concrete.

The application of such strategies to produce actual creative behavior requires, however, special knowledge and skills relevant to the actual area of creativity in question: an artist needs to know how colours can be combined, a scientist must be able to analyze ideas, etc. Also important are more general techniques such as obtaining information or communicating ideas, or the ability to recognize and avoid blocking factors.

Creativity as a facet of personality

Despite the importance of cognitive processes, creativity depends upon more than thinking skills (Barron and Harrington, 1981). People need to be willing to branch out and to break away from the conventional; they need to have confidence in themselves and their ideas; they need to be able to tolerate the anxiety resulting from questioning the commonplace; they need to be able to stand up to pressure to conform to the group; they need to be capable of living with the consequences of being divergently excellent, of accepting and coming to terms with the "loneliness of the long distance runner." Thus, if teachers are to encourage children to achieve excellence (in our sense of the term), they need to know far more about creativity than merely what kinds of abilities are involved.

Many attempts have been made to associate creativity with personality. Relatively recent studies (e.g., Dellas and Gaier, 1970; Foster, 1971; Taft and Gilchrist, 1970) have, like the earlier studies of Barron, Cattell, MacKinnon, Roe and Torrance, suggested that persons such as artists and creative scientists have certain specifiable personality characteristics which differentiate them from the public at large. Farisha (1978) has concluded that personality is consistently emphasized in the literature as a deciding factor in the emergence of creativity.

In summarizing some of the findings, Neff (1975, pp. 75–76), listed the main characteristics of creative people on which there is a good deal of agreement. These include:

1. Flexibility;
2. Sensitivity;
3. Tolerance;
4. Sense of responsibility;
5. Empathy;
6. Independence;
7. Positive self-image;
8. Need for social contact;
9. Interest in getting ahead.

The list has been extended by Heinelt (1974, p. 29), who identified the following characteristics of creative school children: They

1. Are usually introverts;
2. Are more self-willed;
3. Are less dependent upon group support;
4. Are intellectually active, and ask many questions;
5. Are extremely flexible in their thinking;
6. Show wit and a sense of humor;
7. Often remain aloof from their classmates;
8. Prefer to work independently;
9. Are often socially isolated;
10. Feel superior to their classmates and tend to be arrogant;
11. Are not among the most popular in their class.

In addition, certain traits seem to be seen less frequently in creative people than in noncreative, although there is some disagreement in the relevant literature on specifics (Neff, 1975). The list of "uncharacteristics" of creative individuals includes:

1. Feeling of well-being;
2. Willingness to conform;
3. Self-control;
4. Desire to make a good impression;
5. Conformity.

Creativity and motivation

In addition to possessing certain personal traits, creative individuals are characterized by their willingness to expend effort, by what Stanley

(1984, p. 178) referred to as "academic hunger." Some people seem to be able to tolerate uncertainty, or even have a need for novelty (Cropley and Sikand, 1973; Dellas and Gaier, 1970). Associated with this is the willingness of some people to take risks, for instance by abandoning previously held positions or trying strange or different tasks. These factors define "the courage to create" (Motamedi, 1982, p. 84). Finally, as Roe (1963) showed, and later writers have confirmed, successful creative people as a group show high levels of persistence — they stick at something once they have started it. Treffinger, Isaksen and Firestein (1983) give great emphasis to such variables in their discussion of creative behavior and its facilitation. The following list of key characteristics of creative individuals in the domain of motivation is based on their summary. Creative individuals display:

1. Curiosity;
2. Willingness to respond freely in stimulating situations;
3. Openness to new or unusual experiences;
4. Willingness to take risks;
5. Sensitivity to problems and a desire to solve them;
6. Tolerance of ambiguity;
7. Self-confidence.

In his "triad" model of creativity, which has already been mentioned, Necka (1986) distinguished five classes of motives which energize creative behavior:

1. Instrumental motives: creative behavior is a means to an end.
2. Playful motives: creative behavior leads to a state of inner satisfaction. This kind of motivation is also seen as an aspect of the process of self-actualization;
3. Intrinsic motives: creative behavior is an end in itself. The value of creative behavior arises from a sense of duty or the feeling of having a mission.
4. Control motives: creative behavior increases a person's level of competence or strengthens the feeling of having the external world under control;
5. Expressive motives; creative behavior makes it possible to communicate one's own thoughts and feelings to other people.

In the case of actual creative achievements, these motives probably interact and combine, rather than acting singly; for instance, a verbally gifted person might seek fame and fortune through the writing of novels (an instrumental motive), but at the same time have a strong sense of mission (intrinsic motivation) or a desire to "reach" other people (expressive motivation). It is also probable that different people show different combinations or patterns of motives, with different weightings of the various areas in different people. As a result, it is possible to speak of an "individual structure of motives." Furthermore, it is likely that these structures change with the passage of time. The original profit motive of the novelist mentioned about could, for instance, eventually be replaced by the feeling of having something important to say to humanity.

The different kinds of motivation for creativity listed by Necka include a mixture of external and internal factors. Amabile (1983), however, argued that extrinsic motivation (i.e., the desire to obtain rewards offered by the external world and consequent shaping of one's behavior in order to make it pleasing to external authorities such as teachers) is deadly for creativity. According to her, the crucial element in creativity is intrinsic motivation; a certain activity is pursued because is provides internal satisfactions — it is fascinatingly interesting in itself for a particular person, satisfies some internal drive or need, produces a feeling of pleasure or well-being, etc. Amabile goes so far as to argue that the real task in fostering creativity (see Chapter 9) is helping children become immune to extrinsic motivation.

Social factors in creativity

Characteristics such as being self-willed or socially isolated suggest that outstanding creativity might involve a degree of social deviance (see Cropley, 1973, for a more detailed discussion). Cronbach (1968) went so far as to propose that so called "creativity" tests are really personality tests, in which the key characteristic of high scorers is their willingness to offer socially unpopular answers. Such willingness is not necessarily uncommon or unnatural; newborn babies, for instance, display many socially unacceptable behaviors. However, with the passage of time even the hitherto asocial infant comes to confine itself to patterns of behavior which are acceptable to the people around it. Even "difficult" children may come, in adulthood, to stick rigidly to their society's way of doing things. A transformation occurs with the passage of time. The process through which this takes place is referred to as "socialization."

Socialization involves acquiring ways of doing things which conform to the rules of the society in which one lives. This conformity is the result of a process of training; children learn how things ought to be done. Their behavior is modified partly through imitation of important models such as their parents, peers, sports heroes and media figures, partly through deliberate training by parents and teachers with the help of rewards and punishments. Not only are specific forms of behavior learned, such as what to say when introduced to someone for the first time, but also more general values and standards, as well as ideas about where one belongs in a variety of social structures, such as the family, school and community. Children learn, for instance, that it is good, or bad, to deviate from the average, that authority may, or may not, be questioned, that the good opinion of peers is, or is not, of supreme importance, that to stand alone is tolerable, or intolerable, and so on. In other words, they acquire a whole set of norms which not only provide information about how one ought to act in certain circumstances, but also indicate what kinds of thing one may think, what role thinking has in life, and even whether thinking is good or bad in principle.

A relatively high level of unanimity among the members of a particular culture about what is allowable and what is not is useful. People are freed from the need to treat every event in life as though it were a unique isolated occurrence with unknown origins and unknown consequences. The world becomes tolerably predictable, and can be dealt with without excessive uncertainty and strain. However, despite these undoubted benefits, socialization has undesirable side effects in that it encourages thinking in standardized ways; children learn that being like everybody else is highly desirable, and that the world is seen by other people in certain set ways. The result is a high degree of uniformity in behavior and also in thinking. In societies where convergent thinking is greatly prized, then, children learn not only to think convergently, but also that they ought to think in that way and that it is peculiar to think otherwise. They acquire the skills of convergent thinking, they come to value it highly, and they judge people who think divergently as less worthy. The criticism, and even crushing rejection, experienced by many original thinkers is one of the results of this process.

Creativity and nonconformity

The effects of socialization on creativity raise questions about the whole relationship between creativity and nonconformity. To the extent that their divergent thinking is often accompanied by flamboyant nonconforming behavior, creative thinkers frequently show up as highly unconventional. In fact, however, the unconventionality is one of the concomitants of creative thinking — mere unconventionality does not necessarily signal the presence of genuine creativity. Nevertheless, nonconformity is usually cited as one of the chief personality traits of creative thinkers. As long ago as 1955, Crutchfield demonstrated a pervasive and stable dimension of individual differences centering around the fact that some people quickly revise their opinions when they are at odds with those of some larger group, even, in fact, when the group opinion is blatantly inaccurate but has been faked so that there appears to be consensus. Others, by contrast, stick to their guns when the evidence of their senses tells them that the group is in the wrong. Thus, faced with two lines of different lengths, conforming individuals agree that the obviously shorter of the two is really the longer, when they are confronted with a group of people who all agree that it looks longer to them; nonconformers, on the other hand, tend to resist the group's pressure to get their opinions into line. Krause (1972) has concluded that independence of this kind is an important factor in creativity. MacKinnon (1983) related this discussion to real life by showing that gifted architects were less willing to accept guidance than others, while Helson (1983) reported a similar finding for gifted women mathematicians.

Nonconforming individuals are marked, according to Crutchfield, by their willingness to express impulses and by their freedom from compulsion about rules, while conformers are marked by impulse suppression and strict attention to the rules. This dichotomy appears to be a major personality difference from individual to individual. Luria (1961), for example, regards the very essence of development during childhood as centering on the learning of impulse control, and he suggested speech as the key factor in the achievement of control. According to this conception, developing children acquire control of their own behavior through the internalization of adult verbalizations. The child learns, as it were, "stop rules" (Anderson and Cropley, 1966), which channel behavior into courses reflecting what adults regard as "right." These adults in turn, are heavily influenced in their notions of rightness and wrongness by the culture in which they live, so that the general effect of the child's acquisition of control is that behavior is kept within certain limits which are common to the whole culture. Clearly, children who control their own thinking to the greatest degree will display the highest levels of stereotypy, and will be scarcely, if at all, capable of creative thinking. Conversely, creativity will be facilitated by a not too scrupulous adherence to the cultural rules of the game, and by the consequent retention of willingness to express impulses, even when the "right" thing to do is to control them.

Freud (1910) also linked creativity with impulse expression. During infancy, strong pressures are brought to bear on children to suppress natural urges and express them only in desirable ways and at the desirable time — for example, during toilet training. Two outcomes of these pressures are possible; children may internalize parental injunctions, thus acquiring the ability to control their own impulses in a socially approved way, or they may either fail to internalize the external edicts or even deliberately reject them. The first kind of child gets the payoff of social approval through a knowledge of the rules relevant to the culture, but this is achieved at the expense of impulse suppression. The second kind of child fails to learn the rules of the game (or perhaps, learns them, but refuses to be bound by them). In this case, behavior is likely to be nonconformist, original and independent, but this is achieved at the expense of having to resist the culture's pressures to conform, and of the consequent probability of being censured for unconventionality. Barron (1955) has linked the less controlled personality directly to creativity by concluding that what he called "originality" is intimately related to personality traits like rebelliousness, disorderliness and independence of judgement.

In a later study, Barron (1963) showed that highly creative officers in the US Air Force scored significantly higher on tests of impulsivity than did their less creative colleagues. Barron's linking of creativity with impulsivity has been supported by other empirical evidence. For example, both MacKinnon (1962) and Garwood (1964) reported findings which showed that highly creative individuals tended to suppress their own impulses markedly less than did noncreative individuals. Tyson too (1966) has linked creativity to personality traits such as "independence, originality, openness, intuitiveness, playfulness, and a sense of destiny."

However, probably the most convincing demonstration of the relationship between creativity and control was made by Hudson (1966). He pointed out that even highly convergent individuals can be induced to behave in divergent ways by inviting them to pretend that they are artists or Bohemians, or by getting them under the influence of alcohol. In other words, convergent thinkers are capable of making responses of a divergent kind, if only they can be persuaded to let themselves go. There are some people who keep themselves well under control and regulate themselves carefully, in keeping with what is the culturally approved way of doing things. Conversely, there are people who operate in a much bolder way. They are not afraid to give vent to their impulses and do not keep themselves under such strict control. Encouragement of creativity thus requires a good deal more than simply fostering the ability to think divergently. Creative children need to believe that it is good to behave divergently and to have confidence that creative behavior will be welcomed and valued by others. Whether or not creative children manifest their creativity thus depends upon cultural values, group influences and the availability of appropriate social supports. The problem is that youngsters may learn that creativity is not welcomed by other people, especially their teachers and peers; they may come to accept this value judgement, and to reject creativity themselves, and even come to regard themselves as peculiar or as outsiders.

Social rejection of creativity in the classroom may be expressed in the form of sarcastic or humiliating remarks, actual punishment, exclusion of the child perceived as deviant from the circle of favored pupils, exclusion from important peer groups, even rejections as "weird" or "crazy," namecalling, teasing or downright bullying. The result can be that behavior is frozen into set forms. One task for teachers is that of preventing such freezing, or of unfreezing blocked potentials, a task which may well be as important as promoting the growth of divergent thinking abilities. Hare (1982, p. 158) referred to this as "warming up" students in order to get ideas flowing. The teacher and classmates have a crucial role in establishing the social conditions which facilitate the emergence of creative behavior in the classroom: *recognizing* (accepting and acknowledging) the value of creative behavior; *consolidating* (strengthening, expressing in an understandable way, tidying up) creative responses; *reflecting* (exploring limits, showing further applications, testing for weaknesses) creative responses, and finally *communicating* them (passing on to others).

Creativity and play

One characteristic of highly divergent individuals which has struck many observers is their "playfulness." They may, for example, be particularly good at making up humorous story titles, as was the case with the highly creative high school students studied by Getzels and Jackson (1962). They often display a particularly lively sense of humor, and are frequently unusually alert to the funny side of life and especially good at making up humorous responses to tests. So marked is the preference for humor among highly divergent people that Weisberg and Springer (1961) described it as one of the best discriminators between the most and least divergent people whom they studied.

Hudson (1963) explained the significantly lower frequency of humorous responses among convergers than among divergers by attributing it to a general tendency on their part to "compartmentalize" experience. The converger is a person who "achieves a sense of security by restricting himself to a relatively narrow range of impersonal, technical topics" (1963, p. 913). According to psychoanalytic theory (see, for instance, Stern and Stern, 1984, who summarized the importance of play in a number of psychoanalytic models of creativity, including those of Freud, Kris and Kubie), creative individuals are able to relax strict ego control and admit primary process materials into consciousness. Creative people's playfulness may also manifest itself in the ability to "play" with the meanings of words so that they see new aspects to them which have not previously been seen (Gordon, 1961). They may "play" with the meanings of fundamental laws and principles and eventually arrive at unusual solutions to problems, or they may "play" with common objects until they see implications which have not previously been noticed. What such play involves, essentially, is the capacity to look at the familiar in a new light, and to break the set imposed by the stereotypical meaning of any particular stimulus (Gabriel, 1976). Many creative people, among them Einstein (Gordon, 1961, p. 41), have made this point about their own creativity.

Creativity and madness

Associated with the view of creativity as somehow deviant is the idea that it is basically abnormal, or at least associated with abnormality. Nearly a century ago, Lombroso (1891) presented data purporting to show that genius is closely allied to madness; indeed the relationship of creativity to madness is one of psychology's classical issues. Cropley and Sikand (1973) pointed out that the relevant literature seems to suggest that creative people do indeed share certain characteristics with schizophrenics. Their own data showed that there were certain cognitive similarities between a group of creative architects, writers, musicians and the like, and a group of schizophrenic patients. These similarities, which were characterized by an ability to see connections between elements of experience which would normally be regarded as separate, distinguished both groups from "normals" (i.e., people who were neither creative nor schizophrenic).

More recently Jamison (see Holden, 1987) has been reported as having obtained findings on emotional disturbances in 47 British artists and writers who had all either won major awards or were members of the Royal Academy of Arts. She found that 18 had been treated for manic-depressive conditions, a figure six times as high as would be expected in the general populace. In particular, Jamison argued that mood "highs" are essential for creativity; "highs" are characterized by high levels of motivation and self-confidence (affective variables), as well as by fluency in thinking (cognition). Jamison sees the key as lying in the area of faith in oneself, willingness to make the necessary effort, etc., a conclusion closely related to that of Cropley and Sikand. Byron, Shelley, Coleridge and Poe were apparently able to work creatively only when their mood was so elevated that they had the drive and self-confidence needed for creative production. At the same time, it is significant, when considering the position of creative people in our society, to note that it is at precisely these times that they were labeled abnormal.

In reviewing several studies in the area, Holden (1987) concluded that there is now evidence that moderate degrees of mood disturbance are actually favorable for the emergence of creativity. One possible cause and effect relationship is that mood disturbance permits "disinhibition" (being able to "let go") or "absorption" (intense concentration on a task). In terms of the qualitative theory of creativity already outlined earlier (p. 66) disinhibition would permit the necessary creative reorganizations. The importance of intense task commitment has also already been discussed. On the other hand, the connection may not be causal in nature at all: for instance, it is possible that wide mood swings, on the one hand, and rich imagination and willingness to let go, on the other, both result from a common cause, without themselves causing one another. Such a common cause could be what Holden calls "emotional reactivity" (p. 10) — some people react unusually strongly to external stimuli as well as internal mood signals, possibly as a result of possessing a particularly labile or "fine tuned" (Andreasen, 1987) nervous system. Although this may result in clinical mood disturbances in some people at some times, it can also facilitate letting down cognitive, motivational, personal or even social barriers which normally block creativity.

In the study already mentioned, Cropley and Sikand (1973) found that despite the cognitive similarities between schizophrenics and creatives, there were substantial noncognitive differences between the two groups: the creative individuals tended to be excited by unusual associations in their own thinking and tried to build upon them, whereas the schizophrenics were frightened by them, and tried to avoid them. Cropley and Sikand concluded that the relationship between creativity and psychological disturbance is thus more a matter of motivation than of "different" thinking. This view has recently been supported by Andreasen (1987) who showed that the high proportion of mental illness among a group of writers was related to mood disturbances, and particularly to the euphoric phase of manic-depressive illness.

Closing remarks

The concept of "creativity" leads to a broadening of the notion of academic excellence encompassing both high intelligence and high creativity. There is nothing inherently or automatically antagonistic about intelligence and creativity: Laycock (1979, p. 56) rightly cautioned against "assuming that high scoring [IQ] children must necessarily be rigid and unimaginative or that creative children will be rather stupid in mundane intellectual activities." What is needed however is to overcome any tendency to overestimate the importance of either creativity or intelligence at the expense of the other, if we are to encourage the development of true academic excellence.

It is not the purpose of this chapter to imply that any and all instances of unusual humor, impulsive behavior, nonconformity and the like are necessarily signs of creativity, or that this kind of behavior is in some way superior. Obviously, much humor is merely puerile, and excessive impulse expression is infantile; the criteria of relevance and effectiveness must always be kept in mind. Unfortunately it is often difficult, for instance in the classroom, to distinguish between creativity and naughtiness, lack of discipline, unruliness or even sheer rebelliousness. Consequently, and unfortunately, the personal properties which lead to creativity, or which at least frequently accompany it, are often interpreted negatively by creative children themselves, as well as by teachers and parents. There is thus a readiness to try to stamp out any tendency to be divergent, and for many creative people themselves to accept that they ought to conform. Since academic excellence requires unconventional, in addition to conventional, thinking, its growth calls for the tolerance, and indeed the promotion, of a willingness to diverge. For these reasons, the present chapter has emphasized not only the cognitive aspects of the creative component of academic excellence, but also the importance of personality, motivation, self-image and similar noncognitive factors. These factors will be taken up again in chapters on promoting creativity.

5

Measuring Creativity

The broadening of the concept of giftedness by incorporating creativity into its definition, as outlined in the previous chapter, is now widely accepted (see, for instance, Renzulli, 1986, and Sternberg, 1985, for discussions from different points of view). However, capturing the essence of creativity and defining behavioral indicators which give evidence of creative potential has proved difficult; obviously, no indicators are needed in the case of people already recognized by virtue of their creative achievements, but very few school children belong to this group. Furthermore, we are concerned here not so much with after the fact certifying of acknowledged creativity, but with fostering its development and emergence in cases where this might otherwise not happen. This task lies somewhere beyond the boundaries of conventional standardized tests, since creative thinking requires innovation and novelty (which are inherently difficult to express in standardized forms), as well as combining, more strongly than is the case with conventional thinking, cognitive with affective and social components. Despite this, a variety of assessment procedures has been developed, some of them quite strongly resembling conventional abilities tests in certain respects, although there are also striking differences, as will be shown in the next section.

Creativity tests

As might be expected, increasing interest in creativity saw the emergence of a new kind of test, a test of "creativity." Strictly speaking, such tests had already existed for many years. Binet himself had suggested that interpretations of inkblots could be used to assess creativity and, as Barron and Harrington (1981) pointed out, there was "a proliferation of studies" by creativity investigators prior to 1915, adopting Binet's open-ended multiple solution format. Later, Simpson (1922) tried to design alternatives to existing tests which measured creativity; Andrews (1930) designed tests of "imagination;" McCloy and Meier (1931) tested "recreative imagination;" Thurstone employed tests of "Word Fluency" and "Ideational Fluency" in the

1940s; and Welch (1946) tested subjects' ability to combine items in novel ways.

Such tests had largely fallen into disuse, and were exerting little influence at the time of Guilford's address. Some psychologists (including Guilford himself) thus began to construct tests of divergent thinking — usually called "creativity" tests, although the appropriateness of this label will be discussed later in this chapter. The best known among this flood of tests in the 1950s and 1960s were the "Alternative Uses" test, the "Product Improvement" test, and a revived "Consequences" test, seen in their most highly developed form in the work of Torrance and associates. All of these tests were later incorporated into the battery of "creativity" tests published by Torrance (1966), nowadays referred to as the "Torrance Tests of Creative Thinking" (TTCT). An often cited "creativity" test of the same period was the "Remote Associations Test" (Mednick, 1962), although this has since been criticized on the grounds that it is really a test of convergent thinking. The other influential set of creativity tests to appear during this period was that of Wallach and Kogan (1965), whose major contribution was perhaps their emphasis on a gamelike atmosphere, and the absence of time limits in the testing procedure. Since these tests are less well known than the more traditional "intelligence" tests, we will deal with them at some length here.

Scoring creativity tests

The crucial difference between the creativity tests outlined above and conventional intelligence tests is the way in which they are scored. In general, responses to creativity tests are assessed in one of two ways: either the sheer number of responses to some open-ended item is counted, or else an assessment of the quality of these responses is made. Simply tallying the number of responses (for instance to the instruction: "Write down as many interesting and unusual uses as you can think of for a tin can") constitutes a measure of *Fluency*. According to this criterion, the responses "Use it as a kettle," and "Boil water in it," would receive two points, since they constitute two separate answers. By contrast, scoring for quality of responses involves approaches such as assessing how many shifts of category are contained in a list of answers. This is referred to as scoring for *Flexibility*. According to this criterion, the two answers given above would receive only a single point for Flexibility, since they involve only a single main idea (the tin can as a container of liquid which is to be heated). The responses "Use it as a kettle," and "Throw it at an enemy," by contrast, would receive two points for Flexibility (as well as for Fluency), since two distinct categories (container, weapon) are contained in the answer. A further refinement of quality scoring is to give weights to answers, according to how uncommon they are in the group of children to which a particular youngster belongs. Responses which are given by only a few members of the group are rated as "original" and receive a weight for *Originality*. Other scoring possibilities include assessing the degree of *Elaboration* of responses. "use the tin can as a kettle" obviously being a less elaborated response than "Seal any possible leaks with solder, fit a handle so that you don't burn your fingers, then use it as a kettle. Remember to make a lip so that the water pours out well."

Wallach and Kogan departed from the most common assessment procedures to some degree by reducing the scoring to two dimensions — number of responses, on the one hand, and "uniqueness" on the other. A unique response is defined as one which only a single child in a given group of subjects gives to a particular item.

Recent approaches

A very recent creativity test is that of Urban and Jellen (1986). This test, the "Test for Creative Thinking — Drawing Production (TCT-DP)," differs from the tests of Torrance, Guilford and Wallach and Kogan; scores are derived not from the statistical uncommonness of verbal or figural assocations, but from what the authors call "image production." Although respondents are asked to complete incomplete figures, as in several other tests, scoring of responses is based not on unusualness of the figures created but on nine dimensions derived from Gestalt psychology: these include, for instance, "boundary breaking," "production of new elements" and "humor." A major difference between this approach and those discussed earlier in this section is thus that the TCT-DP is based on a theory of the nature of creative thinking, and that scoring procedures derive from this theory rather than simply from the statistical characteristics of answers.

A final approach to creativity testing which can be mentioned here is that of Facaoaru (e.g., Facaoaru and Bittner, 1986). Her basic argument is that the successful carrying out of real life activities requiring creativity depends on a combination of divergent and convergent processes. For this reason, a "two track" testing procedure is needed, which assesses the "area of overlap" between the two kinds of thinking. The "Divergent–Convergent Problem Solving Processes Scale" assesses among others, "goal directed divergent thinking," "flexibility" and "task commitment."

Some criticisms of creativity tests

Some of the main criticisms of creativity tests have been that (a) different creativity tests measure different things; (b) the tests tend to measure much the same trait as conventional IQ tests; and (c) assessed performance is, in any case, too dependent on mere number of responses. A practical complaint is that it is extremely time consuming to score creativity tests for anything except fluency. Scoring for flexibility presents a certain amount of difficulty, while scoring for originality (described by Torrance, Tan and Allman, 1970, as the "essence" of creativity) is extremely laborious — it is first necessary to check every response of each subject and record its frequency of occurrence in the group as a whole; this frequency is then converted to a percentage of subjects who gave the particular response, and a weight is assigned on the basis of that percentage. Less common responses (those given by a low percentage of subjects) receive the greatest weight, because they are deemed to be original.

A technical problem which not infrequently arises is that of deciding when a response is highly original and when it is totally bizarre. It is debatable, for instance, whether the answer given to the riddle below can be regarded as creative.

> Question: "Why is a mad dog like a can of condensed milk?"
> Answer: "Neither can ride a bike."

Even in the relatively straightforward matter of assessing fluency by simply summing the number of answers, the treatment of bizarre responses causes problems. Should a person who makes a large number of nonsensical or irrational responses be given a high score? Similarly, there is the difficulty of deciding if responses are merely repetitions. Obviously, if a person wrote down the same answer 50 times it would be absurd to award 50 points and, indeed, experience shows that people do repeat some responses, probably from sheer forgetfulness in most cases. However, scorers are faced with the problem of deciding what constitutes a repetition; would "a banana" and "a big banana" be two different responses or a repetition? When decisions are left to the discretion of scorers, different scorers might not agree with each other, while it is also possible that an extremely creative subject might be penalized for simply being too original and innovative for the scorers to comprehend!

Development of standardized scoring procedures for creativity tests is inevitably difficult. Since a major idea underlying creativity tests is that there are no prespecified answers, it is logically impossible to develop lists of acceptable answers which are so highly original that they have never before been made. Hence, in principle there ought to be no universal norms, which would mean that it is impossible to administer a creativity test to a single student and calculated "Creativity Quotient" based on data from a nationwide standardization sample, as is done in the case of intelligence. An answer which receives a high score in one context might receive a low score in another, depending on the particular group of subjects and scorers involved; nonetheless reasonably high correlations between judges have been obtained in various studies cited by Torrance (1966). He has also provided lists of common and therefore unoriginal responses, as well as of known but uncommon (therefore moderately original) responses, arguing that all others are highly original.

Creativity tests have also been subject to criticisms of a different kind. These focus on the content of the tests and the kinds of situation in which they are administered. As Dannenberg (1975) has pointed out, the tests are extremely simple when compared with what people usually have in mind when they talk about "creativity." Is the ability to draw diagrams incorporating circles and then think up novel names for them really connected with the thought processes which made da Vinci or Einstein famous? It has further been argued that the tests are banal and incapable of arousing interest; the intrinsic motivation which is said to be so important in creativity does not seem to be aroused by looking at, say, a few simple lines on a page and trying to interpret them in a fanciful manner. It is tempting to speculate that it would be the most highly creative people who would find the tests least stimulating. Torrance himself has counseled against giving his tests twice to the same subjects, because of different levels of motivation upon retesting. Practical experience indicates however, that although many people do reject the tests on these kinds of grounds, many other subjects in research projects have found them to be exciting, stimulating, even fascinating.

Dannenberg suggested that tests bearing upon real life questions would be better measures of creativity. Such tests could ask subjects to attempt to provide creative solutions to genuine problems in science, engineering, art, medicine, etc.; for example, how to eliminate worldwide dependence on oil or how to eliminate a certain disease. However, the problems of scoring, maintaining objectivity, achieving comparability of results from different groups of subjects (some, but not all, of whom might have had specific training in Creative Problem Solving), would be even greater than is the case with existing tests. Thus, although superficially attractive, real-life-oriented tests do not seem to have practical potential for immediate general use.

Technical issues concerning creativity tests

Early studies such as those of Mackler (1962) and Wodtke (1964) concluded that the reliabilities of the Guilford and Torrance tests were unsatisfactorily low. Dewing (1970) administered the Circles and Uses tests on two occasions six weeks apart, and obtained reliabilities of 0.68

for fluency and 0.54 for originality on the Circles test, and 0.51 and 0.39 respectively for the Uses test. Cropley and Clapson (1971) calculated reliabilities over several years for boys and girls separately, for the same tests, and obtained coefficients ranging from 0.33 to 0.58. In a 10-year longitudinal study, Howieson (1981) reported reliabilities for the TTCT ranging from 0.15 to 0.37, according to sex and method of scoring. A tally of the test–retest reliabilities quoted in the manual for the TTCT (1966) is more optimistic, yielding a median value of 0.68. By contrast, Wallach and Kogan (1965) reported reliabilities in excess of 0.90 for their tests, and this has been confirmed by Cropley and Maslany (1969) and by Kogan and Pankove (1972).

The data thus seem to suggest that although the Wallach–Kogan tests have high reliabilities, the Guilford and Torrance tests are seriously defective in this respect. At the same time, it should be borne in mind that reliabilities in the vicinity of 0.50 are similar to many of those reported for the constituent subtests of accepted intelligence tests. Combining scores on several creativity tests in the same way as is done with intelligence test batteries such as the Wechsler scales thus seems likely to yield a satisfactorily reliable composite score. Such a procedure however raises a new problem, i.e., just what does such a composite score represent? Wallach (1985) has emphasized that creativity is domain specific, i.e., a person who is highly creative in, for instance, art might not be especially creative in science or in verbal expression. At a more technical level, Feldman (1980a) has pointed out that the combination of different tests may yield more reliable measures which have, however, no psychological meaning.

Perhaps educators themselves are still too conditioned to think convergently in terms of tests which possess high reliability, and which are standardized with reference to a large national sample. One of the incidental byproducts of the microcomputer revolution is the ease with which tests can be standardized locally, with almost inevitably beneficial effects. Not only is their local validity (i.e., within the school, or local school district) improved, but reliability, which increases when the number of items is increased, can be enhanced by administering extended locally produced tests over several sessions. McLeod has produced an informal test of associational fluency, scored essentially according to the number of words that "go with" eight stimulus words which the child can produce in 15 minutes. A reliability coefficient of about 0.80 was obtained, which could be further increased by using additional stimulus words.

The effect of administration conditions

Krause (1977) has made the important point that the results of investigations into both the reliability and the validity of creativity tests will be affected by the conditions of administration, such as group vs individual testing, the degree of time pressure and similar factors. Hattie (1977, 1980) compared the effect of administering the Torrance and the Wallach and Kogan creativity tests under three different conditions: (a) untimed, gamelike; (b) conventional, testlike; and (c) administration under testlike conditions on two adjacent days, using the second test as the predictor. He found that administering creativity tests under different conditions leads to substantial differences in performance, and his conclusion (1980, p. 87) was that the "conventional test-like condition seems optimal." Cropley (1972a) has shown that a somewhat different pattern of responses emerges under timed and untimed conditions. He administered Guilford–Torrance tests to students under timed conditions, noted what they had done, then permitted them to continue working for as long as they liked. It was found that some children produced original responses only after a lengthy warm-up period, some produced them only in the first few minutes, while some were original right from the start, and continued to be original over a long period. Krause pointed out that the best conditions may differ from age to age; for example, formal group administration might inhibit a 10-year-old but help a 15-year-old.

Interwoven with the problem of reliability of creativity tests is that of their validity. Do they measure creativity? A major problem in answering this question is that of establishing a criterion, i.e., of achieving clear agreement as to what creativity actually is. Just what it is that is regarded as creative varies not only from society to society, but from person to person in a given society, and even from time to time within the same society. In Victorian England it was deemed necessary to expurgate Shakespeare's works, while the 19th century French mathematician Galois left behind a body of writings which were not understood until years after his death. Furthermore, creativity may take many forms: it may even manifest itself in the capacity to energize and crystallize creative effort in others, rather than to produce creative solutions oneself (Barron, 1969). Creativity occurs in a wide variety of fields (Necka, 1986), so that it is necessary to take account of creativity in science, mathematics, engineering and similar fields (scientific/technological creativity), as well as in art, drama, literature and music (artistic creativity). Land's invention of the Polaroid camera and Pascal's mathematical equations represents creativity, just as much as did the painting of the *Mona Lisa*. Manifestations of creativity in an individual person may, however, be domain specific (Wallach, 1985), so that tests may fail to tap creativity, or criteria from other domains may fail to confirm test scores.

The problem of developing a criterion of creativity is further confounded by the intrusion of moral issues. For example, is it creative to apply the principles of electronics in a new and original way in order to develop a device for neutralizing burglar alarms? Would a burglar who achieved this be as creative as an engineer who developed a foolproof burglar alarm. Vernon (1979) confirmed the importance of values and ethics in identifying creativity.

Creativity and intelligence

One major and obvious approach to establishing creativity as a separate ability which is not sufficiently emphasized by conventional intelligence tests has been to compare scores on creativity tests with those on intelligence tests. The purpose has been to show that creativity tests sort people out in a way which differs from that which results when IQs alone are used: this would show that the two kinds of test measure, to some extent at least, something different. It has long been held (e.g., Torrance, 1959) that the selection of talented individuals purely on the basis of IQ scores misses a substantial group of clever people, and it has been suggested that many of these show outstanding creativity. This view has been strengthened by findings, summarized for instance by Wallach (1985), that IQ scores are an inadequate predictor of later outstanding achievements.

When creativity tests and intelligence tests are administered to a group of subjects, and the correlations between each pair of tests computed, some interesting findings emerge. If "creativity" and "intelligence" are different, homogeneous, measurable commodities, then it is reasonable to expect that there will be: (a) relatively high intercorrelations between each pair of intelligence tests; (b) relatively high intercorrelations between each pair of creativity tests; and (c) relatively low intercorrelations between intelligence tests and creativity tests. Research findings, however, have not been at all clear-cut. Cline, Richards and Abe (1962) reported that creativity tests correlated about 0.22 with each other, but about 0.33 with intelligence tests. Torrance has suggested that the correlation of (verbal) intelligence with verbal creativity is about 0.25, while the correlation with figural creativity is about 0.06 (1966, pp. 82f). Other reported correlations between IQ and creativity have shown considerable variability, and have generally been at least as high as the correlation between verbal and nonverbal IQ tests, i.e., between 0.30 and 0.75 (Hasan and Butcher, 1966: Yamamoto, 1965). Studies in Germany (Grote et al., 1969; Krause, 1972) have reported correlations of 0.48 and 0.44, respectively, between composite intelligence scores and composite creativity scores obtained by summing Wallach–Kogan test scores. On the basis of these studies, Krause concluded that creativity tests correlate with intelligence tests as highly as they do with each other. In a later study (Krause, 1977), however, he obtained much lower correlations. Wallach and Kogan (1965) too, using derivatives of earlier creativity tests, found low correlations between creativity and intelligence, a finding which was supported by Cropley and Maslany (1969). Thus, the position is not at all clear, and is well summed up in a report by the Educational Research Service (ERS, 1975):

> Theories have been advanced to the effect that intelligence and creativity are completely positively correlated, somewhat positively correlated, or totally unrelated.

Attenuation

One of the problems that makes it difficult to intepret correlations between creativity test scores and intelligence test scores arises from the fact that many studies do not report the range of ability of the subjects tested. Many educators assume that a correlation coefficient is some sort of constant, independent of the range of scores obtained by the subjects. This is not so, the computed correlation being affected by "attenuation," i.e., the degree to which the ability range is restricted. Readers who might not be statistics oriented can probably get some idea of the phenomenon of attenuation by considering an analogy from basketball. Suppose you were asked to estimate the correlation between people's physical height and ability to score at basketball. If you think in terms of the whole population from four-foot midgets to seven-foot giants, the correlation would be positive and highly significant — assuming other things, such as training, to be equal — because very tall people enjoy an advantage over the very small in this particular domain. But if the population under consideration consisted of people between 6 feet 6 inches and 6 feet 10 inches or so, your answer would probably be that the correlation would be much less, or even insignificant. The reason is that in the very tall population one of the variables — height — has been attenuated. Correspondingly, if a study into the relationship between measured intelligence and creativity tested children within a restricted range of intelligence, e.g., only those with IQ over 120, the obtained correlation coefficient might be artificially depressed. Yamamoto (1965), for instance, reported a correlation as high as 0.88 between creativity and intelligence, after correcting for restriction of range and test unreliability.

Creativity scores and ratings of creativity

Other studies of the validity of tests of creativity have involved asking judges to rate subjects on the trait of creativity and having them compare test scores with such ratings. An early example is Barron's research into the creativity of Air Force officers (1955). However, Gergen and Berger (1965) cast serious doubt on the usefulness of rater studies by showing that ratings of the creativity shown in paintings were related to the prestige of the persons said to have produced the paintings, as well as to the raters' beliefs concerning how much time and trouble had been expended on the paintings. A factor analytic study by Skager, Schultz and Klein (1965) showed that creativity is judged along several dimensions, so that it is also fair to say that creativity may well mean different things to different judges. In two independent studies, McLeod (1983) administered a battery of intelligence tests, creativity tests and rating scales (Renzulli and Smith, 1977) to the complete Grade 5 and Grade 6 population of two Canadian schools. The correlations between creativity as measured by TTCT and teacher ratings of creativity were totally insignificant, at about 0.10. Harrington, Block and Block (1983) also found that teachers' ratings of creativity correlated poorly with scores on creativity tests.

A related approach has been to define certain areas as creative, and to examine correlations between test scores and achievement in these areas. Vaughan (1971) showed that creativity test scores correlated significantly with musical ability. Singer and Whiton (1971) reported a similar result for test scores and ratings of the creativity of children's drawings. Wallbrown and Huelsman (1975) obtained a significant correlation between tests and the creativity of 10-year-olds' clay models, while Amabile (1983) and Milgram (1983) reported similar findings for creative writing and scientific creativity of children.

Longitudinal studies of the validity of creativity tests

To demonstrate convincingly that so-called "creativity" tests really do measure human creativity, it would be necessary to show that they predict not merely achievement on other tests, but also socially valuable creative behavior. The real life behavior of groups of people previously identified as high scorers on creativity tests needs to be examined, to ascertain whether they have subsequently become creative in the real world, i.e., a study paralleling Terman's study of children with high IQs. Evidence that creativity tests are capable of identifying people who later follow creative pursuits or who succeed in creative achievements would be more compelling than the kinds of study that have been cited so far. The study of Wallach and Wing (1969) is very interesting in this regard. They related students' scores on creativity tests administered on admission to college to what were termed "non-academic talented accomplishments" during the high school years. The criterion data on out of school achievements were derived from a self-administered questionnaire asking for information about leadership activities,

activities in art, music, etc., and showed that nonacademic accomplishments, in contrast to academic achievements, were not related to IQ. However, the major finding was that high scorers on the creativity tests had obtained significantly higher scores for out of school achievement in the areas of creativity studied. Despite procedural criticisms of Wallach and Wing (Cropley, 1972b; Maslany, 1973), for instance because the demonstrated relationships were *post hoc* rather than predictive (i.e., the predictor scores were obtained after the criterion accomplishments had been achieved), the study suggests that the Wallach-Kogan creativity tests may be related to real life achievements of a kind which are not predicted by IQ scores.

Some studies of the long-term predictive validity of creativity tests have used the earlier Torrance/Guilford tests. Torrance (1969) calculated multiple correlations between three indices of creativity and a composite criterion involving the writing of books, publishing of music and similar activities, for a sample of 43 high school seniors contacted seven years after high school graduation. He reported multiple correlations of 0.50, 0.46, and 0.51 between each of three creativity predictors and a criterion battery. In a second study, Torrance, Tan and Allman (1970) reported that the product-moment correlation between originality scores and a composite measure of creative classroom teaching behaviors, measured six years after the administration of the creativity test, was 0.62. Still later, Torrance (1980b) reported on a study extending over 22 years, and concluded that creativity tests had succeeded in identifying a group of specially endowed people. Thus, there are some grounds for believing that creativity test scores on a variety of measures can make statistically significant predictions of later, real life activities of a creative kind.

Cropley (1972b) carried out a relevant longitudinal study, full details of which have been published elsewhere. In 1964, a battery of Torrance/Guilford creativity tests was administered to students in a junior high school and scored only for originality. Subsequently, two follow-up studies were carried out with the same group of students, one after five years, the other after seven years. In the first study, the students completed a questionnaire giving information about their nonacademic talented accomplishments during the year immediately preceding the retesting (i.e., the fifth year since the original administration of the creativity tests), nonacademic talent being assessed in four of the areas suggested by Wallach and Wing — art, drama, literature and music.

The relationship between the predictor battery and the criterion battery was then tested for males and females separately, and for the combined sample. In the case of the boys, a marginally significant canonical correlation of 0.52 was obtained $<0.05<p<0.06$ whereas for the girls, the correlation of 0.46 was not statistically significant. For the full sample, there was a statistically significant correlation of 0.51. When IQ was added to the predictor battery, the canonical correlations rose to 0.62 for the boys ($p < 0.05$) and to 0.49 (not significant) for the girls. In other words, the addition of IQ to the predictor battery improved prediction of nonacademic talented accomplishments only slightly.

These findings were cautiously encouraging. However, the results of the seven year follow-up conducted by Maslany (1973) were less optimistic. A preliminary finding was that the conventional IQ score correlated significantly with only one area of creative achievement — music. In view of the inability of IQs to predict creative achievement, Maslany attempted to demonstrate the value of creativity tests by adding creativity scores to IQ as a predictor, and ascertaining whether improved prediction of creative achievement resulted. In fact, this procedure did not significantly improve prediction.

In a more recent study, Howieson (1981) reported the by now familiar pattern of somewhat conflicting results. He found that there was a strong relationship between scores on the TTCT and nonacademic talented accomplishments 10 years later in the case of boys, but not for girls. This finding is similar to Cropley's (1972b) result, and is also consistent with his earlier finding (1967a) that divergent thinking abilities were more highly differentiated among 12–13-year-old boys than among girls of similar age. Vernon (1979) like Maslany, found that creativity tests did not greatly improve prediction of creativity made solely on the basis of IQs. A study by Hocevar (1980) went so far as to conclude that divergent thinking tests are no better than conventional intelligence tests in predicting creativity. Some studies of real life achievement therefore, have cast doubt on the predictive validity of creativity tests. As Tannenbaum (1979, p. 9) put it: "The question of whether instruments for assessing creativity can locate otherwise undiscoverable talent has never been fully settled."

Wallach (1985) has offered a plausible explanation of the apparently contradictory results outlined in preceding sections. The more the tests concentrate on a specific area of creativity (for instance musical, artistic, mathematical, etc.) and the more the criteria come from the same area, the higher the validity of the tests. By contrast, tests aimed at measuring a global dimension of creativity permit only moderate or low predictions of achievement.

What do creativity tests measure?

Evidence concerning the validity of creativity tests is thus equivocal. What then, do they measure? This question was posed by Wallach

(1970) who answered it by reviewing the literature in the area. He showed that two apparently contradictory sets of findings regularly appear. At one extreme are findings reporting high internal consistency within batteries of creativity tests and low cross correlations with IQ tests. At the other extreme are studies reporting relatively low correlations among creativity tests and substantial correlations between creativity tests and conventional IQs. By the time of the Wallach review, a sufficient number of studies of both kinds was in existence to permit an analysis of what is common to the two groups. He concluded (p. 1223) that the relatively unique feature of creativity tests, which distinguishes some of them from convergent thinking tests, is an emphasis on ideational fluency. Where mere verbal knowledge or verbal cleverness is emphasized, the tests correlate with conventional intelligence tests. Where ideational fluency is emphasized, they do not. Stress on the importance of ideational fluency is consistent with Guilford's original description of the mental abilities which make up divergent thinking. Four of the eight divergent productive abilities he listed were in the fluency domain: "Word fluency," "Associational fluency," "Ideational fluency" and "Expressive fluency."

Unfortunately, as Vernon (1964b) pointed out, correlations among the various measures derived from "creativity" tests, e.g., fluency, flexibility, originality, are so high that the enormous expenditure of energy already mentioned in deriving scores such as "originality" scarcely seems worth the effort, when essentially the same ranking of students can be obtained by simply counting their responses. In other words, as Hocevar (1980) put it, there is a danger that many creativity tests "do not reliably measure anything more than fluency."

In view of the material surveyed in the present chapter, it is necessary to ask if so-called "creativity" tests really measure creativity, in the sense in which the term is generally understood. According to Thorndike (1966), it is "difficult to pull together a coherent picture of the validity" of creativity tests, and although there is a great deal of published evidence, it is weak. Even harsh critics of the value of divergent thinking measures such as Cronbach (1968) have conceded, however, that they attempt to sample an aspect of human intellectual functioning which is at least to a degree neglected by conventional tests. More recently, other researchers such as Feldman (1980b), Keating (1983), Kogan (1983) and Perkins (1981), who have carried out intensive reviews of the evidence, have come to a similar conclusion.

Throughout the present chapter, this elusive aspect has been referred to as "creativity," and the tests as "creativity tests." Despite doubts about the degree of overlap between creativity, as measured by "creativity" (divergent thinking) tests, and creativity as manifested by Leonardo da Vinci, Isaac Newton or William Shakespeare, a refusal to use the term "creativity tests" would be excessively pedantic. Regardless of the name given to the tests, they draw attention to one extremely important point: there is a difference between ways of intellectual functioning which are narrow, conventional, limited and essentially reproductive, and ways which involve branching out, seeing possibilities, making novel suggestions or taking a chance on an idea.

Other ways of identifying creativity

Hocevar (1981) has accurately observed that "the impact of the Guilford tradition," which rests on the assumption that test-measured divergent thinking is somehow linked to creativity, has had a considerable impact on the study of creativity. One of these effects has been to establish the idea that creativity is best measured by means of divergent thinking tests. However, Hocevar further contends that indirect methods of identifying creativity (i.e., by tests) have little to do with the real criteria of creativity, and advocates more direct approaches.

Creative products

Among more direct methods of detecting creativity have been important and interesting studies that have involved investigations focusing on people who have actually produced creative products. These studies include Freud's (1910) study of Leonardo, Rossman's (1931) study of patent holders, Roe's (1963) study of famous scientists and mathematicians, Drevdahl and Cattell's (1958) study of successful artists and writers, Cropley and Sikand's (1973) study of artists, sculptors, architects and writers, and MacKinnon's (1983) study of architects who were rated by their peers as highly creative. These investigations, in which creativity was largely determined by expert or peer group ratings, have shed considerable light on the personal characteristics of creative people, and have made a contribution to the development of nontest procedures for identifying creative potential. Wallach and Wing (1969) and Cropley (1972b) attempted to examine real life creativity in young people with the help of data on "nonacademic talented accomplishments," for example writing a book, winning a science prize, being elected to office, having a piece of music performed, etc. From a practical point of view, this approach is important, since it can provide valuable indicators for programs aimed at fostering children's creativity.

Creative traits and interests

A number of approaches exist for gaining a picture of the creativity of individuals which rely on neither tests nor actual creative achievements. Among these are the use of rating scales for detecting the presence of personal traits whose presence enhances the likelihood of creativity (see Chapter 4): these include curiosity, wit, shrewdness, independence, persistence, unconventionality, self-confidence, etc. Such ratings may be carried out by "experts," by teachers, by parents, or even by peers. They may also take the form of self-ratings. The "Scale for Rating the Behavioral Characteristics of Superior Students" (Renzulli, Hartmann and Callahan, 1971) is an example of a teacher rating scale which includes a "creativity" subscale. The "Quest Student Nomination Questionnaire" (Renzulli, Reis and Smith, 1981) has creativity as one of its components, and is filled out by peers. The "Things My Child Likes to Do" scale for parents (Renzulli, Reis and Smith, 1981) stresses originality, flexibility and creativity. An example of a self-rating scale is the "Gifted Inventory for Finding Talent" (GIFT) (Rimm and Davis, 1980). Children indicate the degree of development of characteristics such as flexibility, curiosity, independence and perseverance. A fuller review of a number of instruments focusing on personal characteristics as indicators of creative potential is to be found in Barron and Harrington (1981).

Another approach is to look at children's interests. Renzulli's (1977) "Interest-a-Lyzer" is an open ended questionnaire which is in part an autobiographical report of 35 creative activities and partly a kind of imaginative, projective inventory (e.g., What three persons from history would you bring back to talk to the class if you had a time machine? What 10 personal possessions would you take on a one-year space trip?) Another instrument emphasizing interests is McGreevy's (1982) "Interests Questionnaire." Closely related to this approach is the use of biographical inventories. A well-known instrument of this kind is Taylor and Ellison's (1978) "Alpha Biographical Inventory." As Barron and Harrington (1981) pointed out, this approach has also been used with adults. They make a further important point; studies of the antecedents of creative behavior, especially those which emphasize past events which seem to promote its emergence, are potentially of great value not simply in identifying creative individuals, but also in helping to specify the kinds of conditions which foster the growth of creativity in the individual — i.e., they have considerable developmental psychological interest.

A common aspect of the approaches outlined here is that they look at either the extent to which the person in question has already behaved in certain ways in the past, or at the degree of prominence of special personal characteristics, such as independence, impulsiveness, self-confidence, etc., which have been interpreted as *prerequisites* for the emergence of creative thinking. Creative potential is thus regarded as depending on the nature of the person, rather than upon cognitive processes or creative products.

Hocevar (1981), after making a critical evaluation of "the voluminous literature on the measurement of creativity," concluded that "a simple and straightforward inventory of creative achievement and activities appears to be more defensible than the more commonly used methods." This suggests the desirability of a more informal, or at least unstandardized, identification procedure (after an initial screening, see Chapter 6, p. 113), such as a case study approach. Renzulli and Smith (1977) have indeed suggested that case study approaches based on multiple sources of information might be superior, and much less costly, than the traditional approach which rests heavily on individualized testing.

Closing remarks

During the last 30 years, dissatisfaction with intelligence as a complete definition of intellectual ability has led to increasing interest in rounding out our understanding of intellect by complementing the concept of intelligence with that of "creativity;" we have presented these two elements here as interacting components of intellectual functiong (see pp. 63–66). In the domain of psychological measurement, the interest has been crystallized in the concepts of convergent and divergent thinking, which are usually taken to be more or less synonymous with intelligence and creativity respectively, although the validity of this assumption is open to question. "Creativity" tests, which seek to measure divergent thinking, have emerged and, although these tests have many weaknesses, especially in the area of validity, they serve to expand the assessment of intellectual ability by focusing attention on important aspects of thinking processes which might otherwise have been neglected, e.g., branching out, seeking new ideas, speculating, etc. Nonetheless, nontest procedures such as biographical scales may well be better indicators of creativity, especially when it is understood in terms of creative products.

6

Identifying the Academically Excellent

Birch (1984) asked the crucial question for the present chapter: Is any identification procedure necessary? He drew attention to the fact that formal identification contains "dangerously destructive tendencies." In particular, he criticized the use of intelligence tests, seeing the test approach as "loaded with weaknesses." Among these are shortcomings of an essentially "technical"nature: for instance selection errors arising from defects in reliability and validity. There is also the serious problem already outlined (see pp. 9-10) of "unfair" treatment of certain groups in society when the results of such tests are strictly adhered to, a problem which will be looked at in great detail in Chapter 7. Just as important are more subtle problems involving the very concept of giftedness, the kinds of behavior which are regarded as indicating its presence, and the design of classroom activities for fostering it. The uncritical use of intelligence tests, or even "creativity" tests, trivializes the property they are supposed to identify, by reducing it to an unknown that apparently manifests itself in test scores. A blind dependence on tests can easily lead to neglect of questions such as the nature of the mental processes which underlie test scores or of the developmental processes involved in their formation and crystallization. It is also easy to overlook the way in which tests in effect, demand certain behaviors and ways of thinking, with the result that they actually come to define, even "create" giftedness, rather than serving as helpful tools in its identification. Excessive faith in tests scores can lead to "teaching to" a narrow and rigid definition of gifts and talents (which has the appearance of being scientific and objective, since it can be stated in scores and profiles), with the result that other properties such as those outlined by Baldwin (1985) are devalued or even ignored. Finally, the set of problems just outlined can easily produce a situation in which little attention is paid to the feelings and wishes of the children in question. The result of all this is that practical classroom activities can become banal or trivial, onesided, narrow, rigid and ineffective.

To turn to the individual people involved — those identified as gifted or, in our terms, academically able — a formal identification process encourages the notion of *giftedness as annointment*. The "gifted program" can easily become something which is jealously guarded by its custodians (those responsible for identification), who see their main function as finding the special few and keeping out the rest. This issue has already been touched upon in Chapter 1 from the point of view of giftedness as a source of gratification for parents, teachers, even the chosen few themselves. It will also be dealt with more fully in later sections of this chapter (see pp. 111–117). It is very interesting to ask at this point what it means in a phenomenological sense to a person identified as gifted to receive this label. It is already known that, for instance, children with extraordinarily high IQs not infrequently suffer a variety of personal and social disturbances (see Horowitz and O'Brien, 1986 for a brief summary). Hendrickson (1986) reported a series of case studies of talented young Australian violinists, in which issues such as their feelings of never having had a proper childhood or of always having had to be perfect, are insightfully discussed. A fossilization of our understanding of exceptional ability by reducing it to the achievement of a certain score on a particular test or series of tests raises the risk of ignoring questions such as these, as well as of neglecting the ways in which gifts and talents develop within the personality of an individual child.

In arguing against formal identification procedures, Birch suggests that in appropriately constructed teaching and learning situations able children would identify themselves through their behavior, thus eliminating the need for identification as we now know it. The problem with this point of view, however, is that it takes insufficient account of a special issue presented in a previous chapter — that of unrealized potential, or "blocked" ability, resulting from lack of motivation or interest, lack of opportunity, or the effect of belonging to a particular disadvantaged group (see Table 2.2). Without help going above and beyond simply endeavoring to improve schooling for all, potentials may waste away. As Shore and Tsiamis (1986), for instance, noted, "identification through performance" is only effective when children have had appropriate opportunities. The notion of hidden, blocked or only partially realized potential provides the main impetus for the argument that there is still room for an identification process based on something other than achievement. Nonetheless, this should occur with full knowledge of the weaknesses of standardized test procedures (see following sections), and should be carried out with a sufficient degree of flexibility and an adequate level of safeguards to minimize the effects of both "technical" and practical problems referred to above. Furthermore, a range of alternative procedures to tests offer themselves for spotting potential.

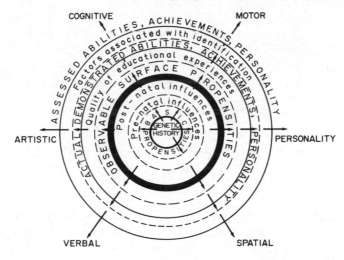

FIG. 6.1. From latent propensities to measured abilities

Special issues in the use of tests

In order to appreciate the dangers involved in the use of tests for identification, it is useful to be familiar with several practical issues in the area; in particular:

1. The relation of test scores to "real" abilities;
2. The accuracy of identification via tests;
3. The difference between vertical and horizontal tests;
4. The difference between level and rate of development.

The relation of test scores to "real" abilities

The dominant attribute which generally springs to mind in identifying academically able children is "intelligence." However, it is important to ask to what extent scores on an intelligence test (or any abilities test) reflect "true" potentials. Figure 6.1 shows how a favorable basic propensity within a person's psychological makeup (for instance a basic potential for a particular skill — depicted as occurring at the center of the figure) must pass through various "layers" in order to be manifested in behavior in the external world (the area outside the circle). Sensory or neurological impairment can impede the realization of innate potential, as can extreme malnutrition or lack of adequate linguistic stimulation. Such impediments — and also adverse emotional factors, poor motivation or inappropriate teaching — can result in demonstrated achievement falling short of potential. The identification of gifted children through tests concentrates only on events beyond the

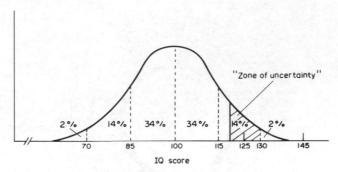

FIG. 6.2. The "zone of uncertainty"

outer rim in Figure 6.1, in the area of actual behavior in real life, and thus measures only what remains after all the layers between potential and external world have been negotiated. Even then, the reliability and validity of measuring instruments, the competence of assessors, lack of precision, and errors of measurement lead to the possibility of future errors in detecting the child with exceptional ability. In other words, the relationship between test scores and potentials within a child is by no means clear, but is obviously far from perfect.

Accuracy of identification

Mental and academic assessments are never perfect, partly because assessment instruments are not perfect and partly because children themselves do not perform with perfect consistency. Figure 6.2 demonstrates the implications of imperfect assessment for the identification process. Suppose that children were being selected for a program designed for the most able five percent. The IQ score which cuts off the top 5 percent in Figure 6.2 is 125, but it should be recognized that a "zone of uncertainty" exists around this cutoff score. If the extent of this zone is conservatively estimated to be from five points above to five points below 125, it will encompass some seven percent of the total group of children, or almost half as many children again as the number actually needing to be identified. It is relatively easy to spot those children who obviously should be accepted and those children who obviously should not be, but the task becomes much more difficult when it comes to deciding who should and should not be accepted among those who score around the cutoff level (i.e., the "zone of uncertainty").

Table 6.1 summarizes the performance of 1000 children on two different administrations of the same test battery. The test–retest reliability of this test battery, represented by a correlation of 0.90 between scores obtained on the two occasions, is extremely satisfactory

TABLE 6.1. *The distribution of the IQ scores of 1000 children on two administrations of the same test*

		Second testing		
		Identified as "nongifted"	Identified as "gifted"	Total
First testing	Identified as "gifted"	7	14	21
	Identified as "nongifted"	967	12	979
	Total	974	26	1000

— indeed substantially higher reliability would be difficult to achieve in practice. But imagine that children with a score higher than 130 were being selected for a special program. If selection had been made on the basis of the first administration, 21 children — those in the two upper quadrants — would have been chosen. If selection had been made on the basis of the second administration, 26 children would have been chosen — those in the two right-hand quadrants. Only 14 children — those in the top right quadrant — would have been selected on both occasions. At least one third of the children identified as being in the top two or three percent on one occasion would have been passed over on the other — and this with an identification procedure whose reliability was 0.90!

If the scores on the second test administration depicted in Table 6.1 are regarded as "correct," the data can be used to illustrate a further important point. We have, in effect, a set of predictor scores (the scores on the first administration) and a set of criterion scores (the scores on the second administration). We can now pose the question: "How accurately were we able to sort out the children on the first testing?" (Remember that for the purposes of this example, we are treating the second testing as containing absolutely "true" information.) Table 6.1 shows that of the 21 children selected as exceptionally able by the first testing, only 14 "really" belonged in this group in that they obtained exceptional scores on the second testing. In other words, seven were identified as exceptionally able, although they were not (upper left-hand quadrant). At the same time, 12 of 26 children who really were of high ability, were not identified (lower right-hand quadrant). The selection procedure had an *efficiency* quotient of 0.67 (14 out of 21 selected really were gifted) and an *effectiveness* quotient of 0.54 (14 out of 26 gifted youngsters were actually detected). In addition, of course, there were two quadrants where the children were correctly identified by the predictor: the upper right-hand quadrant contains 14 children who were predicted to be exceptionally able and who really were, and the lower left-hand quadrant contains 967 children who were correctly identified as being of unexceptional ability. This huge quadrant creates an artificially high reliability for the first testing. In fact, reliability would still have been high had the test failed to identify a single unusually able child! The efficiency and effectiveness coefficients are much more informative.

Whenever predictive decisions are made on the basis of some selection procedure, four possibilities exist — children may be:

1. Correctly identified as exceptional (i.e., true positives);
2. Incorrectly identified as exceptional (false positives);
3. Correctly classified as nonexceptional (true negatives);
4. Incorrectly classified as nonexceptional (false negatives).

The particular significance of these four categories lies in the fact that the different kinds of error (false positives vs false negatives) have different consequences for children who are incorrectly classified, and also for the school system and for society. For instance, is it more serious for a truly exceptional child to be passed over, and thus to receive no special treatment, or for a nonexceptional child to be incorrectly classified as unusually able, and thus possibly exposed to expectations and demands which cannot be met? At the system level, the presence of inappropriately identified children in a program for the gifted can pose special difficulties for the teacher, as well as costs and problems for the school, parents and community — not to mention the children themselves. The question of how concerned we should be about false decisions raises a number of issues. What kinds of cost can be tolerated and which do we regard as intolerable (e.g., monetary costs, costs related to individual morale, intellectual costs to individuals and to society)? Whose welfare is paramount; individual exceptional children, the great mass of nonexceptional youngsters, society as a whole? What kind of error do we wish to avoid: over- or under-identification, over- or under-representation of certain groups, over- or under-emphasis on certain kinds of excellence? One thing is inevitable; no matter what identification instruments or procedures are employed, there will be errors.

Vertical and horizontal tests

In assessing school achievements in, let us say, arithmetic, a test can be constructed containing questions derived from the curricula of several different grades. On this test, a child in Grade 1 who achieves a Grade Equivalent of 4.1 has demonstrated competence not only in arithmetical questions based on the Grade 1 curriculum, but also in those based on the curricula of Grades 2 and 3, and could even deal with some Grade 4 mathematics. This type of test is termed a *vertical* test. Following the practice that had been developed for recording performance on intelligence tests, Grade Equivalents are often translated into quotients, by dividing the average age of students in the grade level achieved by a particular student by that student's actual chronological age. An Arithmetic Grade Equivalent of 4.1 is converted to an Arithmetic Age of 9.1 years, for instance; in a child of 6.5 years this corresponds to an Arithmetic Quotient of 140 (the actual quotient of 9.1/6.5 being multiplied by 100 to remove the need for decimals).

Unfortunately, it was found that quotients based on vertical tests meant different things at different age levels (Terman and Merrill, 1937; Wechsler, 1944) and so *vertical* standardization began to be replaced by *horizontal* standardization. A horizontally standardized test is one in which the raw score of a student on a set of tasks is translated into a standardized score by comparing the individual person's score with the performance of children in the same grade. In order to assess how thoroughly Grade 1 students have assimilated the Grade 1 curriculum in arithmetic, a *horizontal* test of arithmetic achievement has to consist of questions which are based on the Grade 1 curriculum only. Standardized scores might still be expressed as "quotients" based on the mathematics of the normal curve. These *deviation quotients* indicate how far an individual's test score deviates from the average (100) of her/his peer group. Thus, an Arithmetic Quotient of 140 for a Grade 1 pupil indicates that the child scored well above average in comparison with other first graders (in fact, among the top 0.5 percent), but it does not necessarily indicate mastery of material from grades higher than Grade 1.

Level vs rate of development

Whether a student's achievement is evaluated by means of an unstandardized test, by a standardized test which does not take account of the student's actual age, or by a teacher, an assessment is being made of that student's current *level* of development. IQs and Educational Quotients, on the other hand, attempt to assess a child's *rate* of development, since they relate achievement to the child's age at the time of testing. It is rate of development rather than actual level achieved that ought to be the criterion for judging whether or not a child is exceptionally able (or retarded). To demonstrate the obvious validity of this proposition, suppose that it had been decided that a child should have a Mental Age of 12 years and an overall Grade Equivalent achievement of 7 to qualify for entry to a program for able students — in other words, suppose that developmental level only is specified. Clearly, an eight-year-old child would have to be of exceptionally high ability to satisfy this criterion, but it is equally clear than an average 12-year-old and a dull 16-year-old would also qualify. However, one would hardly consider the 16-year-old as being as able as the 8-year-old, because the 16-year-old would have taken eight extra years to reach the same level; i.e., the 16-year-old's rate of development would have been much slower.

The age-within-year effect has been noted at the other end of the educational achievement spectrum from that occupied by the gifted. Dipasquale, Moule and Flewelling (1980) analyzed the number of children referred to an educational clinic according to their month of birth. Whereas the incidence of referrals on account of behavioral problems was relatively constant, i.e., independent of the child's date of birth, children born between September and December (i.e., young for their grade) accounted for almost double the number of referrals for learning problems than did the older children born between January and April.

There are good reasons for advocating that unusually able children should be identified early. If, however, it is decided to rely on Mental Age rather than IQ for identification (e.g., Newland, 1976, p. 244), the age-within-year-group effect can produce some remarkable and disturbing consequences. Suppose that a qualifying instrument consisting of tests, checklists and/or ratings scales is constructed to assess the developmental level of school beginners with an average chronological age of 6.0 years, and that those with a "Developmental Age" of 8.0 years are to be accepted into a gifted program. Older children aged about 6.5 years would need to have a Developmental Quotient (Developmental Age required for admission divided by actual age — 8.0/6.5) of about 125, which would be attained by about one child in 30. On the other hand, the youngest children, aged 5.5. years, would require a Developmental Quotient of 145, the chances of which are less than one in a thousand! This effect can lead to overidentification of "average but dutiful old in grade students" (Hawaii Department of Education, 1977, p. 25).

If students are selected for a special program for the gifted on the basis of achievement level, it is probable that the receiving teachers in the special program will perceive selection as more valid than they would have regarded a procedure based on rate. The reason is that these teachers' assessments of performance will be here and now evaluations of students' levels of achievement without the "bonus" accorded to younger children when rate of development is considered. The dilemma is whether to seek apparent predictive validity (in which case, assessment of developmental level will probably yield the results most acceptable to teachers in the gifted program), or whether to emphasize fairness (in which case, rate should be used).

Specific identification instruments and procedures

Many different methods have been proposed for the identification of able students. Traditionally, examinations calling for essay type answers had been used, but these were to a great extent replacd during the present century by objective, short answer achievement tests. Achievement tests, of course, place at an advantage those who have enjoyed good teaching, parental encouragement and opportunity. Consequently, for the commendable goal of reducing environmental disadvantage and assessing "true potential," the intelligence test came into favor, either to augment or replace achievement tests. Teacher nominations and rating scales, tests of creativity, ratings by peers, self-rating scales and case studies are among the methods that have also been advocated and used for identifying able students.

Achievement tests

No identification instrument acts like a crystal ball, i.e., it does not predict the future without any reference to the past. Even when the intelligence test was considered to be a measure of innate "potential," the test had to use evidence of development prior to the administration of the test to find the average rate of past development, which was then extrapolated into the future on the assumption of constancy of relative rate of development. Thus, if a boy or girl had reached the achievement level of an average 12-year-old at eight years of age, it was assumed that the same child would achieve at the level of an average 18-year-old by the age of 12.

Past attainment *is* the best single predictor of future achievement, assuming that the nature of the future learning task and the circumstances in which it is carried out are essentially similar to those of the past, as has been known for many years (Gallagher and Moss, 1963). Stanley (1976), on the basis of his experience in the Search for Mathematically Precocious Youth Program (SMPY), is in no doubt concerning the value of tests, holding that "high scores on standardized aptitude and achievement tests are probably the *best single* clue to high potential," although the information they provide must be "supplemented by other evidence." Humphreys (1985) pointed out that if college entrance were to be based exclusively on achievement test scores and grades, the advantage of middle-class students over those from working-class homes in admission to college would be reduced by one third. However, a child must have had the chance to demonstrate achievement, and many children — not only the socially deprived — would not have had this opportunity before attending school. Those children who have not enjoyed linguistic stimulation at home, or who have not enjoyed the best teaching in school, are at a disadvantage on achievement tests so that, at the very least, the tests need to be augmented by other means of assessment in order to detect those children who are high in promise but not so high in actual performance.

Care must also be exercised in interpreting the results of achievement tests. If the test is a horizontal test (see p. 101), a seven-year-old child who is doing exceptionally well in mathematics in Grade 2 might be at the 99th percentile, with a level of performance which might be interpreted in the test manual as corresponding to a Grade Equivalent of 4.5 or so. It could be disastrous if this child's mathematical competence were assumed to be at the level of an average student halfway through Grade 4, on the basis of a test made up of Grade 2 items. In order to prepare for the possible acceleration of this child into mathematical work at a higher level, either a vertical test should be administered, or else horizontal tests at Grades 3, 4 and, perhaps, 5 levels, to find out what the child can actually do, and what supplementary material needs to be taught if gaps in skills and knowledge are to be avoided. This is essentially the procedure adopted by Stanley in the SMPY project, and similar to what Renzulli refers to as "compacting."

Intelligence tests

Intelligence tests can be cross classified into four main types. They may be *individual* or *group* tests and they may be *verbal* or *nonverbal*. Individual tests, as their name indicates, are administered personally to a single individual and might take an hour, or even longer, to administer. However, as they are in effect a standardized interview, they can provide a skilled tester with more information than simply an IQ score. Group tests, on the other hand, can be administered simultaneously to all the children in a class, or to greater numbers if a large enough room is available. Group testing can frequently be carried out in less time than it would take to administer an individual test to a single student. Generally, however, the only information provided by the group test is the IQ, possibly augmented by some additional analysis of performance on constituent subskills.

Verbal intelligence tests require the use of words, written words in the case of group tests for the most part, and primarily spoken words in the case of individual tests. Test items typically call for knowledge of vocabulary, synonyms and antonyms, ability to answer questions involving inductive and deductive reasoning, analogies, etc. Because academic learning is predominantly verbal in nature, a verbal intelligence test will usually predict academic success better than will a nonverbal intelligence test. But, as with achievement tests, children with an impoverished language background will be at a disadvantage if tested on a verbal intelligence test. Nevertheless, performance on an intelligence test is less affected by school learning than is performance on an achievement test. Thus, if identification were by intelligence test only, there would be a tendency for some children to be identified who appear to possess unrealized academic potential. In the judgement of the teachers in the program for the academically gifted to which children are transferred, therefore, there is a likelihood of a reported excessive number of false positives among children identified on the basis of intelligence test performance.

Ideally, a nonverbal test ought to require no use of spoken or written language; the instructions ought to be presented by mime and the responses ought to involve some sort of motoric action only, e.g., drawing, pointing, arranging objects, etc. Some intelligence tests, particularly those designed to assess the intelligence of severely hearing impaired children, satisfy these criteria, but a typical nonverbal intelligence test has instructions which are given verbally. Test items are similar in nature to those found in verbal intelligence tests — analogies, classification, completing sequences, etc., even though the items are expressed in the form of pictures or diagrams rather than words. Verbal thinking can also help to solve many nonverbal test questions, so that there can be a real or latent verbal element in socalled nonverbal tests.

A culture free test, or as it is often more modestly expressed nowadays, a "culture fair" or "culture reduced" test, is one which is as appropriate for children raised in one particular culture (e.g., Western Europe) as for those from a quite different culture (e.g., South-East Asia). There is conflicting evidence about the claims of tests which are said to be culture free. However, the average performance of Inuit (Eskimo) children on the Raven's Matrices Test has been found to be comparable with that of the Scottish children on which it was originally standardized (Jensen, 1981, p. 134). Another test which has been claimed to be relatively culture free is the Leiter Intelligence Test. Possibly the best culture reduced individual test, according to some experts, is an Australian instrument — the Queensland Test (QT).

Creativity tests

There is conflicting evidence about the reliability and validity of creativity assessments, and there is only modest correlation between the different methods of assessment. In a study of ninety-four 10- and 11-year-old children extending over a complete range of regular school ability, McLeod (1972) obtained intercorrelations between different methods of assessing creativity which showed that there was a lack of significant relationship between demonstrated fluency (e.g., TTCT and Word Association) and ratings of creativity (Renzulli and sociometric). A low relationship between creativity as assessed by teachers and genuine creativity has been implicitly recognized by Torrance (1976), who observed that "certainly, there seems a great deal of evidence to support the belief that creative individuals . . . are being overlooked and even undermined psychologically for lack of widespread use of whatever detection instruments . . . are available." It is inevitable, therefore, that if a test of creativity is used to identify students, and if teachers' evaluations are used as criterion, or vice versa, there will be a considerable number of false positives and false negatives. Nevertheless, a child's responses to a test designed to measure factors such as fluency of ideas can provide useful qualitative insights that might otherwise be difficult to obtain.

Teacher nomination

The teacher is in the most advantageous position to identify a student with outstanding ability or special talents, and teacher opinion should certainly be sought to augment and check other identification procedures. However, a number of problems arise if identification relies on teacher nomination alone; these are well summed up in the publication of the State Advisory Council for the Gifted and Talented of the Hawaii Education Department (1977) already mentioned.

Following a widely quoted article in the immediate post-*Sputnik* period (Pegnato and Birch, 1959), it has become commonplace to criticize teachers as being incapable of identifying gifted children. Using the Revised Stanford–Binet scale, Pegnato and Birch tested 1400 students in grades 9–12 in a large high school in Pittsburgh, and identified 91 as gifted according to the criterion that their measured IQ was 136 or higher. Several screening procedures, including teacher nomination, were then evaluated by noting how many of the 91 were correctly identified, and by further noting how many of the students nominated were, in fact, gifted according to the criterion. The teachers nominated 195 students, of whom only 41 proved to have IQs of 136 or higher; thus there were 154 false positives and 50 false negatives. The teachers achieved an effectiveness level of 0.45 (and an efficiency level of a mere 0.21). However, apart from the dubious practice of accepting an IQ of 136 + as the criterion for giftedness, the teachers' predictions correlated about 0.65 with the IQ criterion (due, of course, to the large number of correct rejections) — statistically highly significant. If only Pegnato and Birch had presented their results in the form of correlation coefficients, rather than recording the actual number of "hits" and "misses," their findings would perhaps have been interpreted as a vindication, rather than a depreciation, of teacher nomination as a method for identifying academically able students! Despite the low efficiency reported in this study, after a comprehensive survey of the relevant literature Hoge and Cudmore (1986) found "little basis for the negative assessments so often associated with [teacher judgement] measures." However, they observed that it is curious that we concern ourselves so much with the reliability and validity of standardized tests and observational measures, and yet adopt such a casual attitude when it comes to judgemental measures.

Teacher ratings

Teachers' ratings of students are a potential improvement over teacher nomination. An extensive study by Pedulla, Airasian and Madaus (1980) found that there is only moderate correlation between teacher ratings and test results, but that teachers' judgements tend to reflect academically related behaviors such as attention span and persistence, which are not so heavily sampled by tests, despite their importance; in other words, teacher ratings open up the possibility of expanding the criteria taken into account in estimating potential excellence. Denton (1985), reporting on a study of teachers in the UK, concluded that they are capable of identifying unusually able youngsters in their classes. However, it is necessary for giftedness to be defined in terms of specific traits or characteristics, not in global terms. Furthermore, teachers' ratings are most valuable when they focus not on level of achievement, but on personal traits such as enthusiasm, dedication, etc.

Teacher ratings can be improved by ensuring that the instructions accompanying the scales are clear and unambiguous, while teachers can be taught how to improve the efficiency of their ratings. For example, instead of proceeding alphabetically through a class list of 30 names, they should first pick out the most outstanding children on the trait being assessed, then the least outstanding. Thus, the top and bottom three children might first be rated A and E respectively. Then the next best six or so should be rated B and the six least outstanding who are left D. The middle 12 would then fall into the C category. The number to be allocated to each category is not hard and fast, but the above procedure provides a guideline to an effective and reliable rating method.

For legitimate system-wide use of teacher ratings, the assessments of different teachers must be rescaled in some way, in order to render them mutually compatible. If the assessments are of achievement, the task is comparatively straightforward (McIntosh, Walker and MacKay, 1962) and can be accomplished by scaling the ratings of each class so that the mean teacher rating and the range of ratings are the same as those for scores on an achievement test which has been administered throughout the system, and which is used as a common yardstick. Because a common index of motivation is not immediately obvious, the task of scaling teacher ratings of student motivation is more tenuous. However, McLeod (1986) developed a procedure which holds promise for the effective scaling of teachers' ratings of student task commitment or motivation.

Rating by peers and parents

During World War II, officer selection techniques were developed (Vernon and Parry, 1949) which depended in part on candidates' ratings of each other and which appeared to be successful. On the analogous assumption that students are in a position to gain insights into their fellow students' abilities and leadership qualities which are unavailable to teachers and other adults, the use of peer nominations or ratings has been considered (Martinson, 1975) but apparently little used (Yarborough and Johnson, 1983). The most practical procedure of obtaining fellow students' opinions, especially in the elementary grades, is by use of a modified sociometric technique. For example, for peer assessment of general academic ability, all students in the class could be asked to write down the names of three students who always seem to have the correct answer to the teacher's questions, or with whom they would like to work on, say, a science project. For children's assessment of originality and creative thinking, they could be asked to write the names of three students who often have a lot of ideas that no one else seems to think of. The number of choices received by a student is the score on the trait being assessed. Correlations between choices received and other measures of ability or creativity tend to be low over the whole range of students, but students who receive the highest number of choices are usually among the top scorers on ability tests, or receive high teacher ratings for creativity (McLeod, 1972).

If teachers are in a more advantageous position than standardized tests to appreciate some of the more subtle signs of giftedness, parents are in an even more advantageous position to detect abilities in their own children. Jacobs (1971) found that parents in a school in Michigan were able to identify 16 out of 21 children in kindergarten identified as gifted (WPPSI IQ above 125), and misidentified only 10, whereas teachers were able to identify only two. Without replication, however, the findings of this rather inadequately reported, isolated study should be regarded as no more than tentative.

Viewed in a wider perspective, parents do not generally have the opportunity to judge their own children in comparison with other children; on the one hand they are susceptible to overrating their own offspring, but on the other some may underplay the accomplishments of their children, especially if they themselves are very bright (Martinson, 1975, p. 47). Martinson (1975) observed that teachers of young children are likely to acquire information which will alert them to giftedness if they have regular conferences or informal contacts with parents. It is probable, however, that teachers are more likely to have regular contacts with middle-class parents than with minority group, working-class or unemployed parents.

Biographical analysis

It has already been emphasized in several places that academic excellence involves not merely intellectual ability in the IQ sense, but other cognitive traits (see Chapter 4, in which an extended model of cognitive functioning was presented), as well as a range of noncognitive factors such as motivation, determination, self-confidence and the like; to a considerable degree these are the traits Renzulli (1978) probably had in mind when he emphasized the importance of "task commitment." Cropley (1988) summarized these characteristics under the heading "personal preconditions," and saw them as either necessary for the realization of potentials, or at the very least highly favorable to this realization. The basic idea underlying the application of biographical analysis to the identification of potential academic excellence is that children who have already displayed appropriate personal preconditions in their behavior are likely to continue to do so. This element can thus be assessed by examining the past life of a particular child for appropriate examples: for instance long sustained, concentrated work, faith in one's own ability to succeed on difficult tasks, fascination with a particular content area and the like. Naturally, a past history of high achievement is also highly relevant, but less urgent, since such achievement is often identified in school. This is, however, by no means always the case, so that unsung but extraordinary achievement in, for instance, a hobby area is of great importance in biographical analyses. In particular, great creativity in an out of school activity can go unnoticed by the traditional judges, especially teachers. Examples of instruments for the biographical analysis of children's lives include diaries or self-descriptions such as autobiographical sketches, life event inventories and biographical questionnaires. These are most frequently filled out by children themselves, but can also be completed by parents or others with intimate knowledge of a child's life history.

Personality assessment

It has already been mentioned that teacher assessments are most useful when they concentrate on special traits and characteristics such as high attention span, persistence, enthusiasm, etc. In the previous section this list was expanded to include further characteristics such as self-confidence; these can be seen as aspects of the personality which are necessary for the realization of potentials. In Chapter 4, we went in some detail into the role of personality characteristics in the emergence of creativity, while in the chapters on teaching and learning activities we again discussed personality traits which seem to be more typical of outstanding youngsters than of others. Without reproducing this material here, it is possible to say that certain personality constellations are apparently closely bound up with academic excellence — this is because they predispose some people to become excited by a problem, marshal the energy needed for intensive, sustained effort, find the courage to keep going when a solution proves elusive, communicate results to other people in an effective way, and so on. This view of giftedness as encompassing not only ability, but also personality, opens up further approaches to identification through the application of existing personality scales. In addition, special instruments have been constructed specifically for use with unusually able individuals. In a study in Holland, for instance, Mönks, van Boxtel, Roelofs and Sanders (1986) used measures of the general personality traits of self-image, curiosity and locus of control as part of a battery of tests for identifying unusually able students. In addition, however, they collected data on the youngsters' personal characteristics by means of an instrument specifically designed for use with the academically able; this was the "Scale for Rating the Behavioral Characteristics of Superior Students" (SRBCSS) developed by Renzulli, Hartmann and Callahan (1971).

Advantages of different procedures

The result of the various approaches outlined in this section of the present chapter is that a multiplicity of alternative procedures and instruments exists for identification of properties and characteristics related to exceptional ability, many of them departing markedly from the traditional IQ approach. Passow (1985) has given a compact but comprehensive summary of these procedures. It is apparent that no single test or rating procedure is foolproof: achievement scores lead to the lowest proportion of false positives, but may produce a large number of false negatives (i.e., they may be relatively low in effectiveness, while highly efficient). They emphasize traditional school skills and are highly susceptible to opportunity and motivation. Intelligence tests go beyond achievement to some degree (although they too are influenced by opportunity and motivation), but they lead to an increased number of false positives (i.e., they are not especially efficient, although more effective). Other test procedures (for instance, creativity tests) expand the criterion further, but are still subject to some of the problems associated with tests. Teachers tend to give greater emphasis to factors in the cluster of properties Renzulli referred to as "commitment," or which Cropley referred to as "personal preconditions." Peer and parent ratings expand the criterion even further, by taking account of social factors. Biographical analyses focus on actual achievements, and thus provide the only identification instruments which attempt to assess the criterion directly and in a concrete way. In a sense, biographical analyses are a special form of achievement test, so that the wheel has come full circle.

Table 6.2 summarizes a number of the advantages and disadvantages of the various procedures outlined to date.

The crucial point here is that all identification procedures have defects and weaknesses. However, as one moves from achievement tests to ratings of various kinds, the criteria of giftedness change: we progress from strict measurement of the present level of achievement on the criterion itself (achievement) to assessments which are more abstract, broader and more oriented towards identifying *potential* for academic excellence. In other words, we move away from demanding that all four conditions in Figure 2.1 be satisfied (ability, motivation, opportunity and achievement) and consider some of the other conditions, such as ability and motivation without opportunity (and hence with restricted achievement), etc. Adoption of instruments which give major emphasis to elements other than school achievement and cognitive ability thus makes it possible to raise efficiency and effectiveness of identification, with the intention of avoiding errors. However, different selection criteria lead to different patterns of performance in a gifted program; high previous achievement, for instance, most frequently predicts high achievement in the program, whereas other factors, such as high motivation, have a different predictive power. Thus, in addition to use of alternative instruments other than achievement scores or IQs, selection strategies are needed which make it possible to deal with different responses to the gifted program.

Selection strategies

Approaches to selection often concentrate on the need to identify a sufficiently high number of students to ensure that the desired proportion of the total school population (frequently five percent) receives special attention. Not infrequently, a number of students who score below the official cutoff point are also admitted to the program, in order to compensate for dropouts. This approach may satisfy administrative criteria, but it is not well designed from the point of view

TABLE 6.2. *Procedures for identifying exceptional ability*

Procedure	Advantages	Disadvantages
Standardized achievement tests	Part of routine assessment Comprehensive, i.e., given to all Reflect demonstrated ability Yield relatively few false positives Results from different schools may be compared	Cannot be used until child has achieved Susceptible to effects of differential socioeducational opportunity Need augmenting with more individualized information
Intelligence tests	Depend less on school learning than achievement tests Results from different schools may be compared Yield fewer false negatives	May produce false positives
verbal	Better predictors than nonverbal IQ tests	Children from language deficient homes at disadvantage
nonverbal	More "culture fair" than verbal IQ tests	Yield more false positives than verbal IQ tests
Teacher nominations	Can be more insightful than tests	Likely to be biased in favor of quiet, older conformers
Teacher ratings	More sensitive than teacher nomination Often take account of factors neglected by tests Reliability can be improved through training — personal properties Variability between teachers can be eliminated by scaling	If unguided, retain tendency to bias Subject to sex stereotyping (eg., boys–math; girls–art, etc.) May produce false negatives Tend to miss the culturally different Tend to miss the creatively gifted Different teachers have different standards
Parent ratings	Some evidence that parents can identify better than teachers Can permit focus on real life behavior	Parents do not have a wide background against which to judge Likely to be SES selective Likely to be distorted by parent's ambitions, etc.
Peer ratings	Some evidence that classmates can identify better than teachers Give due weight to social factors	Some problems (not insurmountable) in quantifying assessments appropriately

of the need to deal with the human and social costs of selection or nonselection. These include disappointment, feelings of failure, self-doubt, frustration, even resentment or hostility on the part of the children who are not selected. On the part of those who are selected, perhaps incorrectly, many of these reactions are seen, but also anxiety, fear of failure, perfectionism or arrogance, smugness and the like. In recent years, a number of approaches to selection have emerged which are aimed at reducing or avoiding these problems.

Screening

In order that identification of children for a special program for the gifted should be comprehensive, and in order that it be seen to be comprehensive, all children should be considered initially. At the same time, economics and commonsense dictate that the selection process should not involve unnecessary expense. Thus, not all children can be subjected to a detailed identification procedure, but some preliminary sorting must be carried out (screening). This can involve successive steps with screening out at each stage. For jurisdictions where a battery of group ability and achievement tests are administered to all students, the data provided by these present an excellent starting point (Stanley, 1984). Highest achieving students across the whole jurisdiction, or within individual schools, can readily be identified. Their number can also be augmented, if required, by the names of students who have — in the opinion of their teachers — been missed by this approach. The next step is to carry out a more intensive assessment of this pool of students, for instance with the help of various test or rating procedures. In practice, this typically means with an intelligence test! This process of screening should be accompanied by intensive monitoring and study of children in the border zone, whose identification as gifted is not self-evident. The several types of procedure which are available for this more intensive study have already been surveyed.

Use of multiple criteria

An extensive of this approach is to use existing achievement and/or IQ scores as one indicator, but to supplement these with other ratings, personality scores, teachers' opinions and the like. Parents' wishes may be taken into account, or those of the children in question themselves. In order to take greater account of disappointed feelings or even the possibility of selecting children who do not want to participate, it is possible to start by inviting interested parents to nominate their children if they wish. It is also possible to accept self-nominations from the students themselves. This initial group can also be enlarged by teacher nominations. Youngsters who conform to some prestated profile can then finally be selected. For instance, they might need to be in the upper 25 percent on school achievement, at or above the 80th percentile on an IQ test and high on certain personality dimensions. In this way, a combination of characteristics is defined as identifying the unusually able, an approach which is consistent with previous discussions of the multidimensional nature of "true excellence."

A recent example of the use of an unusually extensive set of multiple criteria is to be seen in the study by Mönks and colleagues mentioned earlier (Mönks et al., 1986). Accepting Renzulli's three ring definition (see Chapter 2, pp. 27-28), they set out to measure conventional intelligence, creativity and task commitment. Initially, they made use of standardized tests (to the extent that they are available) for measuring these traits, including Raven's Matrices for the IQ score, parts of existing "creativity" tests such as "What kind of person are you?" (Khatena and Torrance, 1976), and the "Questionnaire for Measuring Inquisitiveness" (Lehwald, 1985). In addition, however, they asked the pupils to rate themselves on intelligence, creativity and perseverance. Peers filled out the "Quest Student Nomination Questionnaire" (Renzulli, et al., 1976), while parents rated their own children on the questionnaire "Things my child likes to do" (Renzulli, et al., 1976). Finally, teachers filled out the "Scale for Rating the Behavioral Characteristics of Superior Students" (Renzulli, Hartmann and Callahan, 1971), as well as providing information about achievement and unusual skills and abilities of students. To a considerable degree, this wide range of criteria reflected the emphasis laid by Mönks et al. not only on the three ring approach, but also on their conviction that academic ability does not develop in a vacuum, but is greatly affected by the three major social domains of children's life (school, family, peer group). It is thus not to be seen as a simple "shot gun" approach, according to the principle that if enough scores are obtained the truth must eventually out, but reflects the model of giftedness already spelled out (it requires a combination of cognitive and noncognitive factors) and acknowledges the influences which guide the crystallization of unusual ability and its manifestation in the form of exceptional achievement.

McLeod (1986) has developed a procedure for standardizing and systematizing the multiple criteria approach. In addition to standardizing teachers' ratings on subjective dimensions, such as enthusiasm or persistence, so that they are similarly distributed from teacher to teacher within a school or a school system, his approach involves a rudimentary expert system: a computer program is provided with parameters such as minimum and maximum number of students who can be accommodated in a gifted program, minimum levels of each criterion which can be accepted and so on. The program then selects the desired number of participants, by "juggling" the levels they display on the various criteria, keeping standards as high as possible.

Noncustodial approaches

It cannot be stressed too strongly that *any* method of identification, formal or informal, standardized or unstandardized, is less then 100 percent reliable or valid. It follows, therefore, that any decision about a specific child should be regarded as dynamic and fluid, not static and fixed for all time on the basis of a single identification procedure. At the same time, children are thinking, feeling human beings with a need for self-respect. Just as it is — or should be — a positive experience to be selected for participation in a special program for the unusually able, it can be a devastating experience to be ejected from such a program. Even children who have shown sufficient ability to have been identified as gifted are unlikely to appreciate the subtleties of educational measurement to the extent of accepting with equanimity that they might not be in the top two percent after all, but only in the top five percent. These children are much more likely to perceive the situation as dichotomous; i.e., if they are not smart, then they must be stupid.

The approaches outlined to date rest on the basic assumption that selection is necessary in order to limit participation: those making the selection decisions exercise a gatekeeper function (Birch, 1984), in order to keep out all but the right people. In terms of the four possible results of decisions depicted earlier, they emphasize efficiency (avoiding false positives by selecting only "truly gifted" youngsters) at the expense of effectiveness (finding all able youngsters, even at the risk of a large number of false positives).

We believe, however, that identification procedures should place more emphasis on effectiveness — especially in view of the fact that the methods and instruments employed are known to yield errors which are weighted to the disadvantage of special groups in society. If these children are to be well served by efforts to promote excellence, we must be willing to tolerate false positives, on the grounds that these are far less a problem than false negatives (rejection of children with high — if hidden — potentials). However, in order to avoid the problems associated with being dropped from a program, it is essential that selection be fluid, in the sense that movement backwards and forwards, into and out of the program, is possible without feelings of failure and rejection.

Renzulli's (1984) *revolving door model* of identification is a step in the right direction. It entails the establishment of a talent pool made up of about a quarter of the students in a school, about a fifth of whom (i.e., five percent of the school population) would be receiving special educational treatment from a resource teacher at any given time. The talent pool is made up of students who have above average ability and who "show interest in a particular topic or area of study" (Renzulli, Reis and Smith, 1981, p. 648). The students receive special educational treatment until the end of a specific contract, "at which time the student steps aside to make room for another child." Acceptance by a child that a stint in a resource room is temporary makes it possible to ease the child painlessly out of a gifted program if it appears that the original identification was in error. On the other hand, where monitoring of progress via the child's project shows that selection was justified, he or she may return to the special program.

In the earlier descriptions of the revolving door model by Renzulli and his collaborators (e.g., Renzulli, Reis and Smith, 1981), a picture emerged of a procedure whose aim is to distribute the benefits of special programming to a quarter of the school population in turn, rather than progressively to increase confidence that the most able children have been validly identified. The possibilities offered by a revolving door model were made more explicit by Clarke (1983) who, in a "dynamic cyclical model," illustrated how observation of a student's response to "enriched" or "improved" provision generates progressively more valid assessments of ability, so that the child may either graduate to more and more advanced or enriched studies, or be withdrawn from the program at the end of a particular cycle — with greatly reduced likelihood of damage to self-respect. The additional information which provides feedback on pupils' reactions to the special program is conceptualized by Mönks et al. (1986) as involving "signals" (p. 47). These are behaviors on the part of students which indicate unusual interest, skill or motivation for particular activities. These should be detected by teachers and used in the making of decisions about further treatment. Renzulli, Reis and Smith (1981) referred to "action information messages" (AIM) — brief written records of "signals" kept by teachers. In the application of the revolving door model they recommend using AIMs as the starting point for discussions with pupils and as a basis for planning further activities.

The most important aspect of such approaches is the acceptance of identification as an ongoing process after the initial (or "first level") identification. A further step in extending admission procedures, however, would be to go beyond the revolving door to an *open door* admissions policy. Shore and Tsiamis (1986) attempted an approximation of this with a group of Canadian youngsters who were accepted into a special program simply on the recommendation of a parent, teacher or other adult, without test scores being taken into account at all. A second group was admitted on the basis of conventional criteria — teacher selection via a scale for identifying superior students plus achievement at or above the 90th percentile on a test of basic skills, or a high IQ plus approval by teachers and psychologists. Comparison of the groups on a variety of measures, including IQ, creativity test scores, personality scores and self-concept indicated that there were virtually no differences between them. The group selected simply by nomination had obviously been the subject of a considerable degree of informal selection on the part of the nominators, something which supports the value of such nominations in identifying unusual ability. The findings suggest that at least with middle-class families, as was the case in this study, an open door policy may be a promising and elegant solution to the problem of selection. Whether this is true for children from social outgroups remains to be seen.

Closing remarks

The task facing any educational administrator who is trying to identify unusually able students is to find those children who are most likely to benefit from the special program. But there is something ambiguous about this criterion. On the one hand, it may be argued that those "most likely to benefit" are those who are most likely to succeed (i.e., those who are least likely to drop out and are the most likely to demonstrate the highest achievement). On the other hand, it may equally be argued that those children "most likely to benefit" include those who appear to have high potential but who, for a variety of reasons, do not always appear among the highest achievers. Taking into consideration the age-within-year-group effect described earlier in the present chapter, one can discern two broad approaches to the identification of academically gifted students, one of which is highly efficient in locating those children most likely to succeed, the other more equitable in ensuring opportunity for those whose gifts and talents exist more as potentials, frequently but not always because of lack of opportunity. For high predictive validity, identification should stress verbal tests of ability and achievement, buttressed by teacher and parent nominations, and test results should focus on the *level* of current performance. For a high level of fairness, achieved at the cost of less-accurate prediction of subsequent success, actual educational achievement would be downplayed and ability assessed through nonverbal tests, whose results would be expressed in the form of quotients relating level of achievement to age (i.e., emphasizing rate of development).

Of particular interest to us is that what Bongartz, Kaißer and Kluge (1985) called "hidden" talent should not go unnoticed. As these authors emphasized, practical educators should stress *potential*; their job is to help this potential to emerge and manifest itself. For identification this means that the aim should not be simply to select the happy few, but actively to promote the emergence and recognition of gifts and talents (in this book especially in the intellectual domain), wherever they exist, and even if they have not yet manifested themselves. In other words, identification is seen here as dynamic — part of a general process of fostering intellectual growth. This approach to identification has two practical consequences which can be mentioned here: (1) identification cannot be limited to the observation of school achievement or of high scores on a narrow range of conventional tests; (2) special measures for promoting academic excellence should be made available on as wide a basis as possible.

We accept that achievement and high test scores are, and will continue to be, major indicators of excellence. In the chapter on "Intelligence" we have already gone in greater detail into some of the problems associated with abilities tests and drawn attention to some of their weaknesses. What is needed is recognition of a wider range of indicators of potential for academic excellence, especially by making greater use of observation based on practical settings (biographical analysis, case studies, etc.,). In addition, there is a need for forms of special provision which open up the possibility of exposure to facilitating activities to the widest range of children. The revolving door model and the open door approach are obviously steps in the right direction.

7

Able Underachievers

It is important to remember that not all unusually clever or talented children fail to achieve highly — if they did, it would not be possible to write a book with exceptional achievement as its theme. Indeed, there are many studies (see Freeman, 1979; Tannenbaum, 1979; Vernon, Adamson and Vernon, 1977, for recent summaries) which emphasize the outstanding successes of unusually able youngsters, both in school and in life itself. Even among those unusually able people who have ultimately succeeded in realizing their potential, however, there is ample evidence that they frequently had difficulty in school (Freeman, 1983; Goertzel, Goertzel and Goertzel, 1978; Rawson, 1968). Einstein failed in languages, Schubert in mathematics, George Bernard Shaw could not spell properly and Tolstoy displayed a severe learning disability during his school years. Delius, Ghandi and Nehru showed no promise in school. Edgar Alan Poe and Einstein were actually expelled for serious misbehavior, while Edison was taken out of school after three months, on the grounds that he was "unable."

Of course, it is dangerous to indulge in simplistic diagnosis of persons in another era and in a totally different educational milieu: In modern psychoeducational terms, the school problems of Churchill or Einstein might largely have been attributable to social maladjustment (stemming from the conflict between their strong wills and unsympathetic, inflexible school regimes). What is clear, however, is that school is not always free of problems and difficulties for the gifted: in a recent review, Horowitz and O'Brien (1986) identified the group of underachieving gifted youngsters as a major area of concern. Yewchuk (1986) made an important distinction in this regard by differentiating between highly able youngsters who simply do not achieve well in school ("gifted underachievers") and those who may be regarded as "learning disabled." Children in the latter group display general or specific learning disabilities (such as dyslexia) which may well have a neurophysiological basis. They may even do very well in areas not related to their disability. The members of the former group, however, fail to achieve because of lack of motivation, rejection of school values,

119

anxiety, or other psychological factors (which will be discussed later in this chapter) or even because of simple lack of opportunity. The present chapter concentrates on the former group — youngsters who are, in principle, capable of doing well in school, but do not. Kerry (1981) distilled a list of negative characteristics of such students. They are frequently:

1. Anti-school;
2. Restless and inattentive;
3. Often bored;
4. Verbally fluent but poor in written work;
5. Often lost in a private world;
6. Inclined to be excessively self-sufficient;
7. Excessively self-critical;
8. Given to emotional outbursts;
9. Impatient with slower pupils;
10. Disliked by their peers;
11. Highly skilled at faking bad.

On the other hand, they also display a number of characteristics which would usually be regarded as positive. They are often, for instance:

1. Friendly with older pupils;
2. Diligent and creative when their interest is aroused;
3. Quick to learn routine material;
4. Good at solving problems;
5. Good at abstract thinking;
6. Very inventive;
7. Likely to ask stimulating or provocative questions.

One interesting, although sad, explanation of the phenomenon of lack of school success among the highly able is to be found in the notion of the *persecution of the clever*. As March (1977) strikingly put it, some of them may simply be "too bright for their own comfort" — rejected by their peers, isolated and jeered at. Kerry (1981) gives a striking case study of such a child, and presents two bitter jokes* which portray the situation referred to here with sad clarity. In the first, a teacher glares in outrage at an unfortunate "egg head" pupil with a pile of books and papers on his desk: "Don't try to be clever here young man, this is a school!" In the second, the teacher again glares at the same student,

*We have changed the "jokes" slightly in order to achieve brevity and clarity in the present context.

saying: "This is a democratic school, young man. Sit down and be stupid like the rest." What this can mean for some gifted youngsters is that it is more comfortable to hide exceptional ability. Underachievement then becomes, to state it dramatically, "faking bad," in order to be accepted (Freeman, 1983; Kerry, 1981).

Special disadvantaged groups

At this point it is necessary to make a further distinction — that between "simple" underachievers and those who may be regarded as disadvantaged. Traditionally, disadvantage is seen as arising from unfavorable socioeconomic conditions or membership of a social outgroup, although it is now increasingly accepted that many girls are also "disadvantaged" (see pp. 124–127). Further groups which will be discussed here are the emotionally or physically handicapped and the geographically isolated.

Socioeconomic status and the blocking of achievement

Over the years, many writers have emphasized the importance of the family in the realization of high potential, including Douglas (1964), Coopersmith (1967), Miller (1970) and Colangelo and Dettman (1983). In a definitive study in which 210 children identified as having outstanding potential were followed over a period of 10 years, data from the Gulbenkian Project (Freeman, 1985), showed that the major influence on how potential is realized is family background; the middle-class family is more favorable to the realization of high potential (see also Vernon, Adamson and Vernon, 1977). This phenomenon was noted many years ago and was discussed by Terman (1925) in the classical study already described in some detail; the central question at this point is that of why it exists.

A major part of the process of growing up involves the taking over by children of values, attitudes, habits, ways of behaving and various skills from those with whom they have contact (see Cropley, 1982a, for a more detailed discussion). This learning process occurs partly as a result of coping models to which children are exposed, partly as a result of the giving or withholding of rewards and punishment, with or without conscious intent. Finally, children acquire standards for determining who is a worthwhile person, as well as an image of themselves as competent or incompetent, clever or stupid, active or passive, loved or unloved. The process through which this occurs is that of *socialization*; the results of the process include acquisition of attitudes and values, of skills and abilities, and of a self-image.

The middle-class family tends to transmit to children highly positive attitudes to school and teachers, as well as to intellectual activity itself. The parents' own attitudes and values also lead frequently to a high level of interest in how their children fare in school, with discussions, overt encouragement, etc. Frequently, the parents' own life history provides a model of success (by conventional standards) and actively demonstrates the worthwhileness of school and learning as aids to achieving a satisfying lifestyle. Finally, many opportunities may be offered for the development of necessary skills, for instance through frequent conversations with parents, or through the provision of books and magazines, perhaps a piano or other musical instrument, tutoring, special training, coaching and the like (Horowitz and O'Brien, 1986). In families that are less well endowed financially, by contrast, many of these factors may be missing (or may take a form which differs from the conventional). There is a greater likelihood of, for instance, reduced emphasis on abstract verbal communication, unfavorable parental experiences with the institution school, or lack of money to cover the costs of special facilities or tuition (see Gallagher, 1986b, for a detailed discussion). The cumulative effect of this is to reduce children's chances of realizing their potentials in ways likely to be greeted as "gifted".

The culturally different

Societies normally contain a number of subgroups with differing cultural norms, even differing languages, as a result of different ethnic backgrounds, different levels of education and income (socioeconomic status groups or social classes) or immigration. It usually happens, however, that the culture of one dominant subgroup is widely accepted as "correct" or standard; this is the culture of the schools, of governing bodies, of the law courts, of many social agencies, of the media. The particular language of this dominant subgroup, (usually the middle class), even its particular form of the national language, is regarded as superior. Behaviors, values and norms of nondominant subgroups are seen as less desirable, or even as inferior or ignorant. A society thus contains various subgroups which are "culturally different." Their members are, in a sense, outsiders, even when they are full citizens of the country and enjoy, in theory at least, full equality with the members of the dominant subgroup.

The problem is, in a nutshell, that disproportionately few children from "culturally different" family backgrounds participate in special programs for the gifted (e.g., Preston, Greenwood, Hughes, Yuen, Thibadeau, Critchlow and Harris, 1984). The mirror image of this state of affairs is that a disproportionately high number of culturally different children is to be found in programs for children with learning problems (Salend, Michael and Taylor, 1984). However, according to Ginsberg and Harrison (1977), this is not the result of an absence of able youngsters among culturally different groups, but rather of the fact that only up to 50 percent of such children are recognized as gifted and treated accordingly. Confirming that many clever youngsters from culturally different backgrounds are never recognized, Vernon, Adamson and Vernon (1977) also point out that the disproportion becomes greater as the children's age increases.

Many such children regard education differently from teachers and the successful able. They may receive no encouragement at home, come under pressure to conform to group norms which are antagonistic to school learning, experience no motivation to achieve or see themselves as preprogrammed for failure. The importance of factors such as these is emphasized by the fact that there *are* culturally different groups which produce large numbers of children who are acknowledged as exceptionally able (e.g., Japanese or Vietnamese in the USA). However, these subgroups usually possess group norms highly favorable to school and learning. Furthermore, the relatively few youngsters who are recognized as exceptionally able in subgroups with "unfavorable" norms usually come from the atypical home (for the group in question) where values, attitudes, self-image, etc., resemble those of the dominant social group (Tannenbaum, 1979; Mistry and Rogoff, 1985). Thus, as was the case with children of low socioeconomic status, family background and associated skills, values and self-image are of vital importance in determining the degree to which culturally different groups are underrepresented, or as Salend, Michael and Taylor (1984) put it "underserved," in gifted education.

Language is a particular problem for many culturally different groups. This is most obvious in the case of children who come from home backgrounds where a language other than the dominant or official language is spoken — for instance, children of indigenous people such as Australian Aboriginals or North American Indians, or of immigrant groups such as Turks in the Federal Republic of Germany, or Mexicans and Puerto Ricans in the USA. In such situations, exposure to two languages may lead not to *bi*-lingualism in the sense of mastery of both languages, but to *semi*-lingualism — reduced competence in both — or even to a situation where the dominant language is seen as the enemy of the "mother tongue," something which is to be used as little as possible even by children who speak it well. This problem is not confined to children with a foreign mother tongue, but also applies to youngsters who speak a nonstandard version of the dominant language, one which is regarded with contempt or as a sign of backwardness by the members of the dominant group, including teachers. This problem is to be seen among West Indians in Great Britain or in some groups of Blacks in the USA.

Apart from psycholinguistic conflicts (for instance "interference" of one language with the other, with resulting grammatical errors, wrong spelling, etc.), various forms of psychological conflict may arise. For instance a child may regard Spanish as a proud language and English as that of the oppressor, whereas the teacher may regard mastery of English as a sign of intellectual superiority and the speaking of Spanish as a sign of retardation or ignorance. Linguistic allegiance may cause some children to reject the dominant school norms. Others, by contrast, may accept that they themselves are stupid or backward because they are proficient in a nondominant language; some children may do both. Far from being the blessing it ought to be, therefore, bilingualism (or even multilingualism) can drive a wedge between some culturally different children and the skills, values, motives and self-image required for the realization of hidden talent in the society at large.

Exceptionally able girls

Three facts have been established about able girls in comparison with boys: fewer girls than boys obtain extremely high IQ scores; there have been fewer girls than boys among prodigious achievers; girls as a group tend to achieve in different subjects from boys. Hitchfield's (1973) study in the UK, for instance, showed that there were fewer girls than boys among the youngsters with very high IQs. This finding was confirmed in the USA by Feldman (1984); in a reanalysis of data from the original Terman study, he showed that nearly 60 percent of those with IQs of 150 or more were boys, while no fewer than 19 out of 26 youngsters with IQs of 180 and more were male. In summarizing findings in this area, Vernon, Adamson and Vernon (1977) concluded that the ratio of boys with extremely high IQs to girls with similar scores is about 3:2. (The other side of the coin is that there are significantly fewer girls than boys with extremely low IQs.)

Turning to the specific example of mathematics, the Johns Hopkins group (Stanley, 1978) reported that in their first SMPY (Study of Mathematically Precocious Youth) contest, 19 percent of the boys in that study of the very highest level of mathematics achievement scored higher than any girl, and that in subsequent contests through 1976, the percentage of boys outscoring the *top* girl were 7.0, 1.5 and 5.5. This finding has also been repeated in the Federal Republic of Germany, where two surveys of children in the Hamburg area in 1983 and 1984 yielded an overwhelming predominance of boys among mathematically outstanding children (Wagner, Zimmermann and Stüven, 1986). Stanley observed that if special mathematical instruction were to be provided for the 28 contestants who scored highest on the mathematical reasoning test in the then most recent competition, all the qualifiers would have been male. One cannot escape the feeling that, in the societal climate of the USA in the late 1970s, Stanley and his colleagues had made strenuous efforts to find mathematically precocious females for their program, which has become widely known and respected. Bereiter (1976) commented on a "good bit of agonizing [in the work of SMPY] about the poorer showing of girls and [making] noble efforts to do something about it." Some of Stanley's concern shows through in his comment that:

> simply to assume . . . that a difference between means or a percentage of high scorers (between the sexes) *must* be evidence of bias and invalidity (in the tests) is either naive or pernicious. One cannot get around the implications by refusing to face the facts. (Stanley, 1978, p. 28)

A study by Armstrong (1980) reported that "females start their high school mathematics career with at least the same ability as their male contemporaries .. [but] by the twelfth grade, males have overtaken females." Armstrong's study emphasized *participation* rather than mathematics achievement alone, and was not concerned solely with the ultrahigh achievers. Factors which were found to have the greatest effect on participation were: attitude toward mathematics; perceived need for mathematics for future career and educational plans; influences of significant others, including teachers, parents and counselors.

Fox (1976) carried out a well controlled experiment in which a group of 26 high scoring girls from the 1973 SMPY competition were given a special female oriented accelerated mathematics program "that would work with and not against their social interests." The girls, who were individually matched with students in a control group for mathematical and verbal aptitude and for educational level of parents, were taught in an all girl class by three female teachers. Fox explains that the class was "designed to provide greater social stimulation . . . Cooperative rather than competitive activities were stressed [and] . . . there was a series of speakers, both men and women, who met with the girls to talk about interesting careers in mathematics and science." Eighteen of the 26 starters completed the course, a dropout rate comparable with that for the regular SMPY programs. Analysis of covariance of the posttest Algebra I test scores showed a highly significant superiority in favor of the girls who had taken the experimental program, although this might have been due in part to practice effects; the experimental girls had already been tested on a parallel form of the Algebra test. Fox concluded that "it is possible to motivate girls to come to a special accelerated program when social aspects of the program are emphasized." But she conceded that "not all the girls enjoyed the class and benefited from it."

A second important study is by Benbow and Benbow (1984) who

proposed, after comprehensive consideration of alternative hypotheses, that it is "a combination of both [biological and environmental] factors which cause the sex difference in [precocious] mathematical reasoning ability." They acknowledge that "any hypothesis involving biological differences between males and females will prove to be unpopular and controversial," but maintain that "the scientific method does not always allow one to take the most socially or politically expedient approach."

One of the most persuasive pieces of evidence suggesting at least a contribution by nonenvironmental factors to the lopsided representation of males and females in the very top flight of mathematically able students stems from a study by Benbow and Stanley (1983). In this study, data were collected from 1980 through 1982 from nearly 40,000 intellectually gifted students in Grade 7 (or 8 if accelerated). All of these children (just over half of whom were female) had scored in the upper three percent in mathematical *or* verbal, or overall ability tests; i.e., both male and female talent search participants were selected by equal criteria before entering. They were then given the College Board Scholastic Aptitude Test's mathematics (SAT-M) and verbal (SAT-V) sections, which are designed for above average 12th graders entering college. The Benbows reasoned that, as most of the 13-year-old students were demonstrably unfamiliar with mathematics from algebra onward, a high performance on the highly abstract SAT could only occur by the use of extraordinary mathematical reasoning ability; for environmentally oriented theories alone to account for high performance by Grade 7 students on the college entry test, it would be necessary to hypothesize that "early socialization experiences significantly influence mathematical reasoning ability as measured by the SAT-M." In the event, the ratio of boys to girls scoring higher than 500 on SAT-M (approximately the mean of college bound 12th grade males) was more than 2 to 1. When the data were sifted to find students who had scored 600 or higher on the SAT, the ratio of males to females increased to 4.1 to 1, while the Grade 7 boys who performed at the very high level represented by a score of 700 or more (the top five percent of college entrants), outnumbered similarly talented females by 12.9 to 1.

There seems to be sufficient evidence to conclude, beyond reasonable doubt, that at the very pinnacle of mathematics achievement (i.e., at the level of the "highly gifted" rather than the "typically" gifted) there is a preponderance of males, at least from the middle grades upwards, and that this preponderance cannot be explained in purely environmental terms. However, the purpose in focusing attention on this phenomenon is not to strike a blow for male chauvinism, but to remind ourselves that the incidence of some manifestations of giftedness might differ — at least actuarially — in males and females.

Apart from differences in subject preferences which have just been discussed, there is a general tendency for able girls to realize their potentials less frequently than boys. Tannenbaum (1979) cites data which show that able girls have achieved less well, i.e., made less out of their potential than their male counterparts, over the years. This phenomenon is demonstrated strikingly by Feldman's data already referred to: although five out of seven girls with extraordinarily high IQs (180 and above) obtained a bachelor degree, compared with 17 out of 19 boys, only one girl went on to graduate study, as against 14 of the boys. In a group of youngsters with IQs of 150 and above, only one out of 11 girls went on to a professional career, whereas all the boys did.

The findings cited to date allow little argument — there are marked differences between able boys and girls, in that girls less frequently realize their potentials and realize them in a narrow range of areas. In this sense, girls are "disadvantaged." The question now arises of why this is so. There are grounds for believing that a good deal of the disadvantage suffered by able girls can be explained in terms of restricted opportunity for acquisition of knowledge and skills, unfavorable attitudes and values, lack of motivation, and negative self-image. As Griggs (1984) has pointed out, prodigious achievement seems to require independence of mind, self-direction in learning, and extreme persistence. Girls, on the other hand, are expected to be dependent and yielding (Freeman, 1983). Boyd (1986) reported significantly lower achievement motivation among girls than boys in her sample, and related this to family expectations that girls will not go on to outstanding achievement. In other words, girls *learn* to expect to achieve less well than boys (Freeman, 1983). Their self-image less frequently includes expectations of academic success (Whitmore, 1980).

Even stated in a more positive way, the situation of girls is unfavorable: as Eccles (1985) pointed out, one of the clear differences in values between able girls and similar boys is that gifted females are, as a group, also interested in being homemakers. Thus, the prodigiously achieving girl may be placed in a situation where doing well involves a conflict, or ambivalence about herself; gifted females with a successful career but no family in the traditional sense often display a high level of emotional disturbance (Helson, 1966), but those who accept the traditional role of homemaker as their main form of fulfillment also report low levels of life satisfaction (Feldman, 1984). There appears to be a real danger of a "Catch 22" situation for gifted females.

Children from geographically remote regions

In some ways children from geographically remote areas resemble physically handicapped youngsters in that they experience reduced levels of contact with the stimulating experiences which are required to foster the acquisition of skills and growth of knowledge. They differ in that they do not suffer from an inability to move freely about or from sensory handicap, but as a result of simple isolation. In terms of social contacts, this isolation may result in a scarcity of appropriate role models and contact with other exceptionally able youngsters. At the socioeconomic level, family interests and values may place no great emphasis on academic achievement.

Politically, the community may lack "advocates," i.e., people who regard fostering of unusually able children as a primary goal of the local school system, resulting in lack of recognition of ability, lack of provision of appropriate experiences, lack of opportunity to develop skills and abilities, and lack of motivation or image of oneself as a potential "high flyer." Lack of exposure to other highly able youngsters can also lead to satisfaction with low levels of achievement through ignorance of what outstanding performance really involves.

Even favorably disposed school authorities face a number of organizational problems. It is, for instance, difficult for isolated communities to assemble a sufficient number of exceptionally able children to justify the cost of special measures. What seems to be crucial, and to be common to successful programs for isolated gifted youngsters, is that the program encourages the child to expect to reach a high level of achievement. Practical measures for bringing this about must often be oriented towards individual motivation, because of the scarcity of appropriate peers. Activities which teachers who are sensitive to the position of the isolated able child can put into effect involve a mixture of individual progression, enrichment and acceleration, of a kind which can be tailored to the needs of a single individual, such as work-study programs, supervised research projects and work on out-of-level texts. Everything depends on the sympathy, insight, knowledge and ingenuity of appropriately informed teachers.

The gifted handicapped

Children with motor and sensory disabilities

According to Humes (1985) there are at least 120,000 unusually able children in the USA who are also disabled, and possibly as many as 540,000. This statistic suggests that special legislative provision, such as the Education for all Handicapped Children Act in the USA, or the Education Act on Special Needs in Great Britain, is fully justified. Apart from the fact that their handicap may prevent them receiving the environmental stimulation they (like all children with exceptional potentials) need, such youngsters have the problem that their potential may go unrecognized, so that they may have to struggle more or less alone to realize it. In this respect, they show many similarities with the socioeconomically or culturally disadvantaged.

Children with motor or sensory disabilities, with chronic illnesses such as diabetes, or with recurring debilitating or disruptive conditions which require frequent or even constant medication, such as asthma, eczema or epilepsy, often suffer marked limitations in their exposure to environmental stimulation. The physically handicapped child cannot run and jump, visit new places, or even take part in special events, with the ease enjoyed by the nonhandicapped child. The deaf child is denied access to a whole category of environmental stimuli, as is the blind youngster. A child who is under continual medication may be limited by constant sedation. Such conditions can severely limit access to the experiences needed for the growth of skills or the acquisition of knowledge.

This unhappy state of affairs is further compounded by psychological factors. Handicapped children may be overprotected by parents, teachers or classmates, with the result that they may come to see themselves as less capable than other people, or even as helpless. On the other hand, they may be encouraged to take on tasks which are too much for them, with the result that they experience frustration and a sense of failure. The result can be a negative self-image, lack of task commitment, or a negative image of school (e.g., Karnes, Schwedel and Lewis, 1983). Thus, the danger exists that such youngsters are not only denied opportunities to develop appropriate knowledge and skills, but that they may come to see themselves in an unfavorable way, lacking an appropriate self-concept, favorable attitudes and values, and positive motivation.

As with all exceptionally able children, but particularly those whose circumstances inhibit their opportunities for realization of outstanding ability, self-concept seems to play a vital role. Such children not only have a need for school activities which straddle the fine line between challenging them adequately and frustrating them, but they also need opportunities for contact with other able youngsters, both handicapped and nonhandicapped. In addition, they need opportunities for contacts with the external world to help compensate for the limitations imposed by their disability, not only in the area of self-image, motivation and values, but also in the acquisition of knowledge, skills and abilities. This latter need should be understood in terms of the known characteristics of unusually able children: a thirst for knowledge; fascination with an area of special interest; a tendency to take on difficult tasks; a not infrequent lack of concern for relationships with other people. Some of these characteristics present enough difficulties in the absence of a handicap, but are especially problematic when coupled with a physical condition which tends, of itself, to frustrate their realization.

Emotionally disturbed able children

The relationship between unusual ability and emotional disturbance is one of psychology's oldest research problems; Lombroso (1891), for instance, examined the truth of the belief that "genius is to madness close allied." Although Jamison (see Holden, 1987) argued that manic episodes seem to have made it possible for many famous people to break out of the bonds of everyday life and reach the highest levels of achievement, Freeman (1983) concluded that emotional disturbance is not in itself an inherent part of unusual ability, and may be a hindrance: Cropley and Sikand (1973), for instance, showed that rigidity and anxiety blocked the emergence of creativity in chronic schizophrenics. Getzels and Dillon (1973), Lutz and Lutz (1980) and Maltby (1984), among others, have shown that some highly able youngsters display emotional disturbances and even disruptive behavior in school and at home. Nonetheless, it is important to remember that this is by no means universal — Hitchfield (1973) for instance, concluded that most clever children are well adjusted. Disagreement about the prevalance of emotional disturbance among the exceptionally able may be explained in part by the fact that many youngsters in this group are diligent, friendly and open, but at the same time depressive, nervous and lacking in self-assurance (Tannenbaum, 1979).

According to Whitmore (1980) poor self-image and lack of self-confidence lead to disturbances of behavior among able youngsters: typically *aggressiveness* in the case of boys and *withdrawal* in the case of girls. The risk that disturbances will manifest themselves increases as the level of ability rises, so that the most able are at highest risk, especially the small group of extraordinarily gifted children with IQs over 180 (Horowitz and O'Brien, 1986). A possible explanation of this phenomenon is that the discrepancy between ability or talent (which are highly advanced) and social/emotional development (which may be at the level of an average child) is greatest.

The school is one of the major causes of emotional disturbance among highly able children, who are frequently forced to deal with unchallenging material which they find both elementary and irrelevant to their special interests (Tannenbaum, 1979), with resulting boredom and frustration. In turn, boredom and frustration lead to behaviors regarded by teachers and classmates as antisocial, so that it is not uncommon for teachers to see clever youngsters as disturbed, because they do not fit into the usual framework (Maltby, 1984). The children may even threaten the teacher's self-concept (Vernon, Adamson and Vernon, 1977) by wanting to treat the teacher as a colleague, or even as a fellow learner who is, unfortunately, a little on the slow side!

In addition, unusually able youngsters sometimes find difficulty in forming associations with their classmates; they may show no interest in the usual games and activities and threaten the conventional role structure by failing to fit in anywhere. This can lead to hostility and isolation. This problem was observed over 60 years ago by Hollingworth, who concluded that it is especially children with extraordinarily high IQs (> 180) who often suffer this way (see Hollingworth, 1942). According to her findings, the problem is particularly acute between the age of four and nine, where agemates simply do not possess the vocabulary, concepts or interests to form assocations with outstandingly able youngsters. Hollingworth introduced the interesting idea of the "optimum IQ," which lies between 125 and 155 in her view.

Some unusually clever youngsters have problems with their parents — surpassing those which are commonplace between parents and children. Sometimes parents see an able child as a source of status and prestige, or as a chance vicariously to relive lost chances of their own youth. The result can be "forcing" of a child who is perceived as gifted. Parents should not be condemned for taking an active interest in the intellectual development of their children, but excessive reactions which may take on neurotic proportions are a cause for concern. Some parents, by contrast, try to force their children to behave "normally" (Ginsburg and Harrison, 1977), i.e., to conform to conventional rules. Others show warmth and affection only when the child is successful, reacting with rejection and hostility when the child fails to meet their expectations (Colangelo and Dettman, 1983). Parents may be enthusiastic about a gifted program as long as it it offers them the gratification of being able to bask in their child's successes, but become extremely hostile to it when their child ceases to shine.

The unusually able child can thus be placed in a situation where the teacher, who should be an ally, often regards him or her as a troublemaker, classmates are rejecting instead of providing close confidants and even parents are inconsistent, sometimes supportive, sometimes regarding the child as a nuisance or a burden. The result can be *ambivalence about oneself*, with subsequent nervousness and uncertainty, hostility, withdrawal or isolation.

A special emotional problem in some exceptionally able or talented children is that of "burn out." Early success or unusual promise establish extremely high expectations of a child. These expectations are taken over by the child, so that anything less than absolute peak performance is seen as a failure. Unremitting pressure from parental expectations, from teacher demands, from an image as someone who produces only the best, can result in a narrow focus on excellence in a particular speciality, to the detriment of wider cognitive development. Endless concentration on a single speciality can lead to social isolation and immaturity in interpersonal relations. Emphasis on peak performance at all times leads to fear of failure, which manifests itself in a self-questioning reluctance to take risks and a generally elevated level of anxiety. Hendrickson (1986) describes the growth of "emotional instability" and "an anxiety complex" among musical prodigies, and shows how this can destroy the career of talented young people of prodigous potential. In a similar vein, Lacattiva (1985) described the "tremendous accountability" imposed on exceptionally able young-sters, and the ensuing fear of failure, guilt, anxiety and frustration, which she concluded often lead to "social and/or emotional maladjust-ment."

The whole issue of adjustment problems among exceptionally able children needs to be examined with care. Despite a tendency for advocates of special provision to justify it as a way of avoiding or alleviating maladjustment and personal difficulties, there is a great deal of evidence that clever children as a group have a good grasp of the values and social skills of their societies, usually have little difficulty in getting along with others, and display only about the same incidence of maladjustment as less clever children, or may even show *better* levels of adjustment (see Janos and Robinson, 1985 for a recent summary of evidence). Does this mean, then, that emphasis by proponents of special provision for the gifted on adjustment problems is a red herring?

Despite the fact that unusually clever youngsters are by no means predestined to lives of social isolation and psychological maladjustment, it is clear that there *are* children who experience difficulties. Furthermore, it seems that there are specifiable circumstances which are associated with the appearance of adjustment problems. For instance, children of extremely high ability experience more emotional and social problems, presumably because their deviation from the norm is very large. The incidence of emotional disturbance among the highly able rises in adolescence (Feger, Wieczerkowski and Prado, 1987) and may in this age group surpass the level among less able youngsters, which suggests that the "normal" adjustment problems of this life stage may cause special difficulties for a comparatively high proportion of able youngsters.

Where unusually able students are either "driven" by their parents and/or teachers, or are labeled as different from other children, the likelihood of problems is increased. Although this is obviously an argument against special measures which label and isolate clever students (i.e., against some approaches to gifted education), or which cater to the neurotic compulsion of some parents to bask in the reflected glory of their children's exceptional talents, it also has important implications of another kind. Unusually able children are often, as has already been pointed out, highly motivated, goal oriented, single minded, onesided in interests and the like. Where teachers and peers regard these characteristics as signs of maladjustment and deviance, and label children accordingly, they are establishing conditions in which the likelihood of social and emotional problems is increased. In a similar way, as Janos and Robinson (1985) showed in their extensive summary of knowledge in the area, able children who are blocked from realizing their ability (gifted underachievers) are much more likely to display psychological disturbances, including emotional and social maladjustment, unfavorable self-concept and conflict with the norms of their society.

What this all means is that maladjustment in the exceptionally able is often a reaction to an unfavorable environment (as is the case with all children). School or subgroup norms which reject hard work, dedication to a subject, extreme interest in school learning, unusually high achievement and the like, or simply make it difficult for ability and talent to manifest themselves (for instance through lack of challenge, uninteresting — for the unusually clever — tasks, lack of opportunity to pursue a special interest, lack of recognition and acclaim, lack of opportunity to interact with intellectual equals and the like) increase the likelihood of psychological disturbance in the unusually clever. It is this state of affairs (the possibility that they *cause* emotional disturbances), not an intrinsic relationship between high ability and pathology, which makes it important for teachers and parents to be aware of the special situation of unusually able children.

Some practical considerations

Unrealized potential — causes

Some children are inherently capable of prodigious achievement, but do not manifest it. Some achieve highly, but fail to reach the full levels of which they are capable, while others display outstanding achievement only after surmounting unusual hurdles or at great personal cost. What are the causes of this phenomenon?

Conceptualizations such as Renzulli's three ring model and Sternberg's triarchic approach, which separate giftedness and intellectual ability into components, provide useful approaches. On the one hand, development of *special skills* may be limited by certain background circumstances (we have already mentioned socioeconomic status, physical or sensory handicap, geographical isolation, cultural difference, skin color and gender). Some groups, for instance, suffer "linguistic disability" (Australian Schools Commission, 1980), while others show gaps in other areas of skill, ability and knowledge which their society values and defines as essential for giftedness. In addition, *task commitment*, which is invariably a characteristic of prodigious achievement may be inhibited by unfavorable attitudes, values and self-image. This latter factor is of crucial importance: the realization of potential is enormously enhanced by a child's belief that success is possible, by "expectation of mastery" (Rathje and Dahme, 1985). Conversely, lack of belief in oneself as capable of achieving — low self-esteem (Colangelo and Dettman, 1983) or negative self-image (Whitmore, 1980) — reduces the likelihood that potential will be realized. Other inhibitory factors include acceptance of the view that school is a waste of time, or that it is deviant to be interested in learning. A components approach thus shows that both cognitive and noncognitive factors are important, and that the particular pattern of these and the level of their development are decisive: life conditions which inhibit even one of these areas of development hinder the emergence of giftedness.

Kerry (1981) discussed the factors which are essential for conversion of potential into academic achievement; these include:

1. Parental or other strong social encouragement;
2. A clear plan or goal;
3. A belief that school learning is valuable;
4. Satisfactory personal and social adjustment;
5. A sense that succeeding is worthwhile.

In addition to such fostering conditions, it is also possible to look at factors which actively inhibit the realization of potential. These include:

1. Lack of opportunity for development of special skills and abilities;
2. Restricted exposure to stimulating experiences;
3. Lack of contact with other clever youngsters;
4. Lack of contact with appropriate adult models;
5. Lack of recognition of abilities, talents or exceptional performance;
6. Exposure to group values which denigrate high performance and positive motivation;
7. Exposure to socializing agencies (family, peer group, etc.) whose attitudes to school and school like activities are negative.

Expanding the criteria for recognizing exceptional ability

Different societies, and different subgroups within a society, use different criteria in answering the question "Who are the unusually able in our midst?" Freeman (1983) has made this point in a dramatic way by pointing out that in a Stone Age society giftedness would probably have been defined as encompassing the ability to hunt effectively, in Ancient Greece as requiring skill in rhetoric, and in a modern society as involving mastery of the skills demanded by advanced technology.

Although different subgroups may define exceptional ability according to different criteria, only those of the dominant cultural group may receive recognition in schools (Gallagher, 1986b); in most countries this means emphasis on language, abstract thinking, listening, sitting quietly and attending, dealing with problems through discussions and respect for authority. To take one contrasting example (and admitting the danger of applying a stereotypical oversimplification), working-class values probably give more weight to visual than aural stimuli, to physical reaction than verbal discussion, to concrete rather than abstract content, to immediate reward rather than to remote future possibilities, to clear concrete structures rather than theoretical considerations. Ways of behaving which are highly effective in certain settings may therefore be judged in schools as ineffective, antisocial, or even retarded. Much the same point has been made by Cropley (1983) in regard to immigrant groups, while it may also be applied to girls, who often show greater ability in artistic and linguistic skills or in affective relationships than in numerical and strictly cognitive fields.

One solution, according to Gallagher, is to supplement conventional criteria (abstract thinking processes, delay of gratification, control of impulses, high speed, etc.) with additional criteria which are important to the particular group in question when dealing with special groups. In other words, propensities which are highly valued in a certain group, and are taken as a sign of unusual ability in that group, should be added to the list of criteria used to identify the unusually able. A related approach would be to acknowledge recognition as a leader by the members of a special group as a criterion of exceptional talent. Naturally this approach has its limitations, since it is unlikely, for instance, that many societies would want to acknowledge as gifted a person recognized as an unusually skillful criminal and leader of other criminals. When applied to immigrants, the poor, residents of remote communities, even the physically handicapped, however, it is clearly an approach which merits serious consideration.

Baldwin (1985) drew attention to the importance of developing novel procedures for use with minority groups. What is needed is to specify aspects of the observable behavior of members of minority groups which might be useful as indicators of exceptional ability. On the basis of a combination of her own practical experience as a teacher and reading of the relevant literature she suggested a number of "exceptional characteristics to look for" (p. 233). These would function, in effect, as supplements to IQ, high grades, highly acclaimed performance of a conventional kind, and the like, in identifying the unusually able. These indicators include (Baldwin, 1985, p. 233): sense of humor, intuitive grasp of situations, understanding of compromise, ability to think systematically, insightfulness, flexibility, even good eye-hand coordination or gracefulness and skill in body movements. George and George

(1986) reported the results of a survey of North American Indians, which showed that they placed great emphasis on being a good mediator, being able to keep secrets, showing compassion and the like, in identifying outstanding individuals. The contribution of variables such as these to academic excellence is, however, unproven, and there is need for research aimed at pinpointing appropriate indicators.

Implications for test procedures

If hidden ability is to be fostered, it must first be located. Unfortunately, many able youngsters are missed, or are even regarded as deviant, disturbed, rebellious or otherwise unable to function in the school setting. Cropley (1982a) described the case of a Swedish boy with an IQ of 170 who spoke several languages fluently by the time he started school and was already good enough at chess to defeat the local champion, but who was regarded as disturbed by his teachers — despite the fact that he had gone to school with high hopes, a positive attitude, a thirst for learning, great respect for teachers and a desire to succeed on examinations. The same author also described the case of a boy in the USA who was consistently described to his teachers as behaviorally disturbed, despite the fact that he was industrious at home and seemed to his parents to learn with unusual rapidity. When he was finally diagnosed by the school as having learning difficulties, they referred him to a psychologist, who found that his IQ was 170! Conventional tests of ability lay great emphasis on reproduction of what has already been learned (see Chapter 5), as well as on a relatively narrow band of cognitive skills such as remembering, reapplying, deducing, solving, etc. Furthermore, personal properties such as willingness to follow instructions, attend closely to detail and work at high speed are necessary for high scores. As Tyerman (1985) argued, what is needed in the case of socially and economically deprived youngsters are tests which measure *potential*. These tests would concentrate on properties such as keenness of observation, a readiness to have one's interest aroused, or ability to profit from special instruction. Schubert (1967) applied the latter approach with long-term hospitalized children; youngsters who obtained low scores on a conventional intelligence test were given special training in solving test problems, and it was shown on retesting that some of them (although by no means all) had made large gains. This was interpreted as indicating that the initial low scores of children whose performance improved dramatically were the result not of lack of ability but of lack of skills, motivation, etc., which are necessary for successful performance on such tests.

Schubert (1973) has given an example of what such special identification procedures could look like. On the basis of Luria's (1961) theory of the nature of intellectual development, he has developed the so-called "VRB Apparatus" (Verbal Regulation of Behavior). According to Luria, the behavior of the intellectually immature child is dominated by motor reactions to immediate, concrete aspects of the environment; with intellectual growth, however, the child acquires abstract, internal rules for regulating behavior, and these are stored (and can be called up from the memory banks) in the form of verbal rules. A child whose verbal recognition of behavior is well advanced is, in principle, "intelligent," although he or she may lack specific knowledge, skills, even values and self-image which are necessary for obtaining a high IQ. Schubert has developed a procedure for measuring the degree of development of verbal regulation of behavior, using the VRB Apparatus as the test instrument, and has shown that it is possible to identify those children from disadvantaged backgrounds (for instance, chronically hospitalized or Canadian Indian children) who have high potential, despite low IQs.

Counselling

In addition to the counselling needs of all children and young people, unusually able youngsters need what Congdon (1985) called a "two pronged" approach. This takes into account the normal needs of all children, but also emphasizes the special needs arising from the child's unusual level of ability. This is particularly true of youngsters from disadvantaged backgrounds. Such counselling involves:

1. Application of special identification procedures and skills;
2. Planning and application of appropriate intervention strategies in both the cognitive domain (knowledge and skills) and also the personal (values, self-image, etc.,);
3. Career and vocational guidance which opens up to the child the kind of horizons which its ability makes possible.

These steps involve what Paulsen (1985) referred to as "educational guidance," "personality guidance" and "career guidance." Although the first and last of these are probably familiar to most people, the second (personality guidance) may be less well known. It involves counselling aimed at helping the unusually able to cope with the special personal problems arising from their exceptional ability: perfectionism and fear of failure, ambivalence about themselves, arrogance or extreme self-doubt, social isolation, deviation from family or peer norms, and the whole gamut of problems which, as has already been shown, take on extra significance among the gifted, and especially the disadvantaged gifted.

Janos and Robinson (1985) also suggested a number of areas in which counselling for the exceptionally able would take special forms. For instance, in the area of teaching and learning processes, counsellors would not only help to match students with special resources such as appropriate classes, out of school programs or mentors, but would also identify particular teachers who show unusual sympathy for clever children or work well with them. In the personal domain, able children need help in understanding the distinction between being different from the majority and being peculiar or deviant or crazy — i.e., help in accepting themselves. Parents and children need help in setting realistic goals or in accepting that exceptional talent may have consequences for social development, self-concept, power structure within the family, sibling relationships, identity and the like. Hendrickson (1986) showed how counselling helped an exceptionally talented young musician deal with problems arising from her feeling that her devotion to musical goals (which were not forced upon her by parents or teachers, but arose out of her own fascination with her field) had robbed her of her right to be a child.

Counselling is also often necessary with parents. In the present context, this means not family therapy, marital counselling and the like, although these may be important and valuable, but systematic work conducted with parents with the aim of helping the child. Many parents are disturbed by an able child's extreme interest in a special topic, or are made anxious by the child's apparent ability to get by with less sleep than other children, or are embarrassed by the constant, penetrating questioning. They may even come to accept the judgement of peers that their child is "weird." At the other extreme are the parents who are determined that their children must be pushed ahead at all costs, and that absolutely everything possible must be done to facilitate what they see as a one in a million genius. This attitude can be destructive for family life and the relationship to the school, especially where the child is perhaps very able, but not a second Einstein. Feger and Prado (1986) reported problems of this kind among the parents of able children who had sought help in a counselling center. Not only can both these extreme reactions hamper the acquisition of knowledge and skills, but they may also have disastrous consequences for the psychological development of able children, leading to perfectionism, extreme fear of failure or its converse, fear of success, burn out, faking bad, and negative attitudes to school, to other people and to themselves. A final problem is that parents whose ambitions are frustrated, or who see their child as supported in its weirdness by the gifted program, may turn against the program and become vitriolic opponents of it.

Reporting on practical experiences in a counselling center for the gifted, Feger, Wieczerkowski and Prado (1987) emphasized that those who seek help are mostly children and young people who are experiencing personal and educational problems. Of these, only a very small proportion come on their own initiative. The people making contact with the center are usually parents, who are concerned about the child or his/her future. The problems reported are usually specific: in the case of preschool children the parents usually have no idea how to respond to the thirst for knowledge and desire to learn shown by their children. They are uncertain whether it is better to encourage the child or to hold it back. In particular, they are uncertain about whether they should or should not discourage development of school related skills such as reading, counting and writing. In elementary school children, the school itself is often a source of disappointment, because clever youngsters are obliged to operate at a level well below their potentials. Their thirst for knowledge is both passively and actively discouraged, and they are expected to concentrate on elementary skills which they have already mastered. Such children can quickly become involved in a *spiral of disappointment*, to which they react with withdrawal, aggression and inattention. At the time of puberty a number of children display a fall off in achievement, accompanied by inability to engage in concentrated, goal oriented study. At the same time, many of them display a *distrust of authority* which is not easy to eliminate, even in a psychological counselling session. A major problem is that disturbances of the developmental process also depress test scores. Consequently, it is important to take careful account of such disturbances in the identification process. This is particularly true in the case of children from a blue collar background; they are the very group which needs identification procedures attuned to their special situation.

At the level of knowledge and skills, counseling can encourage parents to provide their children with helpful materials and equipment, to establish contact with appropriate people and agencies in the immediate environment, or travel to interesting places or events. At a more personal level, counseling should be oriented towards helping parents gain insight into the nature of their child's deviation from the norm, towards helping them see certain kinds of behavior for what they are — "normal" ways for an able child to come to grips with his/her environment. Parents also need help to develop realistic expectations for their children, and to cope with the danger that the parent, not the able child, will become arrogant, overbearing or excessively demand-ing. On the other hand, there are parents who are frightened by the thought that their child is unusually able, either because they do not know how to react or because they are afraid that this will alienate the child from family, friends and his or her "natural" place in life. Parents need hints on how to help their children develop their talents, but to do so without ceasing to be parents in the traditional sense and without turning themselves into either taskmasters or servants.

Closing remarks

Some able children experience difficulty in realizing their unusual ability in the form of prodigious achievement because of socioeconomic and cultural factors, physical or emotional handicap, or lack of recognition of special needs. Although it is convenient to consider such factors separately, it is important to remember that they frequently appear together, interact or even condition one another. Common to all conditions which lead to "disadvantages" for all youngsters, and more importantly in the present context for unusually able children, are that they reduce opportunities for developing knowledge and values favorable to prodigious achievement, inhibit motivation and block the development of an appropriate self-image.

The existence of such children calls for development of a more encompassing understanding of unusual ability, better procedures for identifying the child with high potential, and greater sensitivity among teachers to the existence and needs of special groups. Among the necessary practical measures are adoption of appropriate counseling procedures with both children and parents; in addition to the needs and problems of all children, exceptionally able youngsters and their parents have special needs arising from the children's giftedness. Central in all of these practical considerations is the teacher. What is required is an understanding and awareness of the existence of disadvantaged able children, sensitivity to their special needs, insight into how to work with them and their parents, and knowledge of appropriate teaching and learning strategies.

8

Instructional Strategies and Tactics for Fostering Excellence

Bloom's (1985) study of outstanding achievers in many different fields led him to conclude that a major contribution to the recognition and acceptance of these people's unusual ability was often made in childhood by a relatively "ordinary" person, who had no special talent in the child's area of giftedness. The crucial factor, in the early stages at least, was that someone — often a teacher — encouraged the children to strive for the best, and praised them highly when they did well. We turn now to the question of how to offer instruction in ways which have this "energizing" effect. What can the teacher in the regular classroom do in order to encourage the kinds of thinking outlined in Chapter 3 in the context of a discussion of "intelligence," or in Chapter 4 in the context of "creativity?" As will become apparent, much of what is good for the unusually able is good for all children.

General goals of instruction for promoting excellence

Feldhusen and Treffinger (1980) identified nine decisive kinds of school-based activities, several of which have special application in the case of outstandingly able children: for example those concerned with the development of an awareness and acceptance in the children of their own capacities, interest and needs, or with the need to relate effectively to other people. However, in general the activities are important for all children: for example those aimed at encouraging maximum achievement in basic skills and conceptual understanding, providing learning activities appropriate to a student's level of academic ability, or exposing youngsters to a variety of potential fields of study or work. Few educators would be likely to say that "ordinary" children do not need basic skills or that they should not having learning experience appropriate to their level of ability. Even these, however, are areas of particular importance for those who deviate from the norm, and take on

141

a particular form in the case of children whose deviation consists in unusually high ability.

In addition to activities of this kind, Feldhusen and Treffinger listed several instructional goals which are of particular significance for the fostering of academic excellence as we have defined it. These include:

1. Establishing a large fund of information about diverse subjects;
2. Giving opportunities for gaining experience in creative thinking and problem solving;
3. Offering stimulation to pursue higher level aspirations;
4. Promoting the development of independence and self-direction in learning.

These are not separate, discrete goals. A challenging problem-solving exercise is itself generally a task which requires high levels of aspiration; if dealt with adequately it often requires the acquisition of comprehensive information and perhaps exercise of creativity; successful experiences of this kind provide a vehicle for the development of independent thinking. In addition to the more obvious cognitive and motivational goals implicit in the list just presented, exceptionally able youngsters also need special help in both the intrapersonal and interpersonal domains, even if, or particularly if, they remain in the regular classroom.

Interpersonal aspects

Relating to other people is of special significance in the area of academic excellence, since one of the major criticisms leveled at exceptionally capable children is that they frequently look down on those who are less clever than they. At the very least, even if conscious feelings of superiority are not present, able people have an unfortunate knack for making others feel inadequate. Children who become impatient with classmates, or even with a teacher who seems remarkably slow to grasp a point, are unlikely to enjoy high levels of popularity, regardless of whether they really do look down on other people or are merely assumed to do so. Furthermore, such children are likely to be a disruptive influence in the classroom; there is a risk that they will use their ability to the detriment of others. An important aspect of work with exceptionally capable children, then, is to help them to get along with others, to show consideration for the rest of society, and to accept the social responsibilities arising from their high ability.

At the practical level, this can include learning to state their own ideas in terms relevant to other people's goals and interests, or to make sure that they state criticisms in positive and constructive ways. Clever children need to learn to avoid threatening others, or destroying their dignity by making them look small or foolish. Teachers can help such children to "buy" a certain freedom from conformity pressures, or a certain degree of acceptance, by making concessions to the group, for instance by engaging themselves in causes which command group respect. This is not a matter of conformity or hypocrisy, but of learning to respect other people's feelings and needs, and of understanding that these may differ from one's own without necessarily being stupid. One important teacher activity in this area consists merely of an occasional private talk with the gifted student: the teacher's respect for the uniqueness of the exceptionally able child is emphasized, but the needs of other children are also made clear, along with the possibility that they may feel themselves threatened by what seems to the clever youngster to be perfectly reasonable behavior. Teaching aimed at promoting exceptional academic achievement is thus not simply a matter of forcing more and more information into the heads of clever children, so that they can astonish observers by the breadth and depth of their knowledge. It also involves helping the youngsters to live harmoniously with adults and other children, less clever than themselves, without feelings of superiority, condescension or impatience.

Personal aspects

Unusually able children need the *will to achieve* highly — if they are to realize their potential they must be ready to make the necessary effort. Fortunately, it seems that such youngsters are naturally inclined to seek and pursue knowledge, so that the teacher's task is more that of protecting the child against being "turned off." Part of this process is that of acquiring (or perhaps of not losing) *trust in oneself* as being capable of mastering difficult material, of rising to the challenge — in other words of possessing a positive self-image. Put somewhat differently, being unusually able places a child in an outsider position, and behaving brilliantly carries with it many risks — the risk of being rejected by others, the risk of making a mistake in the course of rushing ahead into unkown areas and the risk of not being understood. Consequently, high ability requires possession of the *courage* to be unusual, if it is to be realized in the form of exceptional achievement. Appreciation of the importance of such factors in peak performance helps to explain why some unusually clever children are successful in school and life, whereas many others are not (see Chapter 7). The general goals of instruction for the able thus include not only those associated with knowledge, skills and abilities, nor only those in the social domain, but also those of the kind just outlined.

Classroom principles

The question now arises of how these general goals can be achieved in the regular classroom. In the first instance we will approach this issue by looking at intermediate principles which will serve as a link between the general goals outlined and specific teaching and learning activities.

Establish a favorable classroom climate

The general instructional goals summarized thus far are all very much dependent upon what might be called the "atmosphere" or "climate" in the classroom. The right classroom climate cannot be scientifically prescribed; its creation depends on the art of the teacher, who has to balance a number of considerations. On the one hand, children need clear guidelines about what is expected of them. On the other, independence and self-direction are not encouraged by rigid rules and detailed control of all activities by the teacher.

Various authors have attempted to characterize the general atmosphere of the ideal classroom. Writing in the context of evaluation, Skager (1978) called for "open" goals. Wall (1976) spoke of the necessity for the classroom to provide "a provocative environment." Cropley, (1978) has applied some of this thinking directly to the area of promoting outstanding achievement by distinguishing between activities aimed at reducing blocks to outstanding effort, such as fear of looking foolish or of being misunderstood, and activities aimed at building up readiness or willingness to produce exceptional achievements, such as belief in oneself, desire to excel, pride in achievement, and the like. He went on to describe what he called "opening" behavior on the part of teachers (which fosters readiness for peak performance or breaks down barriers likely to inhibit such performance) and "closing" behavior (which blocks or inhibits favorable attitudes, habits, values, self-image, etc.). A classroom climate favorable to the realization of exceptional ability is characterized by a general air of acceptance, confidence, mutual support, respect for effort and interest in high performance by all youngsters.

Promote self-directed learning

The term "self-directed learning" implies learning in which certain key determinants of the learning process are decided by the person doing the learning and not by some outsider such as the teacher. Examples of such determinants are the content (what is learned), the timing (when it is learned and at what speed), the location (where) and the methods (how). Self-directed learning is a part of everyday life; most people engage in some form of it every day, even if mainly in out-of-school settings. Thus, it is not something new or exotic, nor is it the monopoly of academically exceptional children. On the other hand, it is clear that the typical school setting tends to offer few opportunities for self-direction. Children seldom have the freedom to decide that a particular topic will be covered during a particular lesson, or be taught in a particular way. This is to a considerable degree understandable, since the basic idea of compulsory universal education is that there are specific things which everyone needs to learn; the existence of schools implies a set place of learning, the system of classes implies set times and a set speed. The problem is that the necessity for a degree of external regulation of learning has led to an excessive emphasis on "other-directed learning" in many school settings. The promotion of academic excellence, however, requires the utilization of all abilities and talents of unusually able children, freed — as much as is reasonably possible — from the fetters of learning frameworks which are determined according to the needs of the less gifted majority. The promotion of self-directed learning is an approach which can help make this possible.

Because the idea of external determination of learning is so strong, there is a danger that self-direction will be equated with a number of negative stereotypes. For this reason, it is necessary to remind ourselves at the outset what self-directed learning is *not*. It has already been said that it is not exotic. Nor is it disorganized or unstructured; self-directed learning implies deliberate learning with specifiable goals. It is not *free of all evaluation* but is, in principle, subject to the same criteria of effectiveness and worthwhileness as any other kind of systematic learning. (It may, however, be facilitated by special forms of evaluation, see pp. 147–148.) It is not *isolated or idiosyncratic*. It is not essential that a self-directed learner work without any regard to other people. Indeed, it would be possible to display self-directed learning in tandem with strong elements of other-direction, as for instance when gifted students direct their own learning in order to prepare for an external examination. The learners may decide the time, place, learning modality, tempo, etc., themselves, despite the fact that the content has been determined by a board of examiners and that the evaluation will be carried out without consulting the learners.

Treffinger (1978) has provided useful guidelines for encouraging independent learning. Of these, perhaps the most important is that teachers themselves should present a model of self-directed learning, and not appear as people who have finished learning. Treffinger (1975) has also suggested how the gap between teacher-directed activities and self-directed activities can be bridged in four principal areas of self-directed learning. The four areas are:

1. Goals and objectives;

TABLE 8.1

| | Teacher direction vs self-direction | |
Area	Teacher directed	Self-directed
Goals and objectives	Teacher prescribes for class Teacher provides options or choices Teacher involves student in creating options	Learner controls choice Teacher provides resources and materials
Entering behavior assessment	Teacher tests and makes specific prescription Teacher diagnoses, provides several options Teacher and learner use individual conference; tests employed individually if needed	Learner controls diagnosis, consults teacher for guidance when unclear about needs
Instructional procedures	Teacher presents content, provides exercises and activities, arranges and supervises practice Teacher provides options for learner to employ independently, at learner's own pace Teacher provides resources and options, uses student contracts which involve the learner in scope, sequence and pace decisions	Learner defines projects, activities, etc.
Performance assessment	Teacher implements evaluation and gives grades Teacher relates evaluation to objectives; gives student an opportunity to react and respond Peer partners used in providing feedback; teacher–student conferences for evaluation	Learner makes written self-evaluation, following feedback from peer partners and teacher

2. Entering behavior assessments, or diagnosis;
3. Instructional procedures;
4. Performance assessment, or evaluation.

The differences between teacher direction and self-direction are presented in Table 8.1.

Conventional wisdom in remedial education dictates that the teacher initially pitch a little short of the target, i.e., a little below the level of the student's known capabilities. With academically exceptional students, however, one may be more ambitious and try out self-directed procedures at the outset, as long as one reverts back to an intermediate stage or even, temporarily, to a teacher directed approach immediately it becomes obvious that the initial strategy was overoptimistic. Whether one begins cautiously or ambitiously, however, the aim must be to determine the student's current status with regard to readiness for self-directed learning, and to provide the opportunity, if it is necessary, to advance from that status to the goal of full self-direction.

Encourage self-evaluation

A particularly vexed question is that of evaluation. The obvious inhibiting effects which stem from a fear of doing badly, coupled with the importance of encouraging outstandingly able youngsters to seek new ideas, to develop their own line of thinking and to question conventional wisdom, has led some people virtually to abandon any and all forms of evaluation. Excessive dependence upon assessments made by others could, it is true, be expected to affect adversely the kind of thinking which is necessary for truly outstanding achievement. On the other hand, it is difficult to accept that the translation of extraordinary potential into actual performance requires the suspension of all forms of critical judgement on the part of teachers. Real life exceptional achievers do not type automatically whatever comes into their head, paint on canvas in a random fashion, or simply throw chemicals together; their products represent a unique innovation based, consciously or unconsciously, on a choice between possible alternatives. In other words, it is not reasonable to suggest that evaluation is inimical to peak performance. What is needed is not an abandonment of any kind of evaluation, but rather a change in the methods of evaluation which are carried out. Exceptionally able students need to be able to engage in a process of *self-evaluation*.

In emphasizing the importance of "guided self-evaluation" Cropley (1982a) identified two basic underlying principles: *acceptance* and *acknowledgement*. Acceptance involves a willingness on the part of teachers to take seriously ideas which depart from the everyday or conventional; acknowledgement requires teachers not only to tolerate the efforts of highly able children but also to make it clear that they welcome such efforts and regard them as important, necessary and praiseworthy.

Acceptance and acknowledgement do not mean that everything which highly able students produce should be greeted with unconditional enthusiasm. However, criticism should always be uttered in a context of constructive help, with the twin aims of encouraging the children's self-evaluation, and of making it possible for them to develop their own ideas further. The self-evaluation may be "guided" in the sense that the teacher draws the student's attention to particularly difficult issues or weak spots, indicating what might be expanded upon here, issues that remain unresolved there — without in any way delivering the final word on rightness or wrongness, or assessing penalties for inadequacies. The evaluation is diagnostic, in that it serves as the basis for further steps (i.e., it is formative), it is not an authoritarian assessment of an end product (i.e., it is not summative). This guidance of self-evaluation may be seen as a "trouble shooting" activity in which the teacher offers help in improving an idea, rather than simply indicating that it is valuable or worthless.

Useful intermediate goals in moving towards self-evaluation from solely teacher evaluation were suggested by Treffinger (1975), and have been summarized earlier in the present chapter (pp. 145–146.

Employ a diagnostic teaching approach

The concept of individual differences, in the sense that an academically exceptional student is significantly more advanced than other children of the same age, is only one factor that must be taken into account when planning an educational program. Intraindividual differences have to be taken into consideration in order "to organize an instructional program for a particular child in conformity with his abilities and disabilities, without regard to how he or she compares with other children" (Kirk and Gallagher, 1983, p. 45). Kirk and Gallagher were primarily concerned with educationally handicapped children: mentally retarded, learning disabled, hearing impaired, etc., and they showed how discrepancies in intraindividual growth in an exceptional child may be depicted with the help of developmental profiles. The strategy of diagnostic teaching is to "teach to the profile," i.e., to raise the level of the "valleys" of the profile, exploiting the strengths represented by the "peaks." The same principle is applicable at all levels of teaching, including the teaching of gifted students; the difference is that when we are dealing with the peaks and valleys in the profile of a gifted student it is analogous to being in the Himalayas rather than near sea level.

Stanley's (1978) approach to the acceleration of children showing exceptional precocity in mathematics is a good example of diagnostic teaching at a high level. It has already been pointed out (Chapter 6, pp. 100–101) that although a Grade 4 student who is at the 99th percentile for maths may be rated by the test norms as having a Grade Equivalent of (say) 9.5, this does *not* necessarily mean that he or she possesses the specific mathematical competencies associated with successful achievement by an average student midway through Grade 9. To make such an assumption can be disastrous; what is needed is a preliminary analysis of the subskills necessary for successful attack on the Grade 9 subject matter. The precocious mathematician will undoubtedly possess some, but not all, of these subskills, and it is first necessary to "remediate" — at an advanced level — the deficiencies. Stanley has demonstrated that this can be done in a fraction of the time that the child would take if left to plough through the curriculum at the regular pace. A possible procedure is set out in point form below. Suppose that a student in Grade 3 is finding the maths work very easy, and is clearly not being challenged. The steps in diagnostic teaching require the teacher to:

1. Decide in the first instance, that the student might tackle Grade 4 work. The question is: what important and necessary content of the intervening curriculum has the student already mastered?
2. Select diagnostic tests. If appropriate tests do not exist, construct them by sampling from exercises in the remainder of the Grade 3 book.
3. Administer the tests and evaluate. Do *not* simply count the number of items correct, but use student responses diagnostically i.e., determine what processes, concepts, etc., might be causing problems. (This is good practice in any school testing situation.)
4. "Remediate" any relative deficiences that are identified. The student is now ready to take off at the Grade 4 level.
5. Determine if the student is now being challenged. If not, repeat the process with a view to accelerating to the Grade 4.5 or Grade 5.0 level.

The long established principles of diagnostic teaching may, and should, be applied across the entire instructional spectrum. Renzulli and Smith (1983) refer to the procedure whereby teachers ascertain, by pretesting, what skills exceptional children already have, as "curriculum compacting."

Newland's (1976, p. 289) instructional principles for gifted students provide another encapsulation of the law. According to Newland (p. 289), there are three basic principles:

1. Prethink.
   (a) Goals: immediate (written, operationally defined), distant (subject to modification);
   (b) Facilities;
   (c) Contingency plans for unexpected developments, i.e., when goals prove to have been inappropriate.
2. Match activities to children's ascertained mental levels.
3. Make learning situationally appropriate — essentially motivational — ultimate social significance of some present learning might have to be explained, to render motivation intrinsic.

Classroom activities

Although it is not the intention of this book to list in great detail specific teaching and learning activities which can be directly adopted, it is useful at this point to make suggestions as to how the general ideas just spelled out can be used as a basis for specific classroom practice. Woodcliffe (1977) has suggested a number of useful guidelines, which include provision of opportunities for:

1. Undertaking challenging work independently and in groups;
2. Practising the skill of asking questions;
3. Carrying on discussion with others;
4. Appreciating the need to complete tasks;
5. Enjoying many opportunities for writing.

Challenging activities

To suggest that academically able students should be faced with challenging tasks may appear trite, but it needs to be emphasized — and it further needs to be emphasized that "challenging" is not synonymous with "busy." A project which requires a great deal of work that is different from the regular classroom routine, but equally routine, can be a welcome diversion but hardly challenging in the true sense of the word. The essence of challenging activities is that they "stretch" the able child's ability and help to accustom children to the experience of working at or near their limits. The result is not merely an increase in skill and knowledge, but a bolstered confidence in oneself, joy in confronting the unknown and a thirst for new frontiers.

Some challenging activities are best organized on an individual basis, others through group work. Groups may be formed on the basis of ability, i.e., with a view to establishing homogeneity of ability within the group; on the other hand, in projects which are in a special area rather than of a general nature, grouping on the basis of shared interest might be preferable. Student preferences for group partners can be established through sociometric techniques, which also provide a means of gaining an understanding of the interpersonal structure of a class. The microcomputer makes it easy to analyze the sociometric structure of a class group (see Chapter 10).

Questioning

Questioning is probably the single most powerful method of stimulating effective learning — if the questioning is itself effective.

Questions may be generated externally or internally. Externally generated questions are those asked by the teacher; indeed, the asking of questions that lead to real learning is an art which, for most people, has to be learned. Without deliberate effort, most teachers tend to ask questions which predominantly test factual recall or regurgitation. As a help to teachers in becoming more versatile in their questioning techniques, Bloom's (1956) well known taxonomy of the cognitive domain generates questions at different levels involving knowledge, comprehension, application, analysis, synthesis and evaluation. In order for Bloom's taxonomy to be used effectively, a teacher needs to assimilate it thoroughly so that it shapes questioning style smoothly and naturally. It would be ironic if, in the cause of promoting creative, divergent thinking, a teacher were to be continually looking over her/his shoulder and going to great pains to learn by rote each of the six categories.

An analysis such as Bloom's presupposes adequate knowledge on the part of the respondent, at least for the types of question which involve essentially convergent thinking, i.e., knowledge, comprehension and analysis. Answers cannot be produced out of a vacuum, but they can be coaxed and shaped through prompting and guidance when the student is not completely familiar with the topic, or when the knowledge necessary to give the answer has only partially been assimilated. Even at the relatively low level where a child asks how to spell a word, it is preferable for the teacher not to supply the correct spelling automatically — certainly not with a gifted student — but to counter with "How do you think the word is spelled?" and then prompt the child if and whenever a wrong letter is enunciated. The end result is that the child, with some guidance, has been primarily responsible for working out the correct response.

Discussion with others

It has long been recognized that two heads are better than one, and three heads are usually better then two, but anyone who has served on many committees will probably agree that the law of diminishing returns probably begins to set in shortly thereafter. A creative project or study is likely to be implemented more efficiently if undertaken by a small group; a study of ambitious proportions that requires the efforts of a whole class should be broken down into subprojects, consolidation of which should be the responsibility of a small coordinating committee.

For academically able students, small group work is vital for several reasons. They need to "bounce" their ideas off others and reciprocally, to provide critical feedback to the ideas of others. Implemented in a constructive manner, this helps in the development of a respect for the opinions and ideas of others; it also provides an opportunity for able youngsters to test their own ideas, to sharpen their thinking skills. Working with others should also help gifted students to accept criticism and even acknowledge and learn from failure. Children — all children — should learn in a positive supportive educational climate, but there is nothing incompatible between a positive supportive climate and the inevitable experience of being wrong occasionally. The path to truth and knowledge is paved with checks and balances, thesis and antithesis. When a student (and not only a student) formulates a hypothesis the most effective method of validating that hypothesis is by checking how well it stands up against alternative hypotheses. Abandonment of a cherished opinion does not come easily, and may be nurtured by constructive criticism from one's peers in a seminar/discussion format.

Appreciation of the need to complete a task

An unfortunate byproduct of a totally uncritical approach to gifted students is the stagnation of self-discipline. Students brimming with new ideas may be prone to lose interest — or to shift their enthusiasm to a further new idea — once the initial problem has been understood, when the initial zest has run its course or when tedious details and difficulties present themselves. The writing, for instance, of reports is mundane relative to the thrill of experimental discovery. Nonetheless, as Edison's aphorism that genius is one percent inspiration and 99 percent perspiration emphasizes, it is precisely the slog of organizing one's ideas and communicating them clearly to others which distinguishes effective work from ineffective. As Woodcliffe (1977) put it in a down-to-earth way: "completion of tasks should be a requirement." Precisely this idea was expressed by Sato (1985) when he stressed the importance of "productivity" in the gifted. It is only through such productivity that the highly able can make a concrete contribution to society.

The willingness to complete a task was referred to by Rathje and Dahme (1985) as "persistence," which they linked with the development of "expectation of mastery." In a similar vein, Stedtnitz (1985) referred to "self-efficacy." There is a danger that excessive perfectionism will lead in the able to procrastination, failure in the development of self-efficacy, and a consequent "stifling" of ability. The result of this is not only loss of productivity, serious enough in itself, but also a disturbance of the development of motivation, with the risk of "burn out" (Hendrickson, 1986), or "childlike," "frustrated" or "abandoned" giftedness (Necka, 1986). Unless highly able individuals are able to carry out not only the gratifying "inspiration" of excellent thinking, but also those aspects requiring "perspiration," they are doing little more than playing with their talents, in a way strongly suggestive of mental onanism.

Opportunities for writing

The manipulation of words which verbal expression requires — especially when those words cannot be stuttered in ungrammatical oral speech but have to be committed to paper — has been recognized at least since John Stuart Mill (1873) as stimulating to the intelligence, including creative intelligence, Stanley's (1984) finding that the Scholastic Aptitude Test (Verbal) is the best single predictor of mathematical precocity supports the view that logical thinking demands clear, accurate expression and close attention to the exact meaning of words.

Naturally, practice in writing is of great importance for the emergence of literary excellence. Frequent chances to write also encourage persistence and productivity (see previous section). In addition they encourage fantasy and creativity, self-criticism or even peer evaluation, as well as social contact to readers and other writers. In other words, opportunities for writing are important not merely in the specific content area in whose framework they are usually offered (language arts, creative writing, etc.), but also as a more general way of fostering skills, attitudes and techniques which facilitate the emergence of academic excellence in general.

This view is completely in accord with psychological research and theory on thinking. As Bruner, Piaget and Vygotsky, among others, have emphasized, internal representation of the external world ("thinking" in more everyday language) may occur without the use of abstract symbols, for instance in the form of mental "pictures" of external objects, or even by means of information stored "in the muscles" (a comb, let us say, "means" a series of movements of the arm). Young children, or even animals, may record their impressions of the external world and organize their reactions to it in this way (for instance, a baby which calls for its rattle by making appropriate movements of its hand, or a setter which indicates the whereabouts of a pheasant by "pointing"). However, although other systems are theoretically conceivable, highly differentiated, abstract and extremely flexible verbal symbols are essential for the ability to recognize and specify the principles underlying events, see theoretical connections between these principles, try out in the mind new combinations, communicate new ways of looking at things to other people, etc. In other words, the importance of rich and varied experience with words goes far beyond their role as literary tools (although this does not denigrate the importance of literary excellence) and encompasses the whole area of understanding and storing experience, getting ideas, etc. — in short, of intellectual excellence.

Instructional materials

It is not the intention of the present book to provide a detailed criticism or a catalogue of specific materials designed for academically exceptional children. Indeed, it is not at all certain that such a goal could be achieved, even if it were considered worthwhile. Some years ago, Feldhusen and Treffinger (1980) provided structured critical evaluations of some 50 sets of published material; in furnishing a "gifted resource room," one of the present authors attempted to order most of the materials included in their list, but about a third of the orders were returned "not known at this address." This experience suggests that some publishers in the realm of gifted education do not show the level of "solidity" one might hope for.

A significant proportion of material advertised for use with gifted students is a variety of what Renzulli (1980) has referred to as "patchwork collections of random practices and activities" or "thirty-minute exercises in creative ways to paste macaroni on oatmeal boxes." Sadly, real life experience indicates that academically talented children not infrequently engage in these trivial activities with an itinerant teacher and then evaluate them as "fun," having clearly enjoyed the experience; one wonders just what sort of things they must have been doing in the regular classroom, compared with which these activities are perceived as so attractive.

The best material is likely to be that devised by an experienced and acutely observing teacher. Although appropriate materials are often difficult to devise, a teacher's time is well spent building up a stock of stimulating materials. These might be original creations by the teacher or, more usually, adaptations of existing materials. The British Schools Council Curriculum Enrichment Project (Ogilvie, 1980) used teams of teachers to produce a series of model programs, or "Sceeps," in mathematics, environmental science, humanities and expressive arts. One of the virtues of such programs is that, apart from any intrinsic value in their own right, they are likely to trigger valuable ideas in the mind of a creative teacher. In evaluating any material for use with academically able students, whether or not the material is designated as being for these students, the teacher should actively examine from a predisposition which asks: "Could this material, or an adaptation thereof, act as a springboard for creative, innovative, satisfying activity?" Expressed alternatively, a rule of thumb might be applied which considers — at least in the imagination — how many potential activities per dollar, or how many potential activities per unit of preparation time, may be expected from a particular set of materials, and to prefer those which yield a high ratio.

An excellent example of material which satisfies this rule of thumb is the "Thinkin" program (see Kaplan, 1974). A series of 30 modest task cards listing a number of social and environmental concerns — ranging from world hunger, law and order to fashions — are covered in such a way that research skills, drawing conclusions, report writing and practical creative activities are generated. The potential scope of activities which these cards can set in motion is limited only by the imagination of the teacher and/or student.

The importance of resource materials has been stated very clearly by Henslowe (1986). In introducing a *Handbook of Instructional Materials for Education of the Gifted and Talented*, she emphasized that such a handbook is a "logical complement" to discussions of planning and implementation of special programs for exceptionally able children. Henslowe lists about 150 practical materials (largely printed), suitable for use with able youngsters, and available at the time of writing. These include teachers' guides, activity books and curriculum kits. Many of these concentrate on thinking skills: fostering creativity and productive thinking, encouraging fantasy, promoting the ability to perceive problems, etc. Other materials concentrate on personal properties such as a feeling of self-worth, confidence, or sensory awareness, or an encouraging imagination or eliminating blocks to creativity. In effect, these materials seek to promote the emergence of skills, attitudes and motives which are regarded as prerequisites for academic excellence. A second block of materials focuses on specific content areas such as mathematics, biology, archaeology, ancient history, literature, etc. Finally, some of the materials are intended as self-help guides for teachers, for instance handbooks on developing a learning center, constructing classroom aids or designing curriculum units. Essentially these materials concentrate on procedures for fostering both cognitive and noncognitive aspects of academic excellence.

A separate bibliography in Henslowe's review lists about 75 AV/TV materials including films, audiotapes, videotapes and computer courses. A number of these are intended for use in teacher inservice education and cover topics such as the nature of giftedness, identification procedures, special curriculum arrangements, etc. Many are also suitable for use with parents or other advocacy groups. Others consist of instructional material in fine arts, science, computer studies, politics, literature, geology and many more.

In addition to products suitable for use as resource or enrichment material — teaching aids in more or less the traditional form (although specially prepared with exceptionally able students in mind) — the materials now available also include "do it yourself" guidelines for teachers on how to design special activities for the gifted. Some of them go into how teachers can carry out activities listed earlier in this chapter; for instance, diagnostic teaching or effective questioning. The *Handbook* can thus be seen as an extremely valuable adjunct to the present book, since we focus here on the basic principles underlying special curriculum approaches, and do not attempt to list all possibilities or provide detailed practical instructions.

A major publishing effort in this area has been mounted in the USA in recent years by Trillium Press (PO Box 209, Monroe, NY 10950). This firm regularly distributes a cross between a newsletter and a catalogue containing information on printed material covering thinking skills (problem solving, creative thinking, etc.), future problem solving, leadership and computer applications, to name a few areas. In addition they offer learning material for mathematics, science, art, language arts, geography, philosophy, etc. One interesting feature of their approach is that not only cognitive but also affective issues are considered. Materials include, in addition to learning packages for pupils, teachers' handbooks, texts for the teacher's library, and materials for parents.

Closing Remarks

All children can be encouraged to think and learn more effectively: in other words to make better use of the potentials which they possess. In this sense promoting academic excellence involves helping all children achieve the best of which they are capable, even if this is modest in comparison with the high flyers. Suggestions for changes in classroom teaching and learning methods are thus aimed at all children, not only at those with exceptional potentials, so long as it is assumed (as we do) that fostering the highest achievement is a major goal of the school. Nonetheless, since the unusually able constitute an exceptional group in whose case this general goal requires particular efforts, the suggestions made in this and following chapters take on a special significance for them.

The guidelines offered in this chapter focus not only on the cognitive aspects of academic excellence, but also on social, personal and motivational components: information and strategies for obtaining, storing and applying it are very important, but so are the wish to do this at a high level, the courage to set high goals, faith in oneself, and the ability to do this without alienating peers. A number of general principles (as against, for instance, specific concrete classroom practices) suggest how to go about fostering the aspects of excellence just mentioned. Among these are establishment of an appropriate atmosphere, encouragement of self-directed learning and evaluation, use of diagnostic teaching and the like.

Various classroom techniques can also be listed. These include provision of opportunities for independent work on challenging activities, placing stress on the importance of completing difficult tasks and fostering discussions among students of different approaches to the solution of such tasks. Many kinds of curriculum materials already exist, often in commerical form, which can be applied to the promoting in students of appropriate knowledge, skills, attitudes, values, self-image and the like. Despite a tendency for the market to be cluttered with material of unproven worth, we offer in this and other chapters guiding principles aimed at helping teachers evaluate such materials, as well as develop their own.

9

Fostering the Emergence of Creativity

In keeping with the definition of academic excellence developed in Chapter 4, i.e., that creativity is one of its integral parts, it follows that the promotion of creativity should be one of the major components of programs aimed at fostering outstanding achievement. In this chapter we will look first at general issues in"training" creativity, before proceeding to a discussion of its promotion in the classroom.

Training children to be creative

Defining outstanding academic ability as encompassing not only conventional intelligence but also divergent, innovative thinking, raises the question of whether it is possible to train children to be more creative. The provision of such training would be an indispensable part of any program aimed at fostering academic excellence. Since creativity, as the term is used in the present book, involves branching out from the conventional, seeing unusual implications, recognizing relationships which most people would not notice, etc., training designed to foster creativity would not be limited to transmission of information, but would consist on the one hand of nurturing skills, and on the other of encouraging appropriate attitudes, values, motives and self-image. Furthermore, such training need not be confined to children who have in some way demonstrated high levels of creative potential; *all* children are in principle capable of becoming more willing and able to be innovative, original and the like.

A number of procedures for "training" creativity have been developed in the last 20 years, including both short-term and long-term training programs. The variety of procedures which exist is illustrated by the fact that Treffinger and Gowan (1971) were able to describe nearly 50 different approaches.

Short-term procedures

Davis and Scott (1971) listed more than 20 creativity facilitating activities, including "attribute listing," "idea matrix," "synectic thinking," "creativity toolbox" and "morphological analysis." Endriss (1982) developed a range of brief "games" such as "bridge building," "idea production," "transformations" and "creative connections." All of these are aimed at raising people's level of creativity with the help of simple training procedures requiring only a small amount of time. The idea behind them is that people acquire techniques for getting ideas or going directly to the unusual, that they develop interest in and motivation for thinking of this kind, or that blocking factors such as fear of letting oneself go or lack of trust in one's own ideas are eliminated.

Another approach which can quickly be adopted is "brainstorming:" the members of a group attempt to solve a problem by assembling the largest possible array of ideas on the subject in question, regardless of whether or not these ideas seem to be relevant. A number of studies have concluded that this approach is effective (Luidgrcn, 1967; Mansfield, Busse and Krepelka, 1978; Osborn, 1960; Parnes, 1967). Hudson (1968) even reported that simply giving students ten examples of unusual responses (in this case, unusual uses for an elastic band) greatly increased their scores on a divergent thinking test. Maltzman reported a simple cognitive procedure in which people were required to think up unusual associations to stimulus words. This was said to lead to lasting increases in originality after only a few minutes' training (Maltzmann, Simon, Raskin and Licht, 1960). More recent studies have attempted to improve scores on creativity tests by means of a number of other training procedures: Belcher (1975) showed children a film in which an actor worked on a creativity test, Dansky (1960) allowed children to play with materials similar to those in tests and Ziv (1976) played a tape of a famous comedian to children, in order to increase their willingness to use humor. Glover and Gary (1976) employed the principles of learning and attempted to increase the frequency of divergent responses by the application of appropriate reinforcements.

Despite fairly frequently reported success in the raising of test scores, there is only limited evidence that such approaches actually increase creativity. Rather, they seem to improve performance only on activities which closely resemble the training procedures. In a detailed review of evidence, Rump (1979) came to the conclusion that the effects of training are at their strongest when the criterion closely resembles the training procedure, and at their weakest when this similarity is weak. In the case of personality, interests and preferences, only limited effects are obtained. Consequently, it is possible to conclude that short-term training procedures have little effect on general creative skills, attitudes, values, self-image and motivation. There is even a danger that creative training procedures have the opposite effect from the desired one. For example, children can become aware in the course of training that certain

TABLE 9.1. *Main characteristics of several creativity programs*

Program	Age level	Material	Aimed at promoting
Productive Thinking Program	Fifth and Sixth Grade pupils	Booklets containing cartoons	(i) Problem solving abilities (ii) Attitudes towards problem solving
Purdue Creative Thinking Program	Fourth Grade pupils	Audiotapes and accompanying printed exercises	Verbal and figural fluency, flexibility, originality and elaboration
Osborne–Parnes Program	High school and college students	No special materials	Getting many ideas Primary emphasis on brainstorming, with separation of idea generation and idea evaluation
Myers–Torrance Workbooks	Elementary school pupils	Workbooks containing exercises	Perceptual and cognitive abilities needed for creativity
Khatena Training Method	Adults and children	No special materials; simple teacher-made aids are employed	(i) Ability to break away from the obvious (ii) Transposing ideas (iii) Seeing analogies (iv) Restructuring information (v) Synthesis of ideas

kinds of behavior are preferred by the teacher, and can alter their behavior accordingly. Although children may be encouraged by the training to work hard on the various tasks which they are presented, they can learn that it is easy to give "original" answers if one engages in hair splitting, gives rambling answers without regard to accuracy or relevance, or offers banalities in the name of creativity. In this way, "creativity" can quickly degenerate to a special form of conformity. Commenting on brainstorming, Parloff and Handlon (1964) suggested that, instead of becoming more creative as a result of offering ideas freely, people may simply become less self-critical.

More comprehensive programs

Mansfield, Busse and Krepelka (1978) have reviewed five relevant creativity training programs: the *Productive Thinking Program*, the *Purdue Creative Thinking Program*, the *Osborn–Parnes Program*, the *Myers–Torrance Workbooks* and the *Khatena Training Method*. An overview of the special characteristics of these programs is presented in Table 9.1.

According to Mansfield, Busse and Krepelka (1978) the Osborn–Parnes program and the Khatena Training Method have the most convincing records. A characteristic shared by both of these programs is their breadth of training, while the training is not linked to a fixed set of materials. Mansfield et al., expressed the belief that brainstorming, which is emphasized by the Osborn–Parnes program, has been an effective element. The better evaluative studies of the *Productive Thinking Program* are said to have provided only "modest evidence of the program's effectiveness." The verdict on the *Purdue Creative Thinking Program* is similarly pessimistic: "The . . . soundest [study] provided the least evidence for the program's effectiveness." Of the *Myers–Torrance Workbooks*, Mansfield et al., consider that "the paucity of soundly designed research on the Myers–Torrance workbooks is surprising, considering their popularity . . . There is no evidence that the workbooks improve performance on measures substantially different from those used in the exercises." In other words, it is not at all clear that the effects of creativity training will be reflected in real life creative accomplishments.

Torrance (1972) himself acknowledged that many researchers would be likely to discredit his evaluation of some 142 studies of attempts to enhance creativity. However, he still maintained that many procedures really do have a positive effect, especially those which emphasize not only cognitive (getting ideas, combining information, etc.) but also affective aspects (having the courage to try something different, wanting to reach a novel solution, etc.). Franklin and Richards (1977) demonstrated that deliberate attempts to increase divergent thinking (i.e., formal training) are more effective than simply reducing the level of formality, or exposing children to a wider variety of experience. However, Cropley and Feuring (1971) showed that the results of such training are not necessarily simple, nor direct: what was effective with girls was not necessarily effective with boys, while the effects of training depended strongly on the conditions under which the criterion data were obtained. Thus, it is apparent that there is a need to exercise a certain level of general reservation about the effectiveness of programs designed to foster creativity, even though they represent at least a step in the right direction and can be an enjoyable experience in their own right.

As Wallach (1985) put it, nonetheless, the basic idea of promoting creativity by means of appropriate training procedures is by no means foolish. Unfortunately, however, simply training divergent thinking does not seem to achieve the desired results. To adapt an analogy suggested by Wallach, teaching sprinters preparing for a race how to hammer down the starting blocks is not irrelevant to their chances of running a fast time, but it can hardly be regarded as training them how to run faster. To take an actual example he mentions: students in a creative writing program practised with divergent thinking tests for two years — at the end they were noticably better on such tests, but their writing had hardly become more creative at all! In order to foster

TABLE 9.2. *The three component model of practical creativity*

Component	Examples of contents	Possibility of classroom facilitation
1. "Expertise"	Special talents or abilities	Low
	Thorough knowledge of a content area, special skills	High
2. Creativity-related abilities and skills	Ability to concentrate	Intermediate
	Special thinking skills (e.g. divergent thinking)	Theoretically high*
3. Personal characteristics	Task commitment and courage	All theoretically high*
	Intrinsic motivation	
	"Expectation of mastery"	

*Although these elements are theoretically amenable to training, they run counter to the existing school tradition, so that their practical facilitation is more difficult than might be expected.

academic excellence, it is necessary to develop procedures which relate directly to the area of achievement in which performance is to be improved, and which involve the kinds of activities which are to be carried out better. Thus, we need creativity-fostering activities which can be applied to school work and which relate to the things students do in class. What this means for creativity-fostering instruction in the classroom will be outlined in the following section.

Fostering creativity in the classroom

A three component model of practical creativity

Both the earlier discussions in this chapter and various sections of Chapters 2, 4 and 5 have emphasized that the emergence of creativity in real life settings among more or less ordinary people (what we call "practical creativity") depends on three components: detailed knowledge of an area and, where necessary, special skills or talents in this area ("expertise"); particular *general* creativity-related skills and abilities (including divergent thinking); personal characteristics which bring about readiness to go beyond the conventional and "swim against the current" (fascination for an area, expectation of mastery and so on). These components are listed above in Table 9.2.

Some of the attributes needed for expertise probably have a strong genetic basis (for instance an ability to distinguish between tones with unusual accuracy which would help in musical expertise). For this reason, this aspect of the component "expertise" has been assessed as "low" in the right-hand column of Table 9.2, which refers to the degree

TABLE 9.3. *Stereotypical combinations of components*

	Combination							
	1	2	3	4	5	6	7	8
Expertise	+	+	+	+	−	−	−	−
Creativity related abilities and skills	+	+	−	−	+	+	−	−
Personal characteristics	+	−	+	−	+	−	+	−

+ = high.
− = low.

of ease with which particular elements of the three components can be influenced by teachers in the classroom. Other elements, by contrast, can easily be influenced in the classroom; accumulation of factual knowledge, for instance, is greatly favored in conventional instruction. Skills such as divergent thinking and personal characteristics such as intrinsic motivation are, in principle, strongly influencable by teachers. However, their facilitation runs so strongly counter to the norms of the traditional classroom that a substantial reorientation of goals and favored teaching and learning procedures would be necessary if they were to be enhanced in practice. Providing a rationale for such a reorientation is the task of this chapter.

Different combinations of components

As was done in Chapter 2 in a somewhat different context, it is possible to construct theoretical situations involving various combinations of components. (These should be understood as stereotypes or "pure" types, which probably seldom exist; "mixed" situations are probably more common in reality.) The eight "idealized" combinations are shown in Table 9.3.

It is interesting to return here to a theme which was discussed in Chapter 2 — that of partial realization of exceptional ability (see Table 2.2). In Table 9.3 there are several combinations of the various components of practical creativity, in addition to the central one in which all three elements, expertise, creativity skills and personal characteristics, are present. The combination of expertise and creative skills without personal characteristics (column 2) is typical for a person who is intellectually "well equipped," but lacks the will to turn these into creativity. This could be a result of never having been "set on fire" by an area or topic, of never having had a model of excellence to follow, or even of having been actively "turned off," for instance in a home environment or a school room in which interest and motivation were ridiculed. The combination of expertise and personal properties without creative skills (column 3) is typical for people who are good at convergent thinking and are also hardworking, but are unable to generate ideas, try the unconventional, see unexpected possibilities, etc. It is possible that such people can be encouraged to enrich their thinking by developing creative skills. As studies of science students at an Australian university (Cropley, 1967b) or of secondary school pupils in Canada (Cropley, 1967a) showed, such pupils tend to obtain high grades in conventional educational settings, the lack of creativity not hindering them greatly. A further group consists of those displaying creativity skills and motivation, but without expertise (column 5). The studies just mentioned showed that this combination is extremely unfavorable to school success, to some degree even less favorable than that of people who are low in all categories. Necka (1986) described the practical consequences of these various partial combinations in a very clear manner. The area where expertise, creativity skills and personal properties combine (column 1) can be said to involve "fully developed" creativity, column 2 (task commitment is missing) can be called "abandoned creativity," column 3 (low creativity skills) "mere technical creativity," and column 5 (low expertise) "juvenile creativity."

General goals of classroom instruction

As Williams (1976a) put it, what is needed in the classroom is a "responsive environment" (p. 18) or a "safe psychological base." This promotes fluent, flexible, original and elaborative thinking (Williams, 1976b). The flow of ideas must be "unfrozen" (Hare, 1982, p. 158); this includes not only thinking skills, but also the "courage to create" (Motamedi, 1982, p. 84). Children need help: to resist the temptation to accept the first, plausible answer to a problem; to see ideas in broader contexts; to visualize possibilities; to use imagination (Torrance and Hall, 1980). Such thinking activities are facilitated not only by appropriate knowledge and skills, but also by personal properties such as self-confidence, curiosity, openness to experience, willingness to be provoked and excited by new possibilities (Treffinger, Isaksen and Firestien, 1983). In other words, the promotion of creativity involves both the ability to get ideas, and the *willingness* to do so. Both these properties are desirable and possible, not only in children of unusually high ability but in all children. However, in the case of the unusually able, the practices take on special importance.

To translate these objectives into practice, Williams (1976c) listed a number of teaching strategies. Adapted for present purposes, these include:

1. Giving practice in spotting paradoxes (inconsistencies, apparent contradictions, etc.);

2. Training children to notice discrepancies (gaps, missing links, etc.);
3. Helping children to see analogies (relationships, implications, etc.);
4. Helping children to develop skill in searching for and obtaining information;
5. Helping children to overcome the effects of habit (breaking out of the strait-jacket of conventional thinking);
6. Giving children opportunities to engage in visualizing (seeing a problem from a new angle);
7. Encouraging children to carry out intuitive thinking (making an informed guess, following a hunch, etc.);
8. Fostering communication (both skills and willingness);
9. Showing children how to learn from mistakes;
10. Helping children to accept change and novelty;
11. Helping children to tolerate ambiguity.

These strategies involve more than simply knowledge and abilities. For example, Nos 7, 10 and 11 require flexibility, willingness to try something out and readiness to take a chance. Self-criticism and willingness to risk the possibility of failure are needed for No. 9. No. 8 requires the self-confidence necessary to offer new ideas (sometimes seen by others as arrogance), while it is also impossible without willingness on the part of other people to accept solutions offered by the creative individual (i.e., it involves social or interpersonal qualities). Even in the area of abilities, it is apparent that carrying out the steps listed above is not just a matter of divergent thinking. In particular, the first four emphasize that creative problem solving calls for the acquisition of substantial information. The most economical way of acquiring this is through the application of convergent thinking skills. Creativity thus involves an integration of convergent and divergent thinking, of motivation, of self-image and of interpersonal qualities.

Other writers such as Torrance, Feldhusen and Treffinger have suggested similar guidelines for classroom practice in fostering creativity. These have been summarized by Cropley (1982a), and include the following list of "do's" for teachers:

1. Show that you value creativity;
2. Encourage children to try out new ideas;
3. Show tolerance for "way out" ideas;
4. Avoid forcing predigested solutions on to children;
5. Encourage independent thinking;
6. Offer constructive criticism;
7. Make time and materials available for following up children's ideas;

8. Encourage children to be many sided in their outlook;
9. Show that you are yourself flexible, many sided and interested in creative effort.

The guidelines listed to date are not classroom activities in themselves, but directions of development which should influence planning of lessons, selecting material, organizing its presentation, questioning students and reacting to their answers, setting and evaluating assignments, etc. In every case it is also important to remember that not only a skill or ability is involved, but that motivational, personal and social factors also need to be taken into account.

Classroom activities

Guidelines have already been suggested which are intended as lines of approach which should be used to shape all teaching. Some specific classroom activities which not only offer good opportunities for implementing these guidelines but also have special relevance in the fostering of creativity will now be considered.

CREATIVE PROBLEM SOLVING

An activity which requires productive thinking, and at the same time offers good opportunities for promoting it, is problem solving. It is apparent that the modern world is beset with problems of major dimensions, such as how to achieve world peace, eliminate disease or feed the ever-growing world population. Although these present a fascinating challenge for clever and creative children, they can quickly assume such vast dimensions that they become mere exercises in unverifiable, unchecked, unevaluated fantasy. In keeping with Renzulli's (1982) suggestion that we should concentrate on "real" problems — not that war, disease and hunger are not genuine problems, but they offer little prospect for actual application of children's ideas — it is possible to identify problems of more modest dimensions which still present a challenge and provide an opportunity for exercising the same mental processes as the vast problems just listed. The possibility of dealing with "little" problems has helped make "creative problem solving" a popular instructional activity for exceptionally able students.

Feldhusen and Treffinger (1980, p. 33) identified three phases in the problem solving process:

1. Awareness, a motivating factor;
2. Problem formulation, when the problem is defined and ideas arise for plausible solution strategies;

3. Searching, during which information is gathered to be associated with the formulation of viable hypotheses.

These phases have to be operationalized, and have generally been broken down into a series of steps for the purpose of Creative Problem Solving (Torrance et al., 1978, p. 5) along the following lines:

1. Encounter a problem "situation;"
2. Brainstorm possible specific problems stemming from the situation that has been presented;
3. Operationalize the problem to be attacked, stating it clearly, i.e., in an "attackable" form;
4. Brainstorm alternative solutions;
5. Brainstorm criteria against which to judge alternative solutions;
6. Rank available solutions according to the criteria that have been adopted;
7. Select and improve the best solution, and present ("sell") it for judging or adoption.

There are many positive features about Creative Problem Solving. It encourages cooperative behavior among gifted students and provides them with a methodology for attacking problems which is usable across subject areas and which can be generalized to form lifelong habits for approaching problems; in short, it fosters a sound general methodology. Moreover, it encourages task commitment and affords experience in the need to meet deadlines. It helps to develop ability to present ideas clearly to other people, to listen creatively and to compromise, in a context which is relevant, topical and of high interest to the student.

It is instructive to compare Creative Problem Solving with the traditional scientific method. Before Bacon's *Novum Organum*, published in 1620, science relied on the Aristotelian deductive method, i.e., reasoning from the general to the particular ("If . . . then . . ."), but Bacon sought to substitute induction, i.e., the production of generalities based on observation of many facts, or reasoning from many particulars to the general. The two approaches were integrated into what became known as the hypothetico-deductive method, or simply "scientific method". Kerlinger (1964) provides a more contemporary summary of the scientific approach, based on Dewey's (1910) analysis:

First, . . . the scientist experiences vague doubts, emotional disturbance, inchoate ideas. He struggles to formulate the problem . . . He studies the literature, scans his own experience and the experience of others. Often he has to wait for an inventive leap of the mind . . . With the problem formulated, with the basic question . . . properly asked, the rest is much easier. The hypothesis is constructed, after which the implications are deduced . . . Lastly, but not finally, the relation expressed by the hypothesis is tested by observation and experimentation. On the basis of the research evidence, the hypothesis is accepted or rejected. The information is then fed back to the original problem.

In short, scientific method may be expressed in the following way:

1. Encounter a problem situation;
2. Search the literature, review one's own and others' experience;
3. Isolate a specific problem;
4. Translate (by induction) the problem into an operational hypothesis;
5. Predict (by deduction) the consequences of the hypothesis in defined circumstances;
6. Select an appropriate research design to test the hypothesis;
7. Gather and analyze data;
8. Accept, reject or amend hypothesis and revert to step 1 (or 3 or 4).

It can be seen that Creative Problem Solving closely parallels traditional scientific method, but diverges from it in two important respects. First, the selection of the "best solution" in Creative Problem Solving is an internal check, requiring no validation against objective or even external data. Creative Problem Solving parallels Archimedes' conceiving of the hydrostatic principle by insight and then deducing the conclusion relating to King Hiero's crown; according to the story, he found the insight sufficiently compelling to leap out of his bath shouting "Eureka!" without waiting for verification. Newton, on the other hand, was more faithful to scientific methodology — and incurred less risk of embarrassment — by delaying the publication of his theory of gravitation until he was able to check it against observation.

The "best" solution derived through Creative Problem Solving is always a winner; by failing to expose it to the test of experimental validation students are shielded from the real world of failure or partial success. Not that a real scientific experiment is ever really a failure; if a professional scientist's cherished hypothesis does not stand up to experimental scrutiny, the experience is still of value in that it leads to the posing of better questions and hypotheses. A second difference between Creative Problem Solving and scientific method is that the former terminates after the "best" solution has been "sold," whereas scientific method is a cumulative process, looping back to an earlier stage for subsequent experiments after hypotheses are accepted, rejected or amended.

Basically, there are two elements in scientific activity:

1. A substantive element: a body of knowledge, information and principles that help us to understand the physical, biological and technological world around us;

2. A methodology element: a process or method of enquiry by which new information and principles are uncovered and old ideas discarded.

There is a danger that Creative Problem Solving, as practised by some teachers, might stress the second of these elements, to the neglect of the first. There is also a danger that fixed, defined patterns of attack such as "SCAMPER" (substitute; combine; adapt; modify; magnify or multiply; put to other uses; eliminate or embellish; reverse or rearrange) for modifying ideas lead to activities which are nominally "creative" but degenerate into a convergent reapplication of routine procedures.

FUTURE PROBLEM SOLVING

Future Problem Solving (FPS) was initiated by Torrance in the USA in 1974, and it rapidly gained popularity, being perceived by participating teachers and students as enjoyable and beneficial (Torrance et al., 1978). Future Problem Solving represents a special form of Creative Problem Solving in which the possibility of any external validation is eliminated by the very nature of the exercise — topics for the programs between 1982 and 1984 including UFOs, ocean communities, nuclear disarmament and genetic engineering (Hoomes, 1984). However, Torrance (1978, p. 15) advises "if always dealing with future situations bothers them, occasionally bring out a current situation. The newspaper is chock full of ideas."

The posing of the problem to be attacked is generally of the form "How might we. . .?" or "In what ways might we. . .?" (Torrance et al., 1987, p. 14). Students study the topic mainly through reading books, newspapers and magazines, supplemented by television and talks with available experts. In view of the global, strategic, geopolitical nature of many of the problems tackled, students ought to have direct access to the perspectives of countries other than their own. Short wave radio, foreign newspapers — and, in the not too distant future, overseas TV via satellite — provide excellent means of becoming acquainted with a total spectrum of current political perspectives of many future problems.

BRAINSTORMING

Brainstorming is a technique which can be used at every stage of Creative Problem Solving. Indeed as Feldhusen and Treffinger (1980) note, it "can conveniently be used in nearly every subject area and situation." Perhaps one of the most spectacular examples of the success of brainstorming by extremely gifted people occurred in World War II at Bletchley Park, England, where mathematicians, scholars, crossword puzzle wizards and creative writers such as Ian Fleming, the creator of James Bond, were assembled. Their accomplishments included a contribution to the breaking of the German Enigma code.

Brainstorming is a group activity in which each member of the group is encouraged to put forward ideas, so that as the session develops, ideas flow "fast and heavy." In order for brainstorming to really catch fire, participants must not feel inhibited, and so criticism of any idea — no matter how implausible or wild — is suspended during the production stage of the proceedings. Torrance et al., (1978) list four basic rules:

1. Criticism is ruled out;
2. Freewheeling is welcomed: i.e., the wilder the ideas the better;
3. Quantity is wanted, because the greater the number of ideas produced the greater the probability that original, useful ideas will emerge;
4. Combination and improvement are sought: i.e., group members are encouraged to "hitch-hike" on the ideas of others.

A variety of scenarios is possible for conducting a brainstorming session. If, as some suggest, members of the group are seated in a circle and encouraged to call out their ideas, the session might be dominated by more extroverted individuals, and potentially valuable contributions from students who are more reticent can be lost. One procedure which the authors have found to be practical with groups from Grade 4 to senior university administrators is summarized in point form in Table 9.4. Preferably, the group should consist of between 10 and 12 individuals; larger groups should be divided into subgroups, the results from which are pooled and distributed later by the overall coordinator.

There are various ways to treat the rankings. The simplest is simply to tally how many times a suggestion is included in the list of each group member, and the suggestion which is included the most times is the "winner." Alternatively, the median ranking of each suggestion is determined (with a rank of 11 being accorded to a suggestion each time it is not included in the top ten for any group member). A useful exercise for computer oriented students (and a potential point of departure for a study and discussion of different voting procedures) would be to analyze the rankings according to a "distributed preferences" procedure, such as is used in Australian elections.

SYNECTICS

Synectics is a procedure for bringing together elements which do not seem to belong together. Two major principles of synectic thinking, as outlined by Gordon (1961), are "making the strange familiar" and "making the familiar strange." The idea is that unusual, apparently

TABLE 9.4. *Steps in brainstorming*

1. The group appoints two scribes/recorders:
   (i) One writes suggestions on the blackboard (plenty of blackboard space is needed) or on sheets of paper which can be displayed around the room. Each suggestion is numbered.
   (ii) The other writes the suggestions on paper, for later identification of items.
2. For approximately ten minutes, each person writes his/her suggestions on individual sheets of paper. No talking or discussion occurs during this period.
3. A round robin then takes place during which group members, in turn, read out their most important suggestion, and the scribes record. No comment or discussion of suggestions yet. But hitchhiking is permitted, i.e. members of the group may add to an existing suggestion if their own suggestion represents an extension of one already on the board.
4. Step 3 is repeated. Normally, this procedure will continue until everyone has literally dried up. If time is limited, it might be necessary to limit the procedure to four or five rounds.
5. Group discussion takes place concerning equivalence of suggestions and the merging of different suggestions. Scribes erase, transfer and amend as required.
6. Each member of the group ranks what he or she considers to be the most important ten suggestions on the board, in order of perceived importance. The suggestions are identified by number, i.e. there is no need to write the suggestions in full, as scribe No. 2 has recorded the suggestion numbers.
7. Depending on the time available, the results may be analyzed on the spot, but it will generally be more convenient for each member of the group to hand in the ranked suggestions to a scribe who passes them on to the workshop later.
8. The conclusions are made available later, after analysis.

irrelevant or little-known objects or processes are seen in a new light by emphasizing elements which fit in well with the problem at hand, although they would not normally be regarded as relevant (making the strange familiar), or that well-known objects or processes are looked at as though one does not really know what they are for, although the facts about them are known (making the familiar strange). As in brainstorming, synectics is usually conducted in a group (although the two basic principles can also be carried out by an individual person working alone).

Group members are confronted with some problem to be solved. Initially, members of the group simply suggest objects or processes which actually have some relationship to the requirements of the problem solution, although they would normally not be regarded as related to it — for instance a member of a group trying to develop a form of paint which would never fade mentioned that some algae never lose their colour, thus "making the strange familiar" by redefining something (algae) which has nothing to do with the problem in question (paint) in terms of the familiar. Subsequently, a paint which forms a coat or layer adhering to the surface of the painted object (instead of soaking into it) was developed. Similarly, to invent an example, it would be possible to redefine a window (something with which we are all familiar) as a device for permitting communication through soundproof barriers, thus making the familiar strange.

A synectic thinking session could have the following steps:

1. Group leaders describes the problem which is to be solved;
2. Groups members spontaneously offer key words which reduce the problem to its basic elements;
3. The group leader tries to find abstract definitions of the problem using only two of these key words (i.e., to make the familiar strange);
4. Participants suggest analogies to be found in everyday life, in nature, in industry, or technology, etc. (i.e., they attempt to make the strange familiar);
5. Participants imagine that they are a living example of the analogy mentioned in the previous step, and picture how they would feel in the situation in question.

This approach is, in some ways, related to brainstorming. However, it is particularly interesting in that it seeks to systematize the process of seeing connections between elements of experience and knowledge which are not normally regarded as belonging together. In this respect, it constitutes a procedure for promoting purposeful, goal directed divergent thinking.

"PLAYING" WITH IDEAS

The notion of "playing" with ideas has already been mentioned as both a characteristic of highly creative people and also an aid to divergent thinking. Endriss (1982) has outlined a series of "games" which can be introduced into classroom instruction in order to "unfreeze" or "warm up" ideas. These games are suitable for use with young children, with older students and with adults. They seek to foster the emergence of various thinking strategies such as those developed by Kirst and Diekmeyer (1973, pp. 127ff):

1. Producing (offering a coherent idea or thought);
2. Analyzing (precisely defining the content of objects and ideas);
3. Elaborating (developing a detailed structure on the basis of guiding principles);
4. Pointing up (establishing the decisive, definitive elements of objects and ideas);
5. Associating (seeing connections between ideas);
6. Constructing (combining ideas or objects to form a specified new product);
7. Translating (expressing ideas in different forms, or via different modalities — a word being "translated" into a picture, for example);

8. Revising (breaking away from existing relationships among ideas and suggesting new ones);
9. Seeing analogies (recognizing new examples of the familiar).

The games themselves take only a few minutes to carry out and can easily be played as a warm up before any lesson. However, it is also possible to introduce activities based on these games into the teaching of a large number of subjects. The activities would then be part of the battery of learning and teaching tactics available to all teachers and not treated as discrete events.

In the case of *producing*, for instance, students could be asked to invent the full name of an association identified only by its initials. The associations need not be real ones, but the names derived from the initials must be meaningful, even if exotic. From the initials NPL, for instance, students could suggest "National Peanut League" or "Nameless Parent Lovers," "Nonplussed Learning," etc. A game for *analyzing* involves giving students a list of materials (such as glass, wind, light, sand) and asking them to list as many ways as possible in which these could be put to use, even if this use is unkown at present. *Elaboration* might require students to describe an object, after being given only certain basic principles. The object need not exist at present, but should be rational and at least theoretically imaginable. An amusing game for *pointing up* might be to have students invent nicknames for famous people (not for mutual acquaintances), which summarize as many as possible of the crucial characteristics which make this person a unique individual.

As an *association* activity, students can be asked to invent as many new expressions as they can (these words must have a meaning, even if the word does not actually exist), by joining all or parts of a short list of key words. For instance, they could be asked to find combinations of any forms of "banana," "press" and "break" such as "daybreak banana presser" (a person who works in a milk bar and prepares banana juice before the start of the day's work), or "banana press break" (an exclusive news story about bananas), etc. An exercise for *constructing* consists of giving pupils three random stimuli — such as "a piece of leather," the word "long" and the process "eating." The task is to invent in as elaborated a form as possible an object which could incorporate all three, such as a device for making it possible to eat leather in long strips, etc. *Translating* can be encouraged by exercises such as asking students to do a drawing (other than a drawing of someone eating) which captures the essence of a sound such as "yum yum."

An exercise which helps to promote *revising* is to ask pupils to suggest novel uses for a well-known object, the most common examples (see both Torrance's and Guilford's test batteries) being a tin can or a brick or an empty bottle. A novel idea for how to use a tin can, for example, might be to cut appropriate holes in it and use it as a suit of armour for a mouse, in order to give it a fair chance against the cat! Finally, *seeing analogies* can be promoted by giving students a key word, such as "tree" and asking them to identify as many objects as possible from outside the plant world which could be said to have tree like properties. A fairly obvious example would be "stalagmite," a somewhat more remote one would be "book" (since they both have leaves).

These examples for fostering various thinking strategies through the use of game like activities, and thus capitalizing on the connection between creativity and play, are not meant to be exhaustive. On the contrary, they are simply isolated examples intended to stimulate teachers' imagination. Even more important, they can also be treated not as specific activities to be taken over wholesale, but as tactics or strategies. For instance, a geography teacher could ask students to locate three cities on the world map, given only five facts about the kinds of clothing people wear there (elaborating), or a history teacher could ask students to write down what life would be like in their country if certain fictional events had taken place at a particular time (producing, associating, revising and constructing). In other words, readers are encouraged to point up key ideas, see analogies, construct new exercises and incorporate such tactics into their teaching methods.

DEBATING

One activity that has perhaps received less than its due share of attention in the fostering of academic excellence is the art (and science) of debating. Perhaps this is due in part to its assocation with the frequently dull, predictable and apparently inflexible speeches of professional politicians. Perhaps it has not been "sold" with the same persuasiveness as "space age" activities such as future problem solving.

Debating possesses many of the attributes regarded as important and particularly appropriate for academically exceptional students. Good debating requires plausible, original argument firmly grounded in a sound research base. A debating team should not consist solely of the mover and seconder of the motion; these people are the visible presenters of what is essentially a team effort. Hence, in preparing for a debate, it is possible to envisage brainstorming sessions during which arguments — both positive arguments and rebuttal arguments — are developed and, where needed, research is identified. There is work for everyone on the team, including those who may feel uncomfortable at the prospect of speaking in public.

The process of debate provides practice in organizing, developing and presenting ideas in an orderly and efficient manner. During the debate itself, moreover, there is a need to react quickly to telling arguments by the opposition, but any reaction has to be made in a courteous manner according to the rules, thus fostering self-discipline and a tolerance for the opinion of others. In debating tournaments, a team must both defend and attack a motion (not during a single session, of course!), i.e., its members are required to support a motion with which they themselves might be in total disagreement. This forces them to look at the situation from all sides, and perhaps even concede that there might be some virtue in opinions other than those which they espouse; at any rate, the exercise encourages what, for them, are novel and original ideas. And at the end of each debate they have the opportunity to meet with both success and defeat — and to "treat those two imposters just the same."

The role of the teacher

In a study conducted about 25 years ago, Torrance (1963) showed that teachers had a strong preference for student behavior involving what Cropley (1978) called "conserving activities," such as learning by heart, reproducing, reapplying and the like, and that they placed little value on "innovating activities," such as branching out, inventing, speculating, questioning, etc. This finding reflects the position as it was a quarter of a century ago. However, Howieson (1984) also found that teachers preferred conventional "good" behaviors to "creative" ones, in a study in which he readministered the same "Ideal Pupil Checklist" as had been employed by Torrance in 1960 to a sample of teachers in Western Australia, one of the areas in which the original study had been carried out. Similar findings were reported by Obuche (1986) in a study of the pupil characteristics regarded by Nigerian teachers as defining the "ideal" pupil. Out of a list of 62 characteristics "industrious," "sincere," "obedient," "considerate of others," "courteous" and "does work on time" occupied six of the first ten places. By contrast, "independent in thinking," "curious," "willing to take risks," "critical of others" and "nonconforming" occupied much lower positions. Howieson made a direct link between such teacher preferences and the incidence of creativity among pupils by drawing attention to the fact that Western Australian children obtained very low average scores on so-called "creativity" tests, and suggested that there may well be a direct connection between teacher attitudes and pupils' creativity.

Classroom instruction has traditionally and typically aimed at helping children to acquire facts and techniques which permit them to find the single, best, correct answer to a problem. The function of the teacher has been to decide what is correct and what is not — and then to show children how to arrive at the right answer. Implicit in the exchange of ideas between teacher and students is the assumption that knowledge of acts, the application of laws and an acknowledgement of the importance of rules of conventional logic will always lead to a good solution. The task of the teacher is to present new material in ways which show that it is unmistakably related to what has gone before, and to help children acquire appropriate knowledge, techniques and rules. Such an approach is important. Children should acquire basic factual knowledge and master various socially desirable techniques such as the ability to read, write and reckon, for instance. The school has a clear responsibility to students in this direction, which cannot be overlooked, even by the most enthusiastic advocate of creativity. However, an overemphasis can lead to a situation in which abilities and personal characteristics which are crucial for creativity are forgotten, or even treated with suspicion or contempt. A creative child may be regarded as a nuisance, a troublemaker, or even a major classroom "problem." Cropley (1982a) has reported a number of case studies of children whose behavior does not seem to have been at all undesirable, yet who were severely criticized or rejected by their teachers.

One problem is that many teachers have difficulty in distinguishing between divergent behavior and disruptive or rebellious behavior. This is not altogether surprising when some of the things that creative students do are borne in mind. They may, for instance, ask unexpected, apparently irrelevant or even seemingly foolish questions, give answers which neither teacher nor classmates can immediately understand, or offer outrageous speculations. They may alter test items or classroom materials to make them more interesting or show open dissatisfaction with materials, content or even with the teacher's presentation. They may reveal impatience or exasperation with teachers or classmates, or openly criticize them for being "stupid." These sorts of activity are not conducive to popularity; they may cause a good deal of "time wasting," or may even help to bring about disorderly situations in which classroom discipline is endangered and the orderly conduct of normal teaching activities threatened. A teacher who reacts in a positive, accepting way to apparently disruptive or irrational behavior on the part of an isolated creative child may seem to the other pupils to be tolerating "bad" behavior, or to be playing favorites. The disruption of the orderly flow of events within the classroom which can follow a creative response may be seized upon by genuinely unruly or rebellious students as an opportunity to create disorder. It is thus scarcely surprising that uninformed and inadequately prepared teachers often find it easier to snuff out creative behavior in the interests of good order and well organized instruction.

Blocks to creativity

A number of characteristics of teachers tend to inhibit creative thinking skills or block children's willingness to display their creativity (see Cropley, 1982a, for a fuller discussion). These include:

1. One-sided emphasis on being right;
2. Excessive emphasis on the importance of knowing facts by heart;
3. Insistence on mechanical learning of set techniques for solving problems;
4. Overemphasis of external evaluation and underemphasis of self-evaluation;
5. Impatient insistence on "getting through the lesson;"
6. Insistence on total conformity to the norms of the class group;
7. Strict distinction between work and play, work always being sober and worthwhile, play being frivolous and merely recreational.

It is important that teachers cover the material in the curriculum and that children learn to live with external evaluation rather than regarding their own estimate of their self-worth as unchallengeable. It is also good that students learn simple techniques for dealing with problem situations, that they are able to get along with their classmates and that they understand the difference between hard work and frivolous behavior. "Going overboard" for creativity would represent just as serious an imbalance as that which currently prevails in many classrooms. Thus, avoiding the blocks just listed requires redressing an imbalance, not abandoning traditional skills, habits and values entirely.

Fostering creativity

Teachers need to show their students how it is possible to reapply, transform and reshape techniques or pieces of information which can then be applied to new situations for which they were not originally intended. It is important, too, to emphasize that a given question often has many answers, or that it is possible to react to the same situation in a variety of ways. Major goals of classroom instruction should be to encourage children to recognize new possibilities for solving problems and actively to seek alternative solutions. Such a policy has implications not only for students but also for the teacher, who can no longer function as the single source of all wisdom, dictating what is relevant and what is not, and making all judgements about quality, but must be willing to depart from the lesson plan, to bring new material into the lesson, to look at answers which are not in the textbook and so on.

Teacher flexibility and the encouragement of originality in students are commendable goals for education generally and are not confined to the context of giftedness. However, there are special circumstances which demand special efforts with unusually creative children. One important area where creative behavior in the classroom can be in danger of being blocked is in the social domain. Many creative youngsters get along perfectly well with their classmates, but some experience considerable difficulty, largely as a result of the inhibiting factor of conformity pressure. Teachers can often help these children by "taking them under their wing." A quiet talk about avoiding hurting other people's feelings, or giving everybody a chance to speak up in class, can be a great help. In a similar way, willingness to offer quiet criticism or praise after class or to discuss a special interest of the creative child can go a long way towards demonstrating the recognition which is so important for unusually able and highly gifted youngsters. By contrast, Cropley (1978) has provided several anecdotal examples which illustrate how the teacher can be a major inhibiting influence for many creative children.

Closing Remarks

The promotion of fully rounded academic excellence requires the fostering not only of conventional thinking, but also of creativity. All children can benefit from deliberate efforts to encourage having new ideas, seeing the unexpected, trying novel approaches, etc. Helping children to operate in this way involves not only thinking skills, knowledge and abilities, but also interest, willingness, self-confidence and the like; this means that the fostering of creativity in the classroom is also concerned with affective, and not merely cognitive, development. A number of classroom activities are especially favorable to the promotion of creative thinking; these have in common the elements of arousing interest, encouraging a search for ideas without fear of failure or pressure to hit upon a quick solution, considering all possible solutions as initially of equal potential merit, evaluating ideas oneself and communicating ideas to others and defending them if necessary, without, however, closing the mind to alternatives. Often, elements of speculation, fantasy or even play are involved.

Realizing these general principles demands teaching strategies which focus on "innovating" rather than "conserving." Conserving activities concentrate on speed, accuracy, logic, correctness and the like; these are desirable and important elements, but should not be emphasized to the exclusion of speculating, trying the new, etc. (innovating activities). Many teacher habits, values and attitudes block innovating activities, so that the fostering of creativity consists to a considerable degree of elimination of blocks. Innovative activity does not, however, spring into existence of its own accord, so active facilitation is also needed. A combination of personal properties and adoption of appropriate teaching methods marks out the "creativity facilitating teacher."

10

Computers and Academic Excellence

Possibilities and prospects

The most obvious and visible aspect of the emergence of high technology has been the computer; in particular, the microcomputer has penetrated everyday life to a remarkable degree. Computers are not, however, the only form of high technology with obvious and direct relevance to education: others include the videodisc, slow scan television, videotex, the electronic blackboard and even telephone hookups. Similarly, the implications of high technology are not confined to improving traditional forms of education, but offer opportunities for new perspectives in the educational domain. Advances in video and telecommunication technology, for instance, have led to new impluses in *Distance Education*; much greater masses of information can now be made available to the student *in situ*, discussion groups can include students separated by great distances, etc. Telecourses provide one relevant example of the expansion of teaching and learning methods. Currently, such courses are generally limited to lectures or demonstrations in which the student is an essentially passive participant. However, increasingly sophisticated modes of communication make it possible for students to participate in discussions with other students and to ask questions directly to the person presenting the lesson.

The imminent availability of satellite transmissions from other nations also means that it will be possible for students to learn in a much more direct way about the culture, values and structures of other societies (Lindenau, 1984). In Canada, the province of British Columbia has already used satellite and microwave facilities to introduce a Knowledge Network program. For the cost of installing a satellite antenna, local cooperatives have been able to provide a wide range of academic and technical-vocational programs produced by universities and institutes of technology. The service is augmented by a toll free telephone tutorial service for students in remote areas. Similar networks were described by a number of participants in the Sixth and

180

Seventh World Conferences on Gifted and Talented Children in Hamburg and Salt Lake City respectively.

In addition to an increasingly efficient satellite technology, the use of fibre optic cable has greatly expanded the possibilities of teleconferencing. When the power of the computer is also harnessed to link distant learners to each other in a kind of conference or network, even more possibilities offer themselves. Participants do not need to be logged on all at the same time, but can enter or leave the system when it is convenient, since unlike the telephone the computer will accept and record messages as they take place. Messages are not limited to those passing between instructor and student, but can involve student to student communication between individuals or among groups. Individuals involved in a hookup can consider their replies carefully before transmitting them but, once a reply has been formulated, it can be transmitted extremely rapidly. Finally, linkups with commercial facilities such as databases provide access to a wealth of information which would otherwise not be available.

For academically exceptional students, the prospect of easy communication with peers and intellectual equals who are geographically distant from them (which might mean across the city, across the state or even across the world) has obvious benefits, especially when earlier discussions of the importance of factors such as contact with similarly able individuals, recognition by others and development of a positive self-image are borne in mind. At present, however, experience with such systems is so limited that it is not clear how (or for that matter even whether) hitech communication systems can best be used for fostering learning and personal growth among the exceptionally able.

A second illustrative example of the possibilities offered by hitech is to be seen in the potential of new methods of communication to provide special forms of inservice training for teachers of gifted students. Other professions are already using existing technologies to provide updated information to practitioners in the field. For example, the American Medical Association is currently offering "Med-Video Clinic," an accredited course in diagnostic practice developed by the University of California at Los Angeles. A similar service is also offered in Canada by the Ontario Department of Health, through its "Telehealth" and "Telemedicine" programs (Naisbitt, 1984). An ambitious example of interactive programming has been undertaken by St Joseph's Hospital in London, Ontario. Teaching hospitals are connected by cable and then linked by microwave transmission to outlying hospitals, which are also equipped with transmitting facilities. Doctors in each location can therefore see and hear each other, and are able to present cases of interest and concern, or conduct patient examinations by television monitor. A similar kind of network for teachers is certainly technically possible. Despite the promise, however, costs are currently too prohibitive for implementation on a wide scale. Nonetheless, many scenarios which would have been dismissed as flights of fancy only a few years ago have been demonstrated to be feasible, and the recent history of the "silicon revolution" has been such as to suggest that a few years hence they will be commonplace.

The function of hitech is by no means limited to fostering communication between learner and teacher, or among learners. Cleary, Moyes and Packham (1976) wrote of new opportunities for changing the *quality* of education (and not just its organization), while Cropley (1982b) has argued that recent advances in educational technology provide an important prerequisite for the realization of "revolutionary" models of the whole educational process. Some of these will be outlined in the following sections.

Applying the computer in the classroom

Pedagogical principles

Simply helping people cope with hitech in their everyday life is an educational goal in itself: the production worker who must work with robots, the secretary whose typewriter has become a word-processor, the hairdresser whose equipment now includes programmable machines, even the driver confronted with new controls in the family car, are all examples of people who may need help in dealing with aspects of the environment which have suddenly become unfamiliar. Hitech may also create new educational *contents* such as programming, systems design and the like. However, the present section concentrates not on learning about hitech as an end in itself, but on (a) its use as an aid to traditional pedagogical activities, such as the delivery of information to learners, the diagnosis of difficulties, the maintenance of interest and motivation, etc.; (b) its role in fostering psychological growth in the intellectually able.

Pedagogically speaking, the computer offers, among other things, the possibility of:

1. A high degree of structure in the learning situation;
2. Concrete experience of "reversibility" (the possibility of returning a situation to its original starting point);
3. A high level of self-management of learning (for instance through the repetition of difficult sections or the skipping of easy ones);
4. New or increased possibilities for self-evaluation;
5. The possibility of exploring the unfamiliar without anxiety or threat (for instance by trying an answer and seeing how the computer

system reacts — if the reaction is negative the answer can be "reversed" and the section repeated, as was pointed out in 2 and 3);

6. A great deal of practice in problem solving without penalty for lack of immediate success (see 2, 3 and 4);
7. The possibility of following a project to the bitter end at one's own pace;
8. Various possibilities for group learning, peer evaluation, and the like.

It is properties of this kind which need to be made use of, if the full power of the computer as an instructional tool is to be released.

Psychological principles

From a psychological point of view the functions of the computer as a "teaching aid" may be seen as cognitive, motivational, personal and even social in nature. The cognitive domain includes fostering rapid development of highly differentiated cognitive structures and information processing strategies. In the case of motivation, computer applications have an important role in maintaining interest, developing curiosity and fostering the desire to master problem situations. In the personal domain, interaction with the computer can, among other things, promote development of a sense of control over the outcomes of a learning situation. Computer networks, or even team work at the terminal, open up prospects for communication, joint planning, mutual help and moral support. In the sense just outlined, the computer and related hitech have a general educational function which does not derive from technology itself, but rather from the ability of technological systems to meet psychoeducational needs which existed before the emergence of hitech, and which would continue to be important even if it did not exist.

As is the case in many other areas discussed in this book, this function (encouraging special forms and tactics of learning, fostering motivation, promoting self-confidence, etc.) is important for fostering gifts and talents in all children, but takes on particular significance in certain special situations. In the case of the emotionally disturbed, for example, computer applications offer the chance of learning in an environment free of the threat or distraction offered by other people and makes available an infinitely patient teacher who never shows anger or frustration. Physically handicapped children can benefit not only from the conditions just outlined, but from the possibility of frequent repetition of learning steps or the presentation of material at varying speeds, according to the needs of a particular youngster. In the case of grossly handicapped children, such as quadraplegics, hitech offers previously unknown forms of communication, such as "writing" on a typewriter by means of eye movements: the paralyzed person gazes at a word or letter displayed on a video display unit, the direction of gaze is detected by the system, and the appropriate letter or word is typed. The positive results of being able to communicate via the written word not only on cognitive growth, but on social contacts, desire to learn, the sense of personal competence, and the like, can be enormous. Although less dramatic, the potential of hitech to broaden the range of experience of children who would otherwise have little access to libraries or to people of similar special interests — such as youngsters from isolated locations, or those from poor family backgrounds — is also apparent.

Despite what has just been said, application of computers in instruction has tended to reflect mainly the presuppositions of stimulus–response psychology, generally resulting in programs ranging from simple drill and practice routines to more sophisticated tutorials involving branching. Especially for children with learning disabilities, drill and practice programs are probably very valuable, while gifted students can profit from tutorial programs with branching, as these allow them to control the pace of their own learning. To take a concrete example, a number of promising programs have been developed to facilitate creative, independent writing in highly able children (Wresch, 1984). These programs:

1. Guide those students who profit from concrete, sequential learning to produce a preliminary outline of ideas;
2. Lead those who need help with an assigned topic to generate and structure random ideas;
3. Provide open-ended inquiry approaches for those who enjoy generating ideas randomly or even abstractly.

Such programs provide, in dialogue format, a guided brainstorming experience for the student. However, they are static, in the sense that the program structure is fixed, so that essentially the same path is followed and the same questions asked, irrespective of topic or specific student responses. To a considerable degree, then, the student is required to work towards a solution or end point which has been preordained as correct by the writer of the program, something which has already been criticized in Chapters 4, 5 and 9.

Two important concepts taken from learning psychology which bear upon this point are "individualized learning" and "self-directed learning." In the usual classroom situation a group of learners moves at a more or less fixed speed towards goals specified by the teacher. The computer, however, offers the prospect of actively involving learners in their own learning and permitting them to design learning experiences in accordance with their own preferences. These are, of course, benefits which it can bring for all children although, as Chapters 8 and 9 have shown, they take on special significance in the case of the unusually able. Nonetheless, they are still largely concerned with the organization of otherwise conventional learning processes.

Even as long as 20 years ago Covington and Crutchfield (1965) showed that educational technology could do far more than this. They developed "technological" procedures for facilitating creative problem solving, and showed that these led to significant differences between trained and untrained pupils. The positive effects of the training were still present five months later, and were independent of sex, IQ or prior problem solving experience. The training fostered a mixture of convergent and divergent thinking skills, as well as confident attitudes to problem solving: children were encouraged to ask effective questions, generate ideas, distinguish between high and low quality ideas and make suggestions for solutions, as well as to view problem solving as interesting and stimulating. The level of technology involved at the time the program was developed was rudimentary in comparison with what is available today. Nonetheless, the procedures — telling children detective stories, drawing attention to clues, inviting suggestions for solutions, indicating weaknesses in proffered solutions, etc. — are very suitable for further development with the help of modern hitech. Much more recently Coutant (1985), to take a simple example, described a program for using computers in mathematics instruction not for routine drill but to release "imagination" and "creativity." Jordan and Smith (1985) reported on the use of the computer to increase the output of pupils in a creative writing class; one result was that group discussion of output was facilitated and processes of group evaluation were set in motion.

Burke (1982) suggested that cognitive psychology, through its investigation of information processing and the metacognitive aspects of learning, could revolutionize instruction. Educational technology opens up the prospect of a breakthrough in these areas through the fostering of what Wiens (1977) called "metaskills." These are related to what is often called "learning to learn:" skill in establishing what it is that one wants to learn, in finding the necessary information, in ascertaining whether or not one's own goals have been achieved and the like. The importance of such processes in gifted thinking was emphasized by Resnick and Glaser (1985), and especially by Sternberg (1985), who used the term "metacognition" to refer to processes such as identification of the essence of a problem, selection among possible approaches, self-evaluation, etc. (see earlier discussions). From a developmental psychological point of view, the computer is ideally suited to promotion of the growth of operational thinking in the

Piagetian sense and, in the case of the unusually able, of post formal operational thinking (see Case, 1978, for a more detailed discussion of this concept).

In summary, high technology has considerable potential for improving the learning of both unusually able and also average and below average students. Features of computer application offer the opportunity of fulfilling a number of requirements which take on special significance with exceptionally able students, such as dealing in a creative way with real life problems, testing the effects of brainstorming, trying out many solutions, etc. It also has great potential for individualizing learning and promoting self-directed learning, while at the same time helping in the building of learning groups and in the emergence of group processes — thus providing a way of bringing about the contact with intellectual peers which has already been shown to be important. As Masuda (1981, p. 65) put it, computer technology offers the opportunity of achieving a situation in which "education will be freed from the restrictions of income, time and place." In these ways, computer applications stand to benefit all learners, although they take on special significance with the highly able.

Computers and instruction

While the explosion in microcomputer technology is relatively recent, the idea of using computers to help provide instruction for academically able students is not new. Dover (1983), citing research by Vogelli and Suppes, traced the evolution of such instruction to work done in the USSR during the 1950s. Although informal programs were available in the USA at this time, probably the first formal program (which was aimed at accelerating and enriching the mathematics curriculum for elementary school children) was that of the National Science Foundation in 1963 (Dover, 1983). Early programs used large mainframe computers linked to terminals in the homes of gifted students, but not all met with unqualified success. Reviewing a program which aimed at providing advanced instruction to students with IQs over 165, Suppes (see Dover, 1983, pp. 81–82) noted a high droput rate, which he attributed to lack of program structure and to the absence of formal academic credit for the extra work done.

By 1978, Sisk had identified computer assisted instruction (CAI) as the most rapidly developing educational use of computers, but it soon became obvious that there was a dearth of good instructional software (see Burke, 1982). This situation is beginning to be rectified, partly because of the entry of large publishing firms into the market, bringing with them their own expertise. Some offerings continue to be little more than translations of traditional materials from the printed page to the monitor screen; however, the necessary improvement of courseware cannot be achieved simply through greater sophistication in programming, but must make use of the distinctive capabilities of the computer. Recognition of the special properties of this medium is still developing, both among educators and among the producers of educational materials.

Recent advances in linking the computer with other devices have greatly enhanced its effectiveness as an instructional tool. The ability of the computer to interact with and control a videodisc player, for instance, permits the presentation of material in visual form, while the computer's random access capabilities can be used to select any specific part of a presentation for more detailed treatment. For example, a professional production of, say, *Hamlet* could be shown, and scenes to be examined in greater detail subsequently re-presented. Alternatively, different productions of the same scene could be shown side by side and compared.

The linking of computer and videodisc has also greatly broadened the possibilities for highly sophisticated *simulations*. In essence, it becomes possible for pupils to work on tasks or situations which could not normally be brought into the classroom. Numerous simulations have been devised: for instance, there are programs which simulate chemical reactions, voting behavior for different segments of the population, even moves made by ice hockey or football players. The PLATO system simulates human patients who can be subjected to various "treatments". Computer and videodisc linkups have been used to examine the effectiveness of various alternative configurations suggested by engineering trainees. Using a similar approach based on simulating social, financial or technological systems, it would be possible to explore the consequences of divergent solutions derived from problem solving or brainstorming sessions, such as were discussed in Chapter 8.

Diagnosis of learning needs

The use of the computer to diagnose learners' existing knowledge, aptitudes, interests and even learning styles also seems to offer considerable promise. Indeed, relatively primitive forms of this constituted one of the earliest uses of computers in education (see Knapper and Cropley, 1985 for a fuller discussion), and diagnosis is still a major feature of computer managed instruction. The computer generates diagnostic questions from a large bank of items, pinpoints what learners already know and where their weaknesses are and provides information on appropriate (not necessarily computer stored) materials. This approach seems to have particular promise for unusually able students. It offers a tool which can be used to guide and personalize learning activities in a much more rapid and precise manner than is possible through traditional discussions between teacher and pupil. Unfortunately, however, developing diagnostic test banks and linking these to suggestions for study materials is no simple matter. It is even more difficult to go a step further and guide students on the basis of study habits, preferred learning style and similar factors. Hence, the use of high technology described here does not yet exist in the sophisticated forms which are really needed; further development in this area should be a major goal of research and development activities.

The computer as an intellectual tool

The computer has opened up new vistas for educational contents, extending from electronics, through the application of advanced mathematical concepts, to the very structure and analysis of thought and knowledge. It is therefore appropriate that computer technology should become an object of inquiry for academically exceptional students. Beyond the technological aspects of computing, social and ethical issues such as the impact of computers on society and the privacy of information call for examination by alert minds. Cropley (1982b) has argued that there is a serious danger that the impact of high technology on education will be looked at only from the technical point of view (cost, efficiency, elegance of systems, etc.), with subsequent neglect of the "human" issues (self-image, attitudes to learning, values, etc.). It is important that the most able students do not neglect these aspects.

Up to the present, however, the scope of study into computer technology has generally been less ambitious. It has been commonly accepted that "computer literacy" should be part of the curriculum for gifted students, although the term has been interpreted in widely different ways (Jensen and Wedman, 1983). In view of the fluid state of the computer field, it is hardly surprising that any provisional operational definition of literacy should have undergone changes. A few years ago a person might have been considered computer literate if he or she could switch the infernal machine on, knew how to insert the floppy disk without ruining it and could access and run programs on the disk. Later, familiarity with some of the jargon relating to memory and its capacity would probably have been added, and currently one might add the requirement that to be computer literate a person should have sufficient understanding to be able to amend a program if it does not quite do what the user wants. Such a degree of literacy is hardly sufficient for the intellectual development of academically exceptional students; its acceptance would be analogous to agreeing that competence in basic literacy is sufficient for appreciating the language of

Shakespeare. For an academically gifted student, computer literacy should consist of more than keeping abreast of the latest developments.

Programming

The single most significant contribution of modern technological developments to the education of academically exceptional children is the facilitation of direct interaction between student and computer through the writing of programs. Creating a computer program comes very close to the ideal as a learning experience for these children — and for others — because of a number of intrinsic characteristics:

1. Although programming calls for innovative, original and creative thinking, there is a tangible problem to be solved by the program, in contrast to some creative problem solving activities, which lack external validity checks.
2. There is no single unique solution to a situation, i.e., a problem can be solved by programs which might differ in strategy as well as in detail.
3. Evaluation of a program as it is developing is honest and totally neutral, i.e., the unemotional computer provides immediate negative feedback — but with total lack of any hint of personal animosity or disappointment — when the programmer errs.
4. The completion of a program which works, or even elimination of a troublesome "bug," generates a feeling in the programmer which is little short of ecstasy — i.e., there is powerful positive reinforcement, while noncognitive aspects of learning also play a role.
5. The programmer is able — alone or in discussion with others — to appraise critically and improve existing working programs, rendering them more elegant and more efficient, and to discuss the relative merits of alternative conceptual models and representations (Dover, 1983; Fiday, 1983).
6. As Bailes (1985) emphasized, the swapping of programs is an effective technique for generating contacts among learners, and is an effective way of providing able youngsters with access to intellectual peers.
7. Computer programs have an inbuilt, virtually limitless versatility and capacity for further development. Programming can thus become a process in which elementary programs develop into larger, complex and interrelated schemes, in the same way as cognitive development moves from the preoperational to concrete operations to formal operations. The purpose of programming for the academically exceptional is not simply the learning of a useful additional technical skill, but an opportunity for exploring structural approaches to problem solving in a realistic context (Doorly, 1980).

Approaches which have sought to incorporate programming into teaching the unusually able have done so in a variety of ways. The ability to produce graphic images has proved a popular avenue for introducing students to the technology and for making them aware of their capacity to control and manipulate the computer. In addition to providing relevant practice in skills such as graphing and project planning, the production of simple pictures can stimulate the development of logical thinking, the recognition of multiple solution possibilities and a systematic approach to problem solving (Nay, 1981; Fiday, 1983). Building on educational concepts formulated by Dewey and Piaget, Papert (1980) envisaged the computer as a flexible tool placed at the child's disposal for the exploration of concepts and relationships. He developed a simple, but remarkably powerful, set of commands in the form of the programming language LOGO, which has proved extremely popular. Maintaining that interrelating the structural elements in a LOGO environment fosters intellectual flexibility, Papert (1980) suggested that programming activities lead to growth in combinatorial and self-referential thought. Reports by many who have used LOGO in the classroom as an introduction to computing have generally been enthusiastic, and supportive of Papert's claims (Carter, 1981; Fiday, 1983; Weir, 1981), even emphasizing its value in fostering creativity (Parsons, 1985).

Psychological effects of programming

Among the beneficial effects that have been claimed for computer programming is facilitation of *metacognitive development*: the process of editing or improving a computer program provides an opportunity to reflect on one's own thought processes. Others have maintained that the student masters the material being explored more thoroughly as a result of assuming the *role of teacher* to the machine (Papert, 1980; Overall, Howley and Leventhal, 1981). In the affective domain, Milner and Wildberger (1977) commented on *increased self-confidence* in gifted students working with computers. There is also some indication that, because the computer provides a milieu in which the intellectually able student may explore alternatives with minimal risk, *curiosity and self-initiated exploratory behavior* are enhanced (Milner and Wildberger, 1977). Wavrick (1980) has observed that gifted students who are accustomed to high achievement can develop unrealistic expectations of themselves — especially in educational settings which are generally uncritical — and that the discipline required in computer program development, editing and correction can promote *awareness of their own limitations* and imperfections. Sisk (1978) has suggested that the sharing and helping of others during programming provides an atmosphere conducive to the development of *social interactive behavior*, a view which is supported by reports from Bailes (1985) and Jordan and Smith (1985).

Teachers, enthusiastic about the response from students, parents and some other teachers, are understandably anxious to share their experience and to generate further progress. As a consequence, the claims made by writers in the professional literature on computers as an intellectual tool for academically exceptional students are largely in the nature of enthusiastic testimonials, rather than conclusions from rigorously planned, empirically validated studies. A recent study by Clements (1986) is of great interest in this context. He reviewed research findings on the benefits of both programming and CAI, and concluded that reports often conflict. Accordingly, he carried out an empirical comparison of the effects of learning to program in LOGO with those of exposure to CAI. Groups of six- and eight-year-olds received appropriate training for a period of 22 weeks, one group learning LOGO programming, a second being taught with the assistance of CAI, and a control group learning in the usual way. Prior to training (pretest) and after its conclusion (posttest) the children were tested in four areas: level of cognitive development in Piagetian terms (in two areas — classification and seriation); metacognitive skills (deciding on the nature of a problem, identifying relevant actions, monitoring one's own progress towards a solution, etc.); creativity; achievement. The posttests showed there were no differences between groups in terms of conventional academic achievement. However, the LOGO group showed *accelerated cognitive growth, improved metacognitive skills,* and *greater creativity*. Arguing that LOGO requires reflection and analysis of one's own thinking, organization of knowledge and memory, analysis of one's own errors and the like, Clements came to the important conclusion that programming may well have not *quantitative* effects (solving more problems), but *qualitative* ones (different styles of thinking, different ways of tackling problems, etc.).

A related study, although it did not involve programming, was carried out by Parker and Parker (1986). They investigated the effects of nine months of computer exposure on 30 exceptionally able children in Grades 1–3, who worked with various commercially available software packages (including puzzles and games) for two 75-minute periods a week. A major goal of the project was to investigate the effects of contact with microcomputers on thinking and problem solving. In particular, the authors were interested in "higher order thinking skills" such as analysis of information by breaking it into its constituent elements, resynthesis of these elements into new wholes, application of ideas and solutions in new situations and evaluation of solutions. (These categories are strongly reminiscent of Sternberg's (1985) discussion of metacognition.) The intention of the researchers was not to attempt to train such thinking skills directly, but to offer the children learning situations in which they were strongly incorporated, and where their application led to obvious payoffs. Pre- and post-testing of the children revealed that 25 out of 28 for whom both sets of data were available improved their higher order thinking skills from the beginning of the project in October to its end in June.

On the other hand, Messer (1987) drew attention to the possible negative side of computer use by young children. He found no overall superiority in problem solving capacity of normally gifted ten-year-olds who had access to a computer at home over those who did not. There was even a tendency for the children who had more access to the computer to become dependent on it to offer them hints on how to procede, when they came up against a problem. He stressed that success in problem solving is strongly related to what he called an "independent" approach: this involves personal satisfaction as the main source of motivation, and the setting of personal standards in evaluating one's own work, rather than dependence upon external authorities. Misused, computers may encourage passivity and dependency, and thus foster a one-sided, convergent pattern of intellectual growth. Although this study was not confined to unusually able children, it emphasizes once again the importance of considering noncognitive factors in using computers to facilitate the emergence of academic excellence.

Expert systems

One of the most exciting areas of computer technology is in the creation of "expert systems," a branch of artificial intelligence (AI). In an expert system (ES), the computer "learns". The prospect of computers being able to learn is one which arouses in some people an apprehensive vision of computers achieving independence from human control: optimists anticipate merely loss of jobs, pessimists fear a science fiction scenario where robots enslave the human race. For the foreseeable future, the prognosis is likely to be less spectacular. Many decisions taken by human experts are based on "heuristics" — the application of rules of thumb derived from experience. The major task in developing an ES is to formulate the rules which have (often unconsciously) been developed by the human expert, in such a way that the computer can understand, retrieve and activate them. However, as time passes and real data are accumulated and fed into the computer, these heuristic rules can be tested empirically and, if necessary, amended. There is nothing revolutionary about this; indeed, it is what human experts have been doing for decades, i.e., profiting from experience. The difference with an ES is that development of the rules governing procedure is based on a rigorous, comprehensive analysis of experience rather than on subjective memory and intuitive interpretation.

There have already been some spectacular achievements by the pioneering ESs (Hayes-Roth, Waterman and Lenat, 1983), but educators have been comparatively slow in applying ES technology to instructional and management problems in the schools (Hofmeister, 1985). Some of the first experimental ES applications in education have been to the diagnosis of children with learning problems (McLeod, Colbourn and Robertson, 1984). McLeod (1986) has produced an elementary illustrative ES for the identification of gifted students along the lines of Hallahan and Kauffman's (1978) interpretation of Renzulli's (1978) definition.

In the present context, however, the attraction of the ES is primarily as a vehicle to be developed *by* academically exceptional students, rather than something to be applied *to* them. Currently, an ES generally requries the use of a mainframe computer, although at least two microcomputer based expert system authoring tools are available: "Expert-Ease" and "M 1" (Ferrara, Parry and Lubke, 1985). Developing a program with Expert-Ease employs a four-stage process:

1. Identifying possible answers;
2. Identifying critical attributes for use in discriminating between differing examples;
3. Writing questions which are designed to help the system assign values to critical attributes;
4. Entering examples of problems.

A logical matrix is then induced, which determines and controls the presentation of appropriate questions to the user, whose responses lead to the "expert" conclusions (Ferrara, Parry and Lubke, 1985). The structure of the first three elements of Expert-Ease is sufficiently reminiscent of creative problem solving strategies to suggest that the creation of ESs is a natural evolutionary step in programming for academically exceptional students. Of course, this is some way down the road but, if recent history is any guide, the road is shorter — much shorter — than many of us realise.

Closing remarks

Educators, particularly special educators, have been subjected to many "revolutionary" materials and procedures over the years. They might be forgiven, therefore, for thinking that "computer hysteria" is simply the latest fad, which will disappear after a year or two, or find its niche in an auxiliary capacity, allowing life to continue essentially as before. However, it is apparent that the application of high technology, especially of microcomputers, opens up new perspectives for the fostering of academic excellence; it offers the prospect of learning freed from many of the restrictions of time and place which have traditionally prevailed. The cognitive, motivational, personal and social aspects of computer applications are all central in this function. It is clear that the microcomputer means that life will never be quite the same again. The US broadcaster, Edward R. Murrow (cited by Lindenau, 1984) commented with reference to television that:

> The instrument can teach, it can illuminate, yes, it can even inspire. But it can do so only to the extent that humans are determined to use it to those ends. Otherwise, it is merely lights and wires in a box.

The same sentiments might be applied to many of the aspects of the emerging computer technology briefly reviewed in the present chapter.

11

Organizational Approaches in Schools

Acceleration and enrichment

One of the questions posed at the end of Chapter 1 was that of how exceptionally able children can best be educated. Apart from adaptation of instruction in the regular classroom (see Chapters 8 and 9), wholehearted provision for the unusually able requires organizational and administrative changes at the level of the school, or even the system. One of the major issues which has emerged is that of how to apply the organizational strategies of "acceleration" and "enrichment." "Acceleration" does not mean causing a sudden jump in a child's level of development. Rather, if the school curriculum is viewed as a sequential series of studies and learning experiences, acceleration represents an attempt to place the student at a point on the continuum which will best ensure further growth at optimal speed, even if this means reaching that point at a younger than average age and then progressing unusually fast. "Enrichment" — "true enrichment" as Hildreth (1966) uses the term, or what might be called "pure" enrichment — occurs "when pupils are challenged to undertake problem solving and original work beyond the interests and abilities of the rest of the [regular] class," although remaining with children of the same calendar age. Although often regarded as quite distinct, and even antithetical (e.g., Stanley, 1977), acceleration and enrichment can be, and often are, two sides of the same coin. Enrichment in the form of original work and problem solving beyond the boundaries of the regular curriculum might well involve work from a higher grade, and may therefore be viewed as a form of acceleration; if acceleration is defined as the adjustment of learning time to meet the individual capabilities of students, then as Fox (1979) has observed, "the two terms are complementary rather than conflicting." Passow (1987) expressed his dissatisfaction with the sharp distinction between acceleration and enrichment even more forcefully. Thus, although the two approaches are discussed below in separate sections, this should not be seen as implying that they are necessarily mutually exclusive.

Acceleration

A number of organizational and administrative strategies exist for allowing unusually able children to move through the stages and phases of school curriculum at a pace suited to their ability level. These range from measures adopted at the beginning of the school career to those coming into effect at its end. A number of these are reviewed below.

Early entrance

"Early entrance" is the term used to describe the administrative procedure whereby children under the conventional age are permitted to enter kindergarten, or Grade 1, if they are adjudged to be capable of succeeding. Generally, this decision is based on some kind of readiness tests, not infrequently supplemented by an intelligence test. Because of inevitable facts of psychometric life, described in more detail in Chapter 6, the probability of children whose birthday is more than three or four months below the regular cutoff date being accepted is extremely low. Early entrance is, strictly speaking, not really acceleration at all; it is only an administrative form of acceleration in which the child does not necessarily deal with classroom material at a faster rate than the norm, but simply starts to work on it at a younger age than usual.

Research findings, summarized by Newland (1976, pp. 246–248), have generally been favorable to early admission although, as Newland observes, "research on early admission generally has not involved the use of well planned control groups which would make possible the comparison of well defined early entrants with other children equally qualified for early admission but not admitted early." A study by McLeod, Markowsky and Leong (1972) illustrated the dangers of making generalized evaluations of early admission procedures. Of 126 children who had been considered for early entrance to Grade 1, the 36 who had been admitted and who could be located two years later formed the "early entrants" group. Forty-three children who had not been admitted early, and who attended the same schools as the early entrants, comprised the "rejectee" group. Both groups were tested on the Metropolitan Achievement Tests towards the end of Grade 2 and their performance compared with control groups made up of classmates matched for sex and age. Overall, the selection procedures appeared to have been validated; the early entrants were at least holding their own with their older classmates, while the rejectees were not outperforming their age peers. However, when the results were further analyzed, a different picture emerged. The average performance of the upper socioeconomic status (USES) rejectees was far superior to that of their classmates. The lower socioeconomic status (LSES) rejectees, on the other hand, performed marginally worse than *their* (relatively low achieving) classmates. In itself, there is nothing necessarily remarkable in this finding, except that when the original selection data were examined, it transpired that there was no difference between the Stanford–Binet IQs of the USES and LSES rejectees. It seems that, for quite different reasons, the rejectees from both the USES and LSES groups could have benefited from early intellectual stimulation: the USES rejectees would probably have succeeded academically if they had been admitted a year earlier, while the LSES children would have experienced a certain degree of compensation for their relatively unstimulating home environments.

If early admission is to be successful, it is highly desirable that the receiving teacher be advised, consulted and counselled. Most kindergarten and Grade 1 teachers would probably agree that slow learners should be held back until their mental and emotional development approximates that of other members of the class. Somewhat paradoxically however, many are likely to be against early entrance for faster learners.

Grade skipping, or "gross acceleration"

"Acceleration" is a term borrowed from applied mathematics, or mechanics, where it describes a rate of change of velocity. Just as an instantaneous increase in speed from 20 miles per hour to 30 miles per hour is not possible, so "skipping a grade"— probably the most common (but often undocumented) form of educational acceleration — is not strictly acceleration at all, since it does not involve stepping up the pace at which certain materials are presented, but simply omitting them altogether. Newland (1976) refers to grade skipping as *"gross acceleration,"* which is perhaps an appropriate expression, especially in the early grades. Grade skipping is a simple and superficially effective treatment for the student who is bored and unchallenged. However, there is no guarantee that a child who is bored in Grade 3 will be automatically "turned on" in Grade 4, especially if the Grade 4 teacher is pedestrian and uninspired. Care must be taken when grade skipping is practised in higher grades — especially in cumulative subjects such as mathematics — that important elements of the curriculum, which will adversely affect the learning of more advanced material, are not omitted. Gallagher (1975, p. 286) referred to grade skipping as one of the least desirable methods of accomplishing the acceleration of gifted students.

Whenever a child is moved up a grade, it should be after a full and careful assessment of the total situation, and should be accompanied by appropriate counselling of all parties concerned, including the receiving teacher. A number of factors should be borne in mind. Among these is the ubiquitous age-within-grade effect. If the child is in one of the lower grades and is one of the older students in the class, superior performance represents a combination of ability differential *and* age differential, and as the years pass the age differential becomes less potent. A second, related, issue is that although children who skip a grade will probably do well after the promotion, many of them will be regarded in later years by their high school teachers as simply average or above average for their grade, without being outstanding. The reason for this is what Stanley (1979) has called the "entrenched view" that students of average age for the grade they are in are an advanced pupils' peer group, a view which is, as he correctly observes, a denial of individual differences. For instance, an accelerated student who is outperforming 85 percent of his or her grade peers is probably achieving within the top one percent of *age* peers. One consequence of gross acceleration for many children is that the probability of their carrying off high school prizes and scholarships is reduced; after all, there *are* bright unaccelerated students in the higher grades! This might seem a somewhat mundane factor to the idealistic educator, but could be an understandable concern for parents, and is not irrelevant for the student's future *curriculum vitae* in the modern competitive world. A publication of the National Association for Gifted Children (June 1981) observed that parents tend to dislike children taking more advanced classes because "an A is an A; why opt for a more difficult class where it is less probable that one will get an A?" A sad reflection on our educational system, but not unreasonable.

Selective acceleration

Selective acceleration occurs when students with advanced skills and ability in a particular subject area study that subject with students at a higher grade level, but otherwise remain with their age peers. This arrangement is more likely to be appropriate in the high school, where academic work is departmentalized. In high schools organized on a semester sytem, e.g., where each class is completed during one of two six-month sessions per academic year, selective acceleration can result in a student completing a four-year course in two years. Such a possibility again emphasizes the need for comprehensive planning of programs for the academically able. What is to happen to a Grade 10 student who has completed the Grade 12 course in mathematics? Clearly there must be provision for Advanced Placement (see p. 200), as a result of which such students can go on to college classes; recent advances in Distance Education involving satellite television and computer networks promise exciting possibilities for academically outstanding students who do not happen to live within easy reach of a university (see Chapter 10).

Adaptive acceleration

Advancing a student through four years of study in two, mentioned in the previous paragraph, could perhaps be appropriately interpreted as an example of adaptive acceleration, which according to Newland (1976, p. 258), involves students working within the regular classroom but doing work associated with a higher grade level. This arrangement would be individually prescribed and probably most practicable in the elementary grades, and is similar to what Stanley (1977, p. 95) called "self-pacing" (or "inappropriate neoenrichment"), which he claims is less effective with precocious mathematicians than is group pacing. Adaptive acceleration is a natural extension of the "continuous progress" program implemented in some elementary schools. For children who are well into the Grade 6 program by the time they nominally finish Grade 5 it is a reasonable goal to complete Grade 8 within the next two academic years, i.e., a year earlier than normal. In principle, this time compressing is similar to what Renzulli and Smith (1983) have referred to as "compacting," and for the diagnostic teaching approach of the Baltimore group's SMPY program.

A different interpretation of adaptive acceleration, or at least a different implementation, is to be seen when a whole class of students is grouped together to be accelerated, and covers the prescribed syllabus in shorter time than is customary. For example, it was common practice for English grammar schools, which were already selective, to be organized into "fast streams" and "slow streams," the former taking four years to cover courses which required five years for the slower streams. In the Federal Republic of Germany such classes are referred to nowadays as "express" classes (*D-Zug-Klassen*). They have a long history in the German speaking countries, stretching back to the early years of the present century, and were tried out in several states of the Federal Republic in the 1960s. although they were regarded at that time as not having proved themselves, and had largely fallen into disuse until very recently. In 1986, the State of Niedersachsen (Lower Saxony) adopted a program of special measures aimed at facilitating the educational progress of unusually able youngsters, *D-Zug-Klassen* constituting one of the main procedures recommended: the work of the first five years of the seven-year academic high school (*Gymnasium*) — Grades 7 - 11 — can be completed in four years by intellectually gifted children. In Bayern (Bavaria), on the other hand, the approach adopted has given most weight to enrichment: since 1986 special in-depth classes are offered in *Gymnasia* for pupils with special interests — for instance, additional foreign languages for specialists in this area, philosophy classes for others, astronomy, electronics, etc.   Although perhaps more commonly practised at the high school level, group adaptive acceleration can, and has, taken place in the elementary grades. If only the exceptionally able alone are considered, group adaptive acceleration requires a fairly large school or the congregating of students from several schools. However, if a continuous progress philosophy is truly being implemented, children who are bright but perhaps not "gifted" in the eyes of those who demand a fixed benchmark such as an IQ of 130, or achievement above the 98th percentile, can benefit from adaptive acceleration. For the exceptionally able, there is no reason why group adaptive acceleration should not be combined with cluster grouping (see p. 204) within the accelerated class. Cox's (1983) answer to the question; "how does a school district develop a continuous progress, or a nongraded school model?" is "very carefully!" This serves to remind us of the need for planning, staff preparation and community support.

Advanced placement

The "problem" has already been mentioned of students who complete either secondary school itself, or work in one or more subjects, faster than their age mates. One possibility is early admission to university. This procedure is by no means new, even though it has only recently returned to prominence. In the 1930s the University of Chicago had a well established program of early admission, while in the 1950s admission to higher education of youngsters from Grade 10 or 11 was judged to have been a successful measure (Stanley and Benbow, 1986). The International Baccalaurate, a program leading to high school graduation, even contains specific provision for early admission to higher education, or for advanced study at university while still at school.

In Europe this procedure is rare, although not necessarily forbidden by educational legislation. The best known European case in recent years is that of Ruth Lawrence, who entered Oxford University at the age of 12. She graduated with high honors, and is presently studying for the PhD. Terry Tao passed the South Australian university entrance exam in mathematics at the age of 8 (see Gross, 1986). He then entered secondary school, where he studied Grade 12 physics and Grade 11 chemistry, also taking Grade 8 English and French. In mathematics, he commenced the first year program at a local university, under the guidance of a professor and, late in the school year, began attending certain university classes in physics. At 10 he was spending one third of his time at university studying mathematics and physics, the remaining two thirds at secondary school in Grades 9 (English), 10 (French), 11 (Geography and Latin) and 12 (Chemistry)!

One major concern about such programs is that the youngsters in question will suffer socially and emotionally. Recent governmental position papers in West Germany, for instance, have emphasized the need to consider not only the intellectual, but also the personal and social development of fast learning children. It was considerations of this kind which led Ruth Lawrence's parents to insist that she wait a year before entering university, and which led to the "mixed" program of Terry Tao just outlined — in some subjects he works with people operating at about his mental age, in others with those nearer his social age (although in none with his actual chronological age peers). Although opponents of rapid acceleration often argue that early entrance can lead to psychological harm, Stanley and Benbow (1986) concluded that there is no evidence to support this case; if anything, there are a host of anecdotes suggesting that early entrance is nearly always beneficial.

Research on acceleration

Reports on research into the effects of educational acceleration has generally been favorable (Fox, 1979; Gallagher, 1975; Newland, 1976; Stanley and Benbow, 1986). However, for the most part it cannot be claimed that these conclusions are based on extensive, rigorously designed studies.

One finding that *has* emerged consistently, even in very early studies (Freehill, 1961; Pressey, 1949; Terman and Oden, 1947) is that acceleration does not result in social or emotional maladjustment; if anything, accelerated students tend to be better adjusted than their regular grade peers. Several authors (e.g., Pressey, 1949; Newland, 1976; Gallagher, 1975) have pointed out that the risks of maladjustment in superior students are probably greater if the student is *not* accelerated. Furthermore, there are grounds for believing that special provision does not necessarily lead to resentment on the part of those who do not receive it. In one study of special classes for the academically talented, Gelmon and MacLean (1974) examined, among other things, the effects within families when one child was selected for the program. They found "no hostility on the part of unselected siblings in 79.5 percent of cases." (At the same time, the corollary of this finding is that there *was* hostility in more than a fifth of the families studied.) Stanley and Benbow (1986) mentioned a number of brilliant achievers (e.g., Nobel Prize Winners) who had been accelerated in school. They concluded that counter-examples are rare. They also came to the conclusion that opposition to acceleration as a principle is usually based on emotion and bias, rather then evidence.

Enrichment

Educational enrichment for the exceptionally able involves giving them the opportunity to study in greater depth topics which are part of the curriculum of their actual grade; for example, undertaking original research and solving problems which are beyond the interests and abilities of the rest of the class (Hildreth, 1966), but do not necessarily require knowledge from higher grades. Enrichment has primarily been conceived of as being provided by the classroom teacher; for a teacher who exudes a zest for learning and welcomes the challenge of fostering a similar enthusiasm in an academically exceptional student, enrichment can be an exciting adventure. It is clearly this kind of enrichment that Fox (1979) had in mind when she observed that enrichment and acceleration are complementary, not conflicting. However, alternative sources of enrichment experiences may be itinerant teachers, resource teachers or mentors (these terms will be explained more fully in later sections); these people can provide enrichment experiences directly or in cooperation with the class teacher.

Enrichment is less costly than most alternative methods of providing special programs; perhaps because a nominal, and possibly superficial, "enrichment program" can be provided cheaply, this approach has probably been used as window dressing by some school authorities as an excuse for not providing more comprehensive and costly services (Mordock 1975). Stanley (1984) insists that "the intellectually talented youth's specific academic hunger" be fed directly rather than have the teacher's "favorite enrichment subject" imposed. Unfortunately, as has frequently been observed (e.g., Hildreth, 1966; Renzulli, 1977, 1980; Keating, 1976), so-called enrichment can degenerate into "busywork" or "fun and games activities" which, as Renzulli (1977, p. 6) has commented, can make a mockery out of the reason why the youngsters in the program were selected for special treatment in the first place. Specifically, Renzulli (1980) has criticized overreliance or excessive reliance on programs which are based on the "popular but completely unsupported belief" that the gifted person is "process oriented" rather than product oriented; this view has "undoubtedly resulted in gifted education's overreliance on cute games and situational specific training activities that purport to develop creativity and other thinking skills." As Renzulli goes on to observe, there is a "vast difference between the types of mental growth that result from a thirty-minute exercise in creative ways of pasting macaroni on oatmeal boxes and the kind of disciplined inquiry and task commitment that sparked the work of . . . anyone . . . that history has recognized as a truly gifted person" (Renzulli, 1980, pp. 6–7). Renzulli himself has developed an integrated, progressive model for providing enrichment activities which

TABLE 11.1. *Guidelines for evaluation of enrichment activities*

Enrichment *is*	Enrichment is *not*, or *not merely*
Productive thinking	Reproductive thinking
Applying and associating learning to other areas	Accumulating and regurgitating information about one area
Learning concepts and generalizations	Learning facts
Complex thinking	Harder work
Determined by student readiness	Determined according to age-or grade-level expectancy
Extending and/or replacing traditional learning experiences	Providing more work
Interrelated learning information	Separate entity learning
Critically evaluating	Accepting all data provided
Problem seeking	Answering questions
Stimulating and encouraging the development of talent	Penalizing giftedness and the development of talent
Learning things as they could, or should, be	Learning things as they are
Learning why and how	Learning what

has been widely adopted, and which was described in greater detail in Chapter 6.

Stanley and Benbow (1986) discuss four types of enrichment in detail — "busy work," "irrelevant academic enrichment," "cultural enrichment" and "relevant academic enrichment." Stanley (1977) leaves his readers in no doubt as to his strong feeling that "any kind of enrichment except perhaps the cultural sort will, without acceleration, tend to harm the brilliant student." Stanley (1980) mourns the fact that, as he sees it, many educators have placed "nearly all their gold and energy on the irrelevant enrichment bandwagon . . . This leaves the typically intellectually talented youth unsatisfied because his specific intellectual hungers are not being met. 'Let them eat cake' is as poor advice in this matter as it was in the historical context."

A good deal of criticism and apparent disillusionment with enrichment (Gallagher, Weiss, Oglesby and Thomas, 1983) no doubt stems at least in part from experience with poor quality enrichment programs. There is a tendency to forget that many judgemental questions in education which appear to be one dimensional (merely matters of quantity) have a second, qualitative dimension. The debate as to whether acceleration or enrichment is the more desirable is no exception. A high quality acceleration program is undoubtedly preferable to a low quality enrichment program, but the question remains of whether a poor acceleration program is preferable to a good enrichment program. Table 11.1, adopted from Kaplan (1974), highlights the desirable characteristics of enrichment activities and contrasts these with potential undesirable characteristics.

Laycock (1979) provides a concise closing statement on enrichment, observing that true enrichment (where the child is challenged and constructively busy) can be very stimulating, but that "there can be quite a distance between good intentions and enrichment."

As was the case with acceleration, a variety of organizational strategies exist for the implementation of enrichment. Some of these offer special advantages in terms of the criteria outlined in Table 11.1.

Special classes

Commenting on a program for gifted children which relied primarily on special classes, Laycock expressed the view that full-time special schools and classes are only an interim solution, because:

> If every teacher were a university graduate, and if every teacher had special training in meeting the needs of the gifted, I would have no special classes; but, for most school systems, this is "pie in the sky." (see Laycock, 1979)

Thirty years later, when classes have been reduced to the numbers envisaged by Laycock, and when teaching has for the most part become a graduate profession, it is not at all clear that the necessary conditions for abolishing special classes have been fulfilled. For this reason, it is still necessary to discuss them as one of the administrative options.

Within a regular school, special classes can range from full-time self-contained classes, tantamount to a "school within a school," to classes which meet on a part-time basis and recruit students from a group of neighborhood schools. They are relatively easy and inexpensive to establish, but, unfortunately, this means that they are sometimes set up with little planning as a visible "program for the gifted." Classes which have been little more than window dressing have tended to be short lived (Newland, 1976).

Full-time self-contained classes enjoy essentially the same advantages and disadvantages as separate schools, except that errors of identification that might have occurred ought to be easier to correct. However, if the class or classes are effectively a school within the school, such correction might be more possible in theory than in practice. In a large school, special classes can be made up of students from within that school, but in the case of smaller schools, children will have to be transferred to a central site — on a permanent basis for full-time special classes, and intermittently for part-time special groupings.

Cluster grouping

A number of organizational forms for the provision of special classes exist. Those which meet on a part-time basis and recruit children from a group of schools are sometimes called "cluster groups." In one Australian venture (Gifted Children Task Force, 1982), to take a concrete example, children were withdrawn from a number of schools for at least a half day per week for a series of disconnected enrichment activities, each activity extending over a five- to six-week period. Advantages claimed for cluster groups include maximizing the specialist facilities that exist in schools, universities and the community, facilitating the interaction between children of like talents and allowing students a more realistic view of themselves in relation to their fellow students. Such classes are the direct descendants of the "Colfax Plan," which stemmed from the pioneering activities of the Colfax Elementary School in Pittsburgh (Pregler, 1954), where bright children from several grades were withdrawn from regular classes for two hours each week to take part in "club activities." One advantage of regular part-time, "pull out" classes is that the students in these classes maintain contact with regular classmates, and can report back to these classmates on some of the information and ideas they have learned during the club or cluster group activities, whereas special schools and special classes tend to restrict after-school neighborhood friendships.

Newland (1976) maintains that the activities of special interest groups should (a) be related to conventional school content; (b) be incorporated within normal school times; and (c) not be superficial or merely escapist. Examination of topics successfully dealt with in cluster groups, such as Auto Vehicle Body for 9–11-year-olds, Contract Bridge, Genealogy and Heraldry, suggests that the first of these criteria is not essential, while the experience of organizers of successful "Saturday Clubs" (see next chapter) casts some doubt on the other two. The term "cluster grouping" has also been applied to grouping according to ability within the regular classroom (Kaplan 1974). Learning centers and learning kits are made available to the more able students, often linked with a system of contracting for independent study.

Tracking

Tracking, or "streaming" as it is termed in some countries, assigns students to a particular ability section, usually within a given year group. Thus, there might be an "A" track for the fast learners, a "B" track for the average and a "C" track for the slower learners. At first glance this appears to be a good idea, because the wide range of ability in a typical grade is broken down into more homogeneous, teachable units. However, there are complications.

In the first place, children in "homogeneous" groups show a remarkable ability to remain stubbornly heterogeneous. Within the relatively narrow general ability range of students in the "A" stream, those who are oustanding in literary subjects are not always among the most able scientists or mathematicians. Tracking tends to be self-reinforcing. Apart from the administrative inconvenience of transferring children from the one track to another, especially after a number of years during which the ''A'' stream will probably have moved ahead of the curriculum covered by the ''B'' stream, and the ''C'' stream will have fallen even further behind, there is research evidence (Findley and Bryan, 1971; Vernon, 1957; Douglas, 1964) that tracking helps to confirm and expand the differences in measured ability and self-concept level between students in the different tracks. The rich get richer and the poor get poorer. This effect can have serious social repercussions when the different tracks approximately coincide with socioeconomic and/or minority group divisions, with the result that tracking may be interpreted as an indirect means of effecting racial or social segregation.

In relatively competitively organized systems of education such as those of Europe (although probably less so now than some years ago), tracking can be an integral part of a progressively fractionated program. In Britain, for example, it was common practice for children to be placed into ability ''streams'' on entry to the junior school, i.e., at the age of seven. By the time they reached the hurdle of the 11 plus, it was virtually a foregone conclusion that no children from the ''B'' or ''C'' streams would qualify for a place at the selective grammar school — except from schools in upper socioeconomic neighborhoods. Once in the grammar school, a student would again be directed into an ''A'', ''B'' or ''C'' stream, albeit from an ability range which was usually restricted to about the top 15 percent of the total population — and again, future educational advancement, such as going to university, would be unlikely for those who found themselves in the ''C'' stream.

An alternative to allocating children to different tracks which are semipermanent administrative units is ''multiple tracking'' or ''setting'', whereby students are placed in appropriate ability groups for different subjects. Thus, a student might be in the ''A'' set for mathematics and the ''B'' set for English. Such an organization is facilitated by back to back timetabling, where all students within a particular grade level take the same subject at the same time.

Resource teachers

So far we have been considering administrative options which involve teachers from within an academically able student's own school, whether this be a regular school or a special school. With enrichment, there is, however, the possibility of enlisting ancillary help from others outside the regular classroom. Among these are resource teachers, generally itinerants who serve a small group of schools.

If it is held to be desirable that academically exceptional children should be based with their regular age peers, but should concurrently be provided with challenging opportunities for contact with their ability peers, then "pull out" arrangements offer many advantages: groups of more able students leave their classroom from time to time and spend several sessions per week with other able students under the guidance of a special resource teacher. It is easy for students who have been inappropriately identified or who are themselves not enamored of the experience to withdraw from such a program. But, as with other types of program, the quality will only be as good as the personnel and material resources which are committed. In a school jurisdiction which is only nominally committed to providing for the academically able, itinerant teachers can be grossly overloaded. They are likely to encounter a wide variety of interests and talents among the children they serve, and if these interests are to be fostered — in contrast to imposing some prepackaged, standard fare — the itinerant teachers must have adequate time for preparation. If they are not to resemble traveling salespersons loaded down with wares, the schools they visit must have learning or enrichment centers which are adequately provided with appropriate equipment and instructional materials for the realization of teaching objectives. Moreover, there must be an opportunity for them to consult, cooperate and jointly plan with the students' regular teachers; if these conditions are not met, at best they will run the risk of being regarded as an irrelevant ancillary, and at worst they will incur hostility and resentment.

In recent years, "in house" resource teachers have become a relatively familiar component in many elementary schools, mainly working with less able and learning disabled students. A resource teacher has — or should have — skills in educational diagnosis, prescription and prescriptive teaching. It is perhaps unfortunate that educational literature generally refers to the "resource room" model, which automatically leads to the concept of pull out (of the regular classroom) models, with all the material divisiveness of such a term.

The presence within the school of a resource teacher who carries the full range of relevant duties, but is also in charge of a class, helps regular class teachers to feel included rather than excluded from the planning and delivery of services to students with special needs. The range of the competent resource teacher's activities is illustrated in Table 11.2.

Resource rooms

The work of resource teachers is often linked to activities in a resource room; a room in the regular school building containing specialized or advanced reading materials or other printed resources (newspapers,

TABLE 11.2. *Possible resource teacher involvement with children requiring special help*

Involvement of resource teacher	Level	Description of involvement
Indirect	1	Consultation and observation
	2	Supplying formal and informal test materials
	3	Supplying instructional resources
Direct	1	Tutorial in regular class. Resource teacher helps the child within the classroom with some specific task
	2	Resource room (occasional). Student attends resource room for help on a specific task for a limited period
	3	Contracted services. Resource teacher briefs or trains tutor (aide, post-secondary student, volunteer) to help student for prescribed period on prescribed task
	4	Resource room regular. Daily, one or possibly two periods per day up to six weeks
	5	Resource room regular. Daily, two to four periods per day. Six weeks or more
	6	Referral to community agency

charts, maps and so on), special facilities (videos, slides, films, etc.), information storage and retrieval systems (files, databases, personal computers, etc.), special collections of materials (files, slides, samples and the like), laboratory equipment going beyond everyday needs (microscopes, ovens, etc.), and a whole range of materials permitting an unusually intensive confrontation with topics of special interest. Such a room has something of the function of a library, with elements of laboratory, workshop and studio. It is usually supervised by a resource teacher, while individual students typically spend only a few hours a week working there. Some of this may be free time, after school or during the noon break for instance, but students may also be allotted specific periods during conventional instruction times for the ''subject'' resource room. Sometimes students who complete class work quickly may use the free time they have thus created for visits to the resource room.

Hammill and Wiederholdt (1972) listed fourteen advantages of the resource room approach. These are (slightly paraphrased by the present authors):

1. Pupils can benefit from specific training while remaining integrated with friends and age mates;
2. Pupils have the advantage of a program prepared by the resource teacher which may, nonetheless, be implemented in cooperation with the regular class teacher;
3. Resource rooms are less expensive than tutoring or special class programs;
4. More children can be served under a resource room arrangement;

5. The resource teacher is less likely than an itinerant professional to be viewed as an outsider by other teachers in the school;
6. Young children with mild problems can be accommodated, and hence later severe disorders can be prevented;
7. Pupils are not labeled;
8. The stigma invariably associated with receiving special attention is minimized;
9. Pupils can receive help in their neighborhood school, so that the necessity of busing around the town or county to an ''appropriately labeled'' class or resource room is largely eliminated;
10. Pupils enjoy the benefits of flexible scheduling; i.e., they may work entirely in contact with their regular classroom teacher, with resource teacher support, or in the resource room when necessary, while the schedule can be quickly changed in response to changed circumstances;
11. There is no appreciable time lapse between referral and initiation of services;
12. Medical and psychological services are available when the school decides they are needed;
13. Since resource rooms will absorb most exceptional children, special classes will increasingly become instructional settings for the more extremely exceptional;
14. The resource teacher is likely to become an ''in house'' school consultant.

The resource room model is not without its critics, at least for serving the learning disabled, Gallagher (1975) considering its benefits to be unsubstantiated. Such reservations should serve as another reminder that *no* form of provision is necessarily good or bad in itself, but can be no better than the quality and competence of those who are involved in its implementation.

Closing remarks

Apart from appropriate changes in teaching and learning in the regular classroom — changes which, while especially helpful in the case of unusually able pupils, are potentially of benefit to all youngsters — a variety of special ways of organizing instruction in order to foster the growth of exceptional ability have emerged. These are all characterized by the assumption that separation of exceptionally able and ''normal'' children, at least some of the time, is absolutely necessary. Nonetheless they also have in common that they are carried on within the general framework of the regular school.

A variety of different organizational forms has emerged. Although most of these are entirely, or at least partly, compatible with each other, and may even supplement each other, there is a tendency in relevant discussions to polarize discussion around two apparently conflicting principles: acceleration and enrichment. As is shown in this chapter, this is to some degree a red herring — enrichment frequently involves elements of acceleration, and vice versa. Unfortunately, it appears that enrichment activities can quickly degenerate into busy-work; this emphasizes the importance of well trained specialist personnel. Acceleration, on the other hand, is often criticized as bringing with it the risk of disturbances in social and personal development, although anecdotal evidence does not support this argument.

What is often missing in discussions of special provision for the unusually able is evidence of the effectiveness of the measures in question. Problems of evaluation of measures and programs have already been mentioned. They will be discussed again in more detail in the following chapter.

12

Measures Outside Traditional Schools

One of the most impressive developments in special provision for the academically able in recent years has been the emergence of a range of activities which lie either partly or entirely outside the regular school. Some of these are conducted under cooperative conditions, to be sure: schools may mediate contact between children or parents and special programs, nominate participants, make rooms or other facilities available, or even provide teachers (for instance on a volunteer basis at weekends or during vacation). However, the programs in question are not an integral part of the work of regular schools — this means that many of them result in strict separation of able and less clever youngsters.

Special schools

The "obvious" initial solution for educating children with special educational needs, not only academically able children but also mentally retarded, visually impaired, hearing impaired, physically handicapped or other exceptional children, has been to identify them, group them together and treat them more or less homogeneously. This is essentially the "three D" procedure advocated by Stanley (1977) — "Discovery, Description and Development" — although Stanley was writing within the specific context of mathematical talent.

Special schools for either slow or fast learners have never been in the mainstream American tradition (Kirk, 1960). In Europe, however, such schools, in the form of *Gymnasia* in Germany and mid-Europe, *lycees* in France and *grammar schools* in Britain, have a substantial tradition. They predate compulsory education and historically derive from times when generally (there were honorable exceptions, for instance in Germany and Scotland) only a minority consisting of the well to do, plus a small number of recipients of scholarships from the deserving poor, went to school at all. In the idealism immediately following World War II, plans were evolved in several European nations to move toward apparently more democratic, comprehensive systems of education, particularly at the secondary level. However, separate schools for the more able are still alive and well, not only in Western Europe but also in Eastern European countries (where admission is facilitated if one's parents are not openly cool or hostile to the regime) and China.

There are obvious advantages to the self-contained school for able students. Probably the greatest is that students are taught among their intellectual peers, which makes for mutual intellectual stimulation. Such schools also afford an opportunity to congregate teachers with appropriate qualifications and competencies, rather than having these professionals (who are not always easy to recruit) disperse their expertise over a number of schools. The arrangement also probably makes for the more efficient deployment of equipment. Some of the benefits of the SMPY, as perceived by Stanley (1977, pp. 100–102) are also applicable to special schools and classes; for instance better preparation for college, reduction of egotism and arrogance, or enhanced feelings of self-worth and accomplishment.

But there are attendant disadvantages, particularly if one takes a broader view than simply the interests of the students who are *in* the special school — and who *succeed* there. The beneficial effects of mutual intellectual stimulation which students in selective schools enjoy are inevitably lost to those students "next in order" of ability, who were left stranded in the regular school. There is also the danger of unfairness in the selection of children for special schools. There are always "false positives" and "false negatives" in identification procedures (see Chapter 6), and placements in selective schools are difficult to reverse, partly because of the adverse effects of transferring children out. Even Stanley has to report that "a homogeneously grouped class which is fast paced by the teacher produces astoundingly good result for about *half* of the students enrolled" and that "students who proceed too slowly may have to leave the group." From various reports by Stanley (e.g., 1976) and Fox (e.g., 1974, 1979) the "failure rate" in the SMPY appears to center around 30 percent. This is compatible with "McLeod's Law" (based on totally undocumented experience with selective schools in England ranging from one which creamed off the top one percent of the ability range to others which accepted as many as the top quarter or so): "In the opinion of their teachers, the bottom third of any identified group of intellectually selected students ought not to be in the program."

There is a real possibility of adverse effects on the self-concept of some children who are admitted to a special program but are subsequently demoralized by what they perceive as failure in competition with a group of students who are all at least their equals intellectually. Almost any special program runs some risk of damaging the self-concept of a minority of the children involved; the risk is potentially more serious in the case of self-contained schools because, due to the relatively long-term nature of the treatment, the effects are likely to be chronic and difficult to ameliorate.

Experience, and such empirical evidence as exists, suggests that allegations that separate schools for exceptionally able students produce snobbery and elitism are groundless; indeed, it may be argued — as Stanley (1977) has observed in relation to the SMPY — that the effect is more likely to be the opposite. Nevertheless, it is true that special schools lead to undesirable situations such as the one which arises when a child who attends a special school has less opportunity to make friends with other children in her/his own neighborhood. Although this is not necessarily due to snobbery or elitism, if a substantial number of people in the community *believes* that selective schools (or classes) produce elitism — and even if such beliefs are symptoms of envy on the part of those holding them (e.g., parent of children who fail to be selected) — the situation is less than satisfactory. Despite the problems they raise, it seems likely that in a comprehensive, multifaceted program for academically able students, where confidence in identification is progressively and cumulatively strengthened through diagnosis and observation, separate schools might be regarded as an appropriate "pinnacle" in a hierarchically organized system. Nonetheless, they would have the maximum beneficial effect only in a society with an appropriately informed public and teaching body.

Saturday Clubs

Many part-time programs have sprung up in many parts of the world, out of school hours and largely independent of the formal educational system. Usually parents have been the motivating and organizing force (repeating the pattern in other areas of special education) no doubt often frustrated by what they perceived as inadequate and inappropriate facilities for their children within the public school system. For instance, Pra Sisto (1978) describes the New Jersey Saturday Workshop as existing "solely to fill the void created by the lack of sufficient programs for gifted children in most of New Jersey's public schools." There is almost certainly no single "correct" way of organizing such programs, here generically described as "Saturday Clubs," although examination of the histories of some of the more successful ventures suggests that dedication by a small group of pioneers, imaginative planning and flexibility are probably common necessary ingredients for success.

Two "Saturday Clubs" which not only survived the initial

enthusiasm and successfully stood the test of time, but developed into successful prototypes for others to emulate, were the Saturday Workshop of New Jersey, USA and the Saturday (formerly Sunday) Club of London, England. Although sharing the common basic characteristics referred to above, there are distinctive differences in approach, from what one might stereotypically see as the structured, businesslike, "typically American" organization in New Jersey, to the casual, unflappable, "typically British" venture in London — until one realizes that Grace Armbruster, the original guiding light in London, came from Iowa.

The New Jersey Saturday Workshop was originally organized in 1957 "by a handful of concerned and dedicated parents" but grew to "supplement the educational and social needs" of nearly 500 children between the ages of four and 12 in its Spring and Fall ten-week sessions, and served nearly 10,000 students over an 18-year period (Pra Sisto, 1978). A Curriculum Coordinator was employed to advise a curriculum committee, and three basic guidelines were established:

1. Courses to be offered had to be recognizably different and go far beyond the depth and breadth of courses in the regular school curriculum — "more of the same" had to be avoided;
2. A logical sequence and balance between the sciences and humanities had to be maintained;
3. The courses offered had to recognize and reflect the learning characteristics and needs of gifted children.

The 50 or so one-hour classes offered in each session ranged from "The Sound of Music" and "Secrets of Nature" for four-year-olds to "All that Jazz" and "Macro–micro Biology" for the over-nines. Apart from the intellectual stimulation, children's social needs were said to be supplemented through interaction with others in the nonthreatening atmosphere which prevailed, while parents were able to attend seminars and discussion groups. There was no formal identification procedure used for selecting children for the program but they were required to have a group or individual IQ of at least 120, and their school had to testify that they were mature, well adjusted and likely to benefit from the program. The teachers were formally hired, although all hiring was done by invitation rather than by advertising, and teachers were subjected to quite intensive evaluation. On the basis of observation over the years, the New Jersey Curriculum Committee concluded that not every regular classroom teacher could or should teach gifted children. The committee also identified certain characteristics displayed by the more successful teachers:

1. They are enthusiastic about working with gifted children;

2. They have a broad cultural background with expert knowledge in a specific subject area;
3. They actively involve students through a "hands on" approach to education;
4. They are flexible and willing to incorporate student ideas;
5. They are self-secure and not threatened by the student's ability;
6. They are accessible to students, both in and outside the classroom;
7. They are experienced at working with children, not necessarily as a teacher;
8. They have a good sense of humor;
9. They understand the problems of gifted children, and have patience;
10. They are aware of the special learning needs and characteristics of gifted children;
11. They transmit enthusiasm and a love of learning;
12. They relate to students on an individual basis;
13. They possess the stamina to prepare more and work harder than is normally expected.

The London Saturday Club began in 1971 as a "Sunday Club" which met in the home of the parent who pioneered the venture. After three years as a "very successful, but intimate," club, it was translated into an enlarged Saturday Club, under the auspices of the National Association for Gifted Children and with active support of the Inner London Education Authority (ILEA), who provided suitable premises and some teaching staff. By 1978, 170 children between the ages of five and about 14 were meeting for three hours each Saturday during term time with a staff of 22 teachers (17 volunteers and five sponsored by the ILEA), and "additional helpers to prepare tea" (Berse, 1977).

The principal goal of the London club was to provide greater opportunity for self-fulfillment (rather than specific attainment) than is normally experienced by gifted children in their everyday lives (NAGC/ILEA, 1978). Admission procedures were even more informal than those employed in New Jersey, selection originally being made on the basis of an interview with the child's parents. Sometimes children were referred with an intelligence test score; most often they were not, although an IQ "might be obtained at a later date" (Berse, 1977). Special consideration was given to children presenting problems, such as isolation from peers, vast underachievement, educational and social deprivation, and general unhappiness. One remarkable, and apparently successful, feature about the London Club's admission policy was that membership of the club was open not only to children "in need of 'stretching' to a higher level but also their brothers and sisters if accompanying them" (NAGC/ILEA, 1978).

Many of the activities were what Newland (see p. 204) might have described as "escapist." This reflected a deliberate desire to avoid replicating school curricula, out of concern that some unsuccessful Saturday Clubs probably placed too much emphasis on intellectual aspects and paid too little heed to motivation and social needs. Nevertheless, activities at the London Club covered a wide spectrum, falling roughly into three categories: physical, small motor skills and intellectual development. Activities include trampolining, gymnastics and dance, games such as badminton, basketball, (field) hockey, cricket, etc. and skill areas: woodwork, metalwork, pottery, painting and photography. A third group of activities consists of science, computer work, production of a weekly newspaper, technical drawing and cartography.

Although the Saturday Club approach is perhaps best established in Great Britain and North America, it is also gathering strength in countries with no modern tradition of out-of-school educational initiatives — the Federal Republic of Germany, for instance, has a highly bureaucratic system of education, with centralized control at either state or federal level, not only of funding (which is also the case in other countries), but also of teacher training, working conditions and even of curiculum. At the school level, there is already — officially — provision for exceptionally able students, by virtue of the existence of the selective secondary schools already referred to (*Gymnasium*). However, there is little "payoff" for the gifted, since it is difficult to break out of the system of progression through grades (skipping a grade is theoretically possible, but not common), and it is risky to take difficult subjects in the matriculation exam (*Abitur*); getting into university is highly selective and is decided on the average examination mark, regardless of which subjects are taken, students thus being well advised to take art, sport and religion if they want to get into university, rather than, say, maths, physics and chemistry. (The national press has recently reported several cases of exceptionally able students who took "difficult" Abitur subjects and were therefore crowded out of university by less able people who took "easy" subjects — in one case despite having written a textbook in physics. Some of these people have been snapped up by universities in the United States.) Against this background, it is hardly surprising that out-of-school, parent-led initiatives in the area of gifted education have, until recently, been rare, since it makes more sense, pragmatically, to concentrate on getting very high marks in "easy" subjects. Not only in Germany, an A is an A is an A. Recently, the situation has improved noticably in at least some states: Niedersachsen and Bayern, for instance, adopted programs of special measures in 1986.

In addition to these activities, staff at the University of Hamburg have initiated a multiyear project on identification and fostering of mathematically able school children, which includes regular classes on Saturday mornings (see Wagner and Zimmermann, 1986). The content of these classes is selected in such a way as to avoid simple overlap with the regular school curriculum — it takes up elements of mathematics which are neglected or officially judged to be too difficult or irrelevant for regular schools (e.g., probability, the theory of numbers, the ''human'' aspects of mathematics, etc.), as well as trying to foster mathematical creativity (flexibility in thinking, ability to generate new ideas and the like). Since 1983 sixth grade children have been selected for the program by being nominated by their maths teacher, by their parents or even by themselves. Those nominated are then tested using both a German version of the US Scholastic Aptitude Test (SAT) and also a locally developed test of mathematical creativity, approximately the top 20 percent being admitted to the program.

Very recently, the mathematics project — just described — *Talentsuche Mathematik* — has been supplemented by a similar ''search for talent'' in the area of creative writing: *Talentsuch Kreatives Schreiben*. Although much smaller in numbers, this project has a similar aim: identifying a group of unusually talented youngsters and offering them a special program outside their regular schools, under the aegis of the University of Hamburg. The aim of the program is to facilitate contact with other similarly talented youngsters, expose them to models in their own field, give them feedback about their own efforts, encourage them to be productive, help them develop their skills, build self-confidence and the like. In general, these goals may be seen as the guiding principles of all the activities described in this section.

Cooperation with the community

As was pointed out in Chapter 1, the impetus for developing programs and procedures for fostering the development of children with exceptional academic ability has often come from outside the schools — indeed, many teachers' organizations and individuals working in education actually oppose special provision. As a result, interest groups in the community have frequently been a strong element in the emergence of programs for the unusually able. (One major group is that of parents, whose role in fostering academic excellence will be dealt with more fully in a later section.) In many countries the school system has now adopted, to some degree at least, measures constituting ''Gifted Education.'' In others, however, this is not the case, so that the community itself has had to become the major source of special provision. In France, for instance, the National Association for Gifted Children, the Languedoc–Roussillon Association for the Promotion of

Gifted Children and Young People, the Society for Artistic, Literary and Scientific Talents, and similar organizations offer a range of measures including summer camps for gifted children and workshops for the scientifically talented. In the Federal Republic of Germany, the German Society for the Gifted Child (*Deutsche Gesellschaft für das hochbegabte Kind*), founded in 1978 as a result of the interest of parents, has established a number of regional groups which offer mathematics classes for Grade 3 and 4 students, astronomy for 12-year-olds, art history for 11-year-olds, music for 8- to 11-year-olds, Japanese for 8- to 10-year-olds, and science for 8- to 10-year-olds. These activities may be taught by professional teachers (although on a volunteer basis), but are usually led by knowledgable members of the public, who possess special qualifications and are interested in working with enthusiastic youngsters.

Many other countries also report that the community is the main source of support, or is at least one of the major sources. The examples of clubs, camps, etc., just given provide some insights on how this may occur. However, even in countries with well developed provision in regular schools, the community continues to be a valuable resource for the provision of enrichment for exceptionally able children. Indeed, in view of the importance of the community in fostering or impeding the development of gifts and talents (see for instance Gallagher's (1986b) discussion), it is not unreasonable to see it as a crucial or decisive factor. Some dimensions of its contribution will be discussed below.

Mentoring

Mentor programs, as a way of making special provision for the exceptionally able, have only recently returned to prominence. This may help to explain their low rating in Gallagher, Weiss, Oglesby and Thomas's (1983) survey. A mentor is a person, usually a volunteer from outside the ranks of professional educators, who has special skills, experience or knowledge in a particular area, and makes these available to a learner (protégé) with similar interests, usually on a one to one basis and in an actual work setting. Gray and Gray (1986) traced mentoring back to the original task of Mentor, who was charged with the education of Telemachus, son of Odysseus, during the absence of the boy's father at the Trojan War. The essence of mentoring as a special form of teaching lies in the participation of the protégé in the work of the mentor, and of the mentor in that of the protégé. Learning by observing a master in action and eventually being allowed to take over parts of the actual work was a perfectly normal and natural way of developing mastery of an area before the emergence of the school as we now know it. The function of the modern mentor is to promote both cognitive and affective growth in the protégé; as Gray and Gray put it, this means not only acquiring the skills of a particular discipline, but also "a positive affection for the mentor's area of expertise." To this can be added faith in oneself as a person capable of unusual achievement in the area in question.

Although the mentor–protégé relationship has to be privileged and permitted to run its course as free of accountability to administrative considerations as possible, relatively little is known about the factors which lead to a successful mentoring relationship. Gray and Gray (1986) describe a Helping Relationship Model which can be used for training potential mentors to progress from elementary forms of help such as providing missing knowledge, modeling the role of the successful practitioner, or giving feedback on performance, etc., to the fostering of discovery learning, metacognitive thinking, self-direction in learning and so on. They distinguish between the "directing" level, the "guiding" level, the "supporting" level and the ultimate level, in which the protégé acts independently to initiate activities, creates an end product, presents this to others and carries on a process of self-evaluation. This is similar to what is sometimes referred to as "autonomous" learning.

There are three identifiable steps in the selection process for mentor programs: (1) the student is selected for the program; (2) the mentor is selected for the program; and (3) mentor and student are matched. Criteria for student selection include interest, motivation, demonstrated ability to learn in independent settings and the ability to get along with others — particularly adults. Criteria for mentor selection include a willingness to commit time, enthusiasm, competence, flexibility and, most important, "a commitment to the truth of the tradition being communicated." Mentors themselves may help in the selection of students, and students may be invited to select mentors with whom they would like to work.

An elaborate statewide mentorship program was established along these lines in Victoria, Australia. Personnel from schools, postsecondary educational institutions, industry and "the wider community" were contacted and a large number of them agreed to be included in a Mentor Contact Register. At the beginning of the following academic year, school principals were asked to nominate students worthy of additional assistance with a particular area of research or with a project which demanded expertise unavailable from within the school's resources. Parents and teachers of nominated children were then invited to seek participation and students were matched with a mentor, on a regional basis, by the project coordinator.

In the "Community Laboratory Research Program" in the USA (Huffman, 1985), students work on actual research projects being carried out by scientists in a variety of laboratories, often using highly advanced procedures and equipment. The desired final product is a scientific paper. One theme which is emerging clearly in recent discussions of mentoring is the importance of a tangible end product: Huffman pointed out that in this program no fewer than 15 students a year, on average, succeed in publishing a paper. To take a further example, the "Learning Activity Mentor Program" in Christchurch, New Zealand, serves the needs of the exceptionally able in the early years of secondary school. The program makes available to schools a register of mentors, and offers advice and assistance in implementing mentor relationships, which may be carried out on an individual or a group basis. The aim of this approach, which is strongly school centered, is to offer enrichment within the framework of the regular school, a feature aimed at achieving effective and socially acceptable provision in a strongly egalitarian environment.

Cooperation with industry

Programs in which business and industry cooperate with schools are by no means new. In their commonest form they involve visits by schoolchildren to places of work, not infrequently accompanied by preparatory or follow-up lessons, and often including a guided tour with distribution of samples, the opportunity for a few lucky ones to try out some of the machines or instruments, passing out of brochures, etc. Another frequent form is to be seen in visits to the school by professionals, specialists and the like, who give a lecture on their work, carry out a demonstration, distribute materials, etc. Some of these measures are very well prepared and carried out, and their value should not be dismissed or underestimated, especially where there is careful preparation and debriefing of students. However, especially in the case of exceptionally able youngsters, it is necessary to make such activities considerably more demanding if they are to function as genuine challenges leading to a worthwhile enrichment of school learning.

At a fundamental level, there is a need for cooperation between professional educators and people in business and industry in working out the basic principles of joint programs aimed specifically at fostering the growth of academically able students. These can then be realized in specially designed measures characterized by the fact that, as Frank (1985) put it, "the community becomes the classroom." An obvious example of a relevant program is to be seen in internships and practica during which able youngsters participate in the real work of a firm or business. A mentor relationship between practising business people or industrial scientists and talented students also offers obvious possibilities for fostering the growth of skills, attitudes, values and self-image already discussed in a number of earlier sections. The crucial point is that the joint work must go beyond intellectual tourism and take on elements of deadly earnest.

One comprehensive program has been described by Lane–Smith (1986). Students aged 16 and 17 are nominated by high schools across Canada on the basis of a combination of very high achievement, creativity, motivation and interpersonal skills. Selected students are invited to take part in a four-week residential program conducted on a university campus, staffed by professors of mathematics, engineering, computing science and *business*. The supporting role of business is threefold: the final selection of participants is made by participating firms, which then sponsor their participant by paying all costs associated with participation and commit themselves to providing a six-week work term for the student after completion of the course. A major goal of the program is to stimulate the most capable one percent of secondary school students to develop levels of creativity, initiative and self-confidence beyond those possible in the schools of an individual province. The initial effect is that the participating universities win for themselves a flow of exceptionally capable and motivated students; ultimately it is hoped that society will benefit from the students' ability and drive. Results reported to date suggest that the program is well on the way to succeeding in these goals.

Parents

As Janos and Robinson (1985) pointed out, surprisingly little is known about the precise details of family influence on the emergence of exceptional potentials. A major problem is that studies of individuals who have achieved at high levels seem to reveal a mixed pattern: the parental home and relationships between the people in it display many characteristics which are obviously favorable (warmth, concern, encouragement, etc.), but at the same time others which would not usually be regarded as desirable (tension, rivalry, aloofness and the like). This is typical of findings in the whole area of adjustment/ maladjustment, high achievement/underachievement, social accep-tance/social rejection of unusually able individuals (see Chapter 7 for more details). Janos and Robinson's review of research makes it clear that able individuals who realize their potentials in the form of exceptional achievement differ from both less able people and less successful able people not only in terms of ability (in the case of youngsters not identified as outstanding), but also in terms of drive, dedication and focus of interest (motivation) and what Cropley (1988) called "personal prerequisites" (openness, independence, venture-someness, self-directedness, tolerance for ambiguity, etc.). The importance of such characteristics becomes clearer in studies in which high and low achievers among the intellectually able are compared (again, see Chapter 7). The central question here is that of the role played by parents in the emergence of such properties.

Family relationships

A great deal is known about academic excellence and family *structure* in demographic and sociological terms, starting with the work of Terman. However, as Janos and Robinson (1985) implied, the time is now ripe for focusing on family *relationships*. In a recent review, Gelcer and Dick (1986) developed an analysis of this kind. Since they were writing from a clinical point of view, they concentrated on essentially pathological aspects of family interactions. Nonetheless, as will be emphasized shortly, their approach can be generalized to the nonclinical family situation.

At an early age, exceptionally able children "identify" themselves to their parents as remarkable, by displaying intellectual precocity, extreme verbal facility, acute and accurate observation of the world around them, great sensitivity and insight and the like. This may arouse in the parents, at different stages of the child's development, wonder, fear, a desire to protect the child, dreams of realizing frustrated personal ambitions and even a feeling of reduced personal worth as a result of unfavorable comparison with the child. Various reactions are observed in child rearing behavior: some parents become overprotective, the child being seen as needing shelter from the dangers of the world, the result being that family life becomes closed and rigid. A second extreme reaction is that the child is turned into a "pseudoadult" (Gelcer and Dick, 1986, p. 448). It may be expected to play an equal or, in extreme cases, even a parenting role vis à vis his or her own parents. This reaction requires that parents blind themselves to the normal childlike weaknesses of their offspring such as lack of experience, emotional immaturity, need for guidance, lack of tried and tested values, narrow perspectives, etc. Finally, there is a third form of reaction which, like the previous two, can most clearly be presented by describing its extreme form: some parents, especially those who themselves have, or have had, aspirations to outstanding achievement, begin to compete with their own children. They seek to offset the poor picture of themselves which emerges from comparisons with their child (especially later, as the child begins to become successful in various fields of endeavor), by finding and flaunting areas where they are still superior. The effect on able children of these extreme parental reactions can be weakened self-concept, difficulty in acquiring clearcut values and norms, ambivalence about their own talent or ability, reduced motivation and so on.

It is important to emphasize at this point that the three patterns of parental reaction just described have been presented in their dramatically extreme, possibly pathological forms. They are often associated with a failure to realize exceptional ability by means of outstanding achievement — in a certain sense, the discussions in the previous paragraph could have been presented in Chapter 7. However, the probability is that the three dimensions presented here play a role in relations between all parents and their children: most parents probably experience moments when they would like to protect their children from the harshness of the world, or yearn for reassurance from them, or feel the urge to demonstrate that they can still show them a thing or two. However, this would normally be tempered by "normal" parenting behavior. The whole domain is thus fraught with *ambivalence*. The practical problem for most parents is that of protecting without stifling, giving responsibility without abrogating authority, challenging critically without becoming destructive. This situation becomes acute when children possess exceptional potentials and is further affected by the level of the child's ability, the level of parental education and ambition, the degree to which parents' own dreams have been realized, the personality structures of parents and children and the like. Apparent contradictions in findings are thus hardly surprising!

Practical guidelines

As with the suggestions for classroom practice, the intention of this section is not to provide detailed description of actual day-to-day behaviors for parents of exceptionally able youngsters, but to offer general principles according to which parents may look critically but constructively at the way they interact with their children. A number of "manuals" for everyday behavior exist, however, including Ginsberg and Harrison (1977), Lewis (1979) and Perino and Perino (1981), to take three examples more or less at random. These offer reviews of basic theory at the intelligent lay level, and go into detail on topics such as childrearing, fostering special adjustment, dealing with schools and teachers, choosing special programs and the like.

As has already been pointed out, there are some grounds for believing that exceptional ability tends to manifest itself in excellence in a special area (despite the existence of brilliant allrounders). Not only is fascination with a particular domain typical of unusually able individuals, but extremely intense contact with a field of excellence seems to be something approaching a prerequisite for the full realisation of potentials. The first task for parents is therefore that of *facilitating the pursuit of such interests*. This can be done by oneself showing interest, willingly answering questions, providing learning materials and opportunities, giving the child opportunities to explain its interests, projects, etc., and respecting its expertise. Related to this kind of support is *help in the acquisition of appropriate general skills* such as language facility, logical and divergent thinking, as well as special skills related to the area(s) of intense interest. Baldwin (1985) has pointed out that these skills may include control of bodily movements, sense of justice and similar characteristics which may be more valued in minority groups. In the area of motivation, exceptionally able youngsters need *opportunities to carry out and complete tasks* and judge them according to high realistic standards. Because of the ease with which they frequently grasp the essence of a project, they may slip into the habit of dropping a piece of work half finished, once the adventure has gone out of the confrontation with the task in question. At the same time, it is important to help them *develop independence of thinking and self-evaluation*: a general principle is that (all) children need to be encouraged to attribute the results of actions to their own behavior, to see that consequences — desirable or undesirable — are frequently self-caused. Research has shown that some parents slip into an unwitting compact with their children in which all blame is shoved onto the shoulders of third parties, mainly teachers.

An area in which, according to Janos and Robinson (1985), there is surprisingly little interest, is that of *emotional development*. Many parents of unusually able children concentrate so strongly on the cognitive aspects of high ability that they neglect their children's need to develop a strong identity, a secure self-image, the ability to cope with frustration, stress, even defeat, the ability to enjoy life, treat others with compassion, love and be loved. Development in this area is not fostered by ignoring these aspects, but it is also not fostered by building a cocoon around a child: what is needed is exposure to appropriate opportunities with the backing of supportive but not over-protective parents. A similar principle holds true in the area of *social development*. A problem here involves the interest commonly displayed by exceptionally able youngsters in social contact with children of their mental rather than chronological age. It was earlier supposed that such children would tend to display the social characteristics of children of their own age, rather than ability level, but as Janos and Robinson (1985) pointed out, this is not supported by empirical evidence. Many able youngsters seek and enjoy contact with their intellectual rather than their chronological peers. At the same time, however, this raises problems, especially in childhood — a physically immature child may, for instance, have difficulty in fitting in with others who have already reached puberty, and have developed appropriate interests. A second problem centers on the possibility of (perceived) arrogance or impatience with others. Parents need to offer support in the social area, even to be willing to

discuss the issues, offering insights, making suggestions for com-
promises, etc. A final point in this area concerns the importance of
social contact with other unusually able youngsters. These are the only
people who can offer the combination of being intellectual peers while
also being chronological peers.

Kline and Meckstroth (1986) outlined special problems of exceptionally able youngsters in the emotional/social domain. These include
feelings of alienation, an exaggerated need to be supported and
understood, social and emotional isolation, role conflicts and unrealized
idealism. Parents can help greatly with the solving of these problems,
but run the risk of either "underinvestment" (aloofness, coldness, etc.)
or "overinvestment" (overprotecting, rigidly controlling and the like).
Specific traits and characteristics of able individuals which can lead to
difficulties in the social/emotional domain include desire for high
achievement, creative expression and perfection (which often leads to
conflict with peers and teachers and other adults, who do not welcome
being corrected and managed by precocious youngsters), intense
inquisitiveness, rapid learning, accurate memory and a large vocabulary (which often make them seem arrogant to other people), and a
strong feeling of being different (which may be interpreted by others as
aloofness or contempt). Kline and Meckstroth interpret these and
similar situations as leading to *stress*. They then offer guidelines on how
family relationships may be adapted in order to reduce or avoid stress,
or help children cope with it. These can be summarized as involving the
provision of "PATs" — (power, attention and time). The content of
PATs should focus, among other things, on self-management,
accepting other people's deviations from perfection, choosing appropriate friends, identifying, labeling, discussing and managing feelings and
the like.

As with all parents, advising parents of unusually able children
involves a position in which every piece of good advice needs to be
balanced by a warning against adopting an extreme position:
encouraging independence should not turn into aloofness, coldness,
abandonment of structure, diffusion of values, etc; protecting a child
against frustration should not turn into stifling, cocooning, coddling
and the like. One danger when parents address themselves consciously
to the question of how best to foster their child's development is that
they can become either paralyzed by fear of doing the wrong thing or
else rigidly controlling, even to the point of moral blackmail, carried out
for instance by means of flamboyant self-sacrifice. What this can lead to
is not compliance with the good intentions of the parents, but resistance
to their goals. For instance, provision of opportunities for intense
contact with an area of excellence needs to be carried out in such a way
as to avoid making children feel that something is being forced on them,

since this may arouse hostility and resistance. The role of parents is less that of an external authority imposing demands and more that of a loyal supporter, involved spectator and energetic facilitator. At the same time, however, parents should not be afraid of expressing clear values or of exercising legitimate, persuasive skills — these are part of good parenting for all children.

Closing remarks

The most obvious form of special provision outside the regular school (for all children with special needs) is the special school. In a number of European countries this measure exists within the framework of the state education system. In others, such schools lie mainly or wholly in the private sector. They offer certain advantages, such as concentration of teachers and resources, but also open up a number of risks. especially in the psychological and social domains. For both pedagogical and political reasons, the special school may continue to be only a relatively marginal form of special provision, especially on a worldwide basis.

One form of out-of-school provision which seems to be gaining strength in a number of countries is that of clubs, special interest groups, vacation camps, etc. Many of these activities are organized in the form of "Saturday Clubs," usually set up on the initiative of parents and frequently staffed by volunteers who are not professional teachers. In the Federal Republic of Germany and France, for instance, national and regional associations constitute a strong growth point for special provision for unusually able youngsters.

A further segment of society which might logically be assumed to have a vested interest in the promotion of excellence is industry. Apart from simply making materials such as computers, laboratory equipment and books available to schools, some firms and businesses are beginning to work both with schools and nonschool organizations. In its active form, this involves development of goals, setting of priorities, design of activities and so on, and not merely provision of finance. Another form of community support is to be seen in the willingness of many people with special knowledge and skills to act as mentors. Mentoring, usually involving a one to one relationship, is an old concept, embodying strong elements of what the teacher–pupil interaction was before the emergence of schools and professional teachers as we know them, and offering glimpses of what teaching would be like in idealized schools. The heart of this approach lies in the personal relationship between mentor and protégé, which permits a high level of learning by doing, as well as contact with the "ethic" of intellectual work at a demanding level.

In addition to their role in organizing and conducting courses, clubs, camps and the like, parents, in their traditional role as child rearers, are an important factor in the emergence and realization of the potential for excellence. Although it is well known that occupational and educational status of parents are significantly related to IQ scores, school marks and success in life (as this is traditionally understood), far less is known about the kinds of family interaction which are favorable for the development of unusual ability. In other words, there is a good deal of uncertainty about the kind of child rearing practices which are favorable to the emergence of academic excellence: results even indicate that some undesirable or even unhealthy patterns of interaction between parents and children are favorable. A major psychological aspect of the situation is that the relationship between parents and unusually able children is beset by ambivalence, and by the tendency of parents to adopt extreme stances; these have their favorable, and also their unfavorable sides.

Advocacy of both in- and out-of-school measures for the promotion of unusual ability assumes that such measures really achieve what they set out to accomplish — that they enhance the realization of potentials in ways which simply doing nothing would not. Once again, however, surprisingly little is known, apart from the fact that many people who have participated in special measures have subsequently done well and relatively few seem to have been actively harmed, or that there are often enormous differences in achievement between program participants and other children, which can logically only be consequences of participation. The conduct of strict experimental studies presents a number of difficulties and its seems that either case studies or similar methods, probably without control groups, or studies of processes and moderator variables will be most practicable.

13

Systemwide Issues: Planning and Personnel

Previous chapters described measures for fostering academic excellence, emphasizing that many of these can be of benefit to all pupils. We turn our attention now to the steps through which an educational *system* can go about implementing practices aimed at promoting excellence.

As early as 1968, in an effort to avoid "some of the hastily contrived adaptations that characterized the post Sputnik era — adaptations which, in many cases, suffered an equally hasty demise," Renzulli (1968, p. 217), conducted a well planned survey to identify those features which were considered by experts to be "Keystones of a quality program" for gifted students. A list was drawn up of educators who had made substantial contributions to the field of education for the gifted, and each person on the list was asked to nominate people who were particularly well qualified to judge the adequacy of various forms of special provision for superior and talented students, yielding a select panel of 21 expert judges. The members of this panel were then asked to rank in order of importance those elements which they considered to be the most important for a worthwhile program, and to stop ranking when enough elements to ensure a high quality program had been checked. A weighted "total rank value" for each element was derived, based on its rank order and the number of experts who had checked it. The seven most important features, according to this criterion, each having been checked by over half of the experts, were:

1. The teacher: selection and training;
2. The curriculum: purposefully distinctive;
3. Student selection procedures;
4. A statement of philosophy and objectives;
5. Staff orientation;
6. A plan of evaluation;
7. Approximate assignment of administrative responsibility.

More recently, the Advisory Committee on the Gifted and Talented to the United States Office of Education called attention to the lack of

228

basic facts about special programming available to educational decision makers. A National Planning Effort was established to collect relevant information (see Gallagher, Weiss, Oglesby & Thomas, 1983). A survey form was distributed through journals and newsletters of cooperating associations, in which seven administrative strategies were listed:

1. Enrichment in the regular classroom;
2. Resource room pull-out programs;
3. Consultant support of regular teachers;
4. Self-contained special classes in regular schools;
5. Independent study programs;
6. Community mentors;
7. Special schools.

Respondents were asked to rank these strategies in order of priority and more than 1200 completed survey forms were returned. A third were from teachers, 13 percent from parents and 26 percent from administrators; three quarters of the total group were female. (According to an NAGC survey, over 70 percent of US State Directors for Gifted and Talented Education are female.) Sixty-five percent of the group indicated that they were presently involved in activities with gifted or talented chilren, and 58 percent of them had been involved for between one and five years. The percentage of respondents who ranked each strategy highest, as well as the percentage who ranked it lowest, are very informative. At the elementary level, there was no doubt that resource rooms were the most popular and the least unpopular; the situation was diametrically reversed in the case of special schools. At the secondary level, however, pride of place went overwhelmingly to advanced classes or special subject classes, with independent study and special schools placed second and third in popularity. There seems to have been a polarization of attitudes towards special schools at the secondary level, i.e., respondents were either very much *for* them or very much *against* them; they received the third highest number of first choices, but also the second highest number of last choices. Perhaps the most surprising finding of the survey was the consistent unpopularity of enrichment in the regular classroom. At the elementary level, only ten percent ranked enrichment first, while 30 percent gave it the lowest rating; at the secondary level, enrichment fared even worse, receiving the lowest number of first choices (four percent) and the highest number of last choices.

An extremely comprehensive survey stretching over four years has recently been completed in the USA under the aegis of the Sid W. Richardson Foundation (Cox, Daniel and Boston, 1985). All 16,000 school districts in the country were surveyed about practices including not only the more or less familiar, such as special schools or classes, but also "radical" measures, such as concurrent enrolment in secondary school and higher education by means of advanced placement programs or other procedures, continuous progress and the like. A further important aspect of this investigation is that it broke away from a restrictive definition of outstanding ability, which would reduce the proportion of children given special treatment to a small "super" group, by focusing on the much larger group of "able learners." At present a program has been set in motion to implement the recommendations of this project in a wide variety of large and small school districts.

In the framework of the Fifth World Conference on Gifted and Talented Children (Held in Manila in1983), Roldan (1986) conducted a survey of educational personnel in the Asia/Pacific Region on the forms of educational provision they regarded as most appropriate for their societies. Enrichment in the framework of the regular classroom was the variant most strongly supported, with pull-out programs involving a resource room and independent study occupying second and third positions. As Roldan emphasized, these measures involve a high degree of working on one's own, of going beyond the regular schoolwork. Roldan was also suprised by the relatively high level of support for special schools, which are often rejected in the Asia/Pacific as elitist. The system related measures which Roldan's respondents most frequently called for were provision of earmarked funds for education of the gifted by governmental agencies, establishment of specialist agencies for the implementation of such provision (for instance government departments), provision of financial support by private foundations and development of research and evaluation programs.

This outline of what is needed can be contrasted with the uneven and often sketchy provision which actually exists, even today. The discrepancies between what is and what might be raise the question of how to go about moving an educational system towards more adequate provision. The various phases include:

1. Acceptance of the need to do something;
2. Formation of appropriate policy;
3. Determination of needs and resources;
4. Development of administrative structures;
5. Commitment to appropriate training of the necessary personnel.

Comprehensive planning

Program implementation does not — or should not — occur overnight. Newland (1976) estimates that in planning an adequate

program for gifted students "it is hardly likely that less than one year
will be needed . . . and two years very well may be more appropriate"
(p. 182). Two illustrative examples of comprehensive, directed
planning are afforded by the state of Hawaii and the state of New South
Wales (NSW) in Australia.

The Hawaii State Plan (Hawaii Department of Education, 1977) was
based on a comprehensive assessment of needs that had been
undertaken during the previous year; this had been achieved by
surveying all existing provisions for the gifted and talented and
comparing actual provision with the estimated size and distribution of
the target population. The definition of the target population, the
philosophical basis underlying the program and its overall goals were
spelled out, followed by specific guidelines indicating how these goals
might be achieved at both the elementary and secondary levels. Further
sections of the planning report presented a model for the identification
of superior and potentially superior students, and provided specific
inservice training proposals for professional personnel at all levels for
the next five years. Finally, the report dealt with evaluation procedures,
budgetary considerations and long term implications.

In NSW (Swan, 1982) a statewide evaluation of programs for
"talented" children was conducted by committees in each school,
assisted by representatives from the State Department of Education.
This evaluation process revealed that although few schools had
specifically designed programs for talented children, there was a general
consensus that individual differences must be catered for, including
those created by virtue of talent (Swan, 1982). The evaluation process
also highlighted teacher concerns, such as their own lack of expertise,
their lack of knowledge on how to identify talent, community attitudes
which discourage the pursuit of excellence, etc. "Bottom up" and "top
down" communications were integrated, for "the model . . . required
information to pass from school to district, to region and then to the
centre" (Swan, 1982).

During the following year, inservice courses were conducted in all
regions, a policy document was developed, and working parties were set
up to produce support documents on specific issues relating to the policy
statement. The policy document itself, although couched in terms
which allowed for flexibility in implementation, spelled out the
respective responsibilities of the "Centre" (i.e., State Department of
Education), the "Region" (i.e., school district) and the "School
Community," which included parents and the general neighborhood
community of individual schools. It also provided concrete guidelines
on identification procedures, a definition of "talented," and a section
on rationale, or philosophy, which stated that "the child with special
aptitudes or abilities should generally be educated in his normal school,

[although] in some instances, the school may need to draw on resources outside the school for necessary expert assistance." Thus, advanced classes, acceleration, enrichment and mentorship should be embraced, but presumably not special schools.

The Hawaii and New South Wales experiences illustrate that, with active involvement from the chief administrator to the class teacher, a momentum can be generated which produces practical, effective policy decisions, in contrast to some of the bland "motherhood" pronouncements — often defensive reactions to pressure from parental lobbyists — which emanate from some educational jurisdictions. A key element that has not generally been *explicitly* identified so far but whose pervading presence is implicit, particularly in the two examples of state planning just cited, is *commitment*. Commitment has to percolate from the chief administrator, through district superintendents and school principals, to the teachers. Furthermore, there has to be concrete evidence of this commitment. One form of evidence of commitment, of course, is the allocation of adequate finances, but commitment involves much more than money. Newland (1976, p. 144) stated it well when he observed that:

> Competent and effective teaching, not just of the gifted, is less a function of the amount of money spent . . . than it is of the interest, motivation, commitment, ingenuity, energy, and overall content competency of those teaching . . . By virtue of . . . extra funding, much more can be done for the gifted . . . without it however, much more could have been done than was done.

Senior administrators can demonstrate commitment through effective, structured, realistic planning procedures and operationalized statements of policy with specific time frames. Demonstrated commitment by senior administrators is a necessary, but in itself insufficient, condition for the success of an innovative program (McLeod, 1979a), needing to be matched by commitment — or at least benevolent tolerance — by professionals at other levels of the educational hierarchy. If a new program is perceived by the regular teacher — or, even more important, by the school principal — as having been arbitrarily imposed by the central office, its chances of success are unlikely to be any better than one which is established in the immediate wake of enthusiasm which can result following a two-day workshop from visiting academic evangelists. It has been demonstrated in a not unrelated context, i.e., that of establishing self-contained classes for moderately handicapped students in regular schools, that teachers who have had relevant inservice training are likely to be more accepting of the program than are teachers who have not received it (Dickson, 1975; Sanche, Chapman and Dineen, 1976; McLeod, 1979b). Teachers who have become informed through inservice training are equipped to participate in a planning process where the "top down" guidelines represent a consolidation of "bottom up" briefing; i.e., where the planning process is, and is seen to be, a total team effort.

Planning constraints

It is one thing to plan in the abstract for academically exceptional children, but actual programs have to be developed within the framework of existing legislation and resources. Of course legislation can be changed and resources can be increased, but realistic planning at least has to consider existing circumstances which place a constraint, or which have the potential to place a constraint on program planning. Constraints include such factors as:

1. The legal definition of "gifted" or "talented" or whatever term is used;
2. The financial resources available;
3. The quantity and quality of professional personnel;
4. Liaison (or lack of liaison) between elementary, secondary and postsecondary educational jurisdictions;
5. Availability of, and regulations concerning, student transportation.

"Financial resources available" should perhaps be reinterpreted as "how much are we prepared to pay?" i.e., it is necessary to declare a specific amount of money (initially, probably fairly modest) which will encourage the development of a priority list of things to be done. The quantity and quality of professional personnel available is crucial, but it should be remembered that ability to teach academically exceptional children is a continuum, not dichotomous — i.e., one cannot divide teachers into two groups, those who can and those who cannot. Successful teachers of academically exceptional children do not necessarily have to be gifted themselves, in the sense of having an IQ over 130 or 140, but if they do not have a genuine zest for learning they may anticipate a demoralizing or even embarrassing experience. They must still consider themselves scholars, as searchers after truth and knowledge, and they must be mature enough to be able to admit that they do not have all the answers — but be able to know how to go about finding the answers.

Steps in planning

An excellent example of planning is to be seen in the phasing in in Texas of "Plan A," a comprehensive scheme of special education for exceptional children. The analysis and structure of the planning process has a validity far beyond its original terms of reference or geographic borders. The stages envisaged in the planning process are:

1. Review of constraints on the planning process;
2. Formulation of the philosophy on which the plan is to be based;
3. Comprehensive assessment of needs;
4. Establishment of priorities to ensure orderly and systematic growth;
5. Development of goals and objectives;
6. Development of program elements, i.e, the specific activities necessary to achieve the stated goals;
7. Development of program policies, i.e., delineation of roles and interrelationships of personnel involved;
8. Allocation of resources;
9. Production of an evaluation design.

The planning of special educational services was envisaged as a five-year operation and, although individual schools were permitted to follow their own development guide, they were encouraged to use the model outlined above. Program goals were to be set for each of the five years, but the submitted document could be reviewed at any time, and therefore become progressively more realistic and valid. The general compatibility of format between development plans from different schools means that consolidation at the regional or state level was facilitated. Thus, schools could readily recognize familiar elements in subsequent policy directives emanating from the State Department of Education, a factor likely to increase the chances of active teacher participation and enthusiasm.

Philosophy formulation

The first principal element in the process of setting up programs for the exceptionally able, once the legal and other restraints have been identified, is the formulation of a philosophy which succeeds in being more than a bland benediction. Perhaps the major philosophical consideration in planning educational services for the academically exceptional is summed up in the phrase "Segregation or Integration?" If student segregation is regarded as undemocratic, and therefore unacceptable, then special schools and full-time special classes are automatically excluded from further consideration. If, on the other hand, segregation of exceptionally able students is acceptable, there are implications for provision for students at the other end of the ability spectrum, i.e., the intellectually and socially handicapped, if there is to be consistency in policy toward exceptional students. Grade promotion policy and policy toward disadvantaged students are also relevant to the philosophy underlying a program for academically exceptional students.

Needs assessment

Within the legal and philosophical constraints surrounding the planning process, the next major task is to assess program needs, which can be analyzed into educational data needs, personnel needs, instructional arrangements and facilities, curriculum and materials, and needs associated with student appraisal, identification and diagnosis.

Educational data needs include a breakdown of the number of children to be served at the kindergarten, elementary and secondary levels, and an analysis of the sociocultural characteristics of the district being served, since these may make necessary various modifications to the general pattern of the program. In the light of the estimated number of children to be served, personnel needs, in the shape of administrators, instructors, supportive professionals and paraprofessionals, have to be determined. The need to plan instructional arrangements calls for an examination of existing school plant facilities. Curriculum and materials have to be perused in order to decide how existing curricula can be developed, modified or augmented in order to be most effective; also, decisions must be made as to what special materials must be purchased, and whether any new curricula have to be developed. All existing resources relating to student appraisal and diagnosis should be surveyed and examined for the part they can play in satisfying local needs for the identification and guidance of academically exceptional children.

Priorities

It is clear that, short of a financial windfall and simultaneous unprecedented dedication to the cause of gifted education, actions along all the lines that will have been suggested by an analysis of needs assessment cannot be instituted immediately. If the phasing in of a program is planned over a number of years, priorities — or targets — should be established for each of the intervening years. Such advice is unlikely to commend itself to parental pressure groups who, understandably, demand action at once. Unfortunately, it has not been uncommon for some school districts to set up almost overnight a program, often in response to such pressure, consisting of little more than enrichment activities coordinated by an itinerant teacher/consultant. Either Aesop's fable of the tortoise and the hare, or Christ's parable of the sower and his seed might be cited in support of the contention that "make haste slowly" is useful advice, provided that the progress is slow but sure — and not too slow.

Program goals and objectives

Goals and objectives, stating what is to be accomplished (but not how it is to be done), include the development of administrative and instructional processes, as well as targets for student achievement. For example an administrative process goal might be to establish an administrative organizational structure which would make for the effective coordination and interschool communication of activities relating to the education of academically exceptional students. An example of an instructional process goal would be to increase the number of students in part-time advanced classes to a specified number by a specified date. A student product objective might be that, say, 20 students would be ready and capable of taking a first year university class in mathematics by the end of their Grade 11 year. With an eye to future evaluation of the program, objectives should be set up which can be expressed in operational terms and which, following Wolfensberger's (1972) dictum that one should "plan for success," are realistic and attainable.

Some responsibilities and powers relating to goals fall within the sphere of the state or provincial legislature. One such responsibility is determining whether a particular educational program shall be *mandatory* or *permissive*. Mandatory legislation requires that local school districts *shall* provide the program. At first glance, mandatory legislation requiring school districts to provide special educational progress for the academically exceptional seems highly desirable, but further deliberation suggests that it is perhaps not such a good idea — at least, not initially. As has been well documented (e.g., Martinson, 1972), there is still opposition on the part of many teachers, administrators and taxpaying parents to the idea of special programs for the gifted. Apart from possible backlash effects of premature mandatory legislation, what will be the probable quality and effectiveness of a program which is forced upon an unwilling school administration? Permissive legislation should not be viewed in a totally negative light, i.e., as providing a devious device by means of which a program can be "accepted in principle" as desirable but at the same time offering a loophole for less enlightened school districts to opt out. At the very least, permissive legislation establishes the legality of spending public money on programs for academically exceptional children, and it may be safely assumed that school districts who are enthusiastic about such programs, i.e., those school districts where programs are most likely to succeed, will take advantage of permissive legislation and provide less enlightened districts with models to copy.

Program elements

For each program objective or goal, there must be corresponding "program elements." Central to the development of program elements is a plan for instructional arrangements, under which the proposed function of classroom teachers, resource teachers, paraprofessionals and non-school personnel are specified. The degree of collaboration and the number of cooperative units to be established need to be spelled out, with attendant implications for staff development training. It is at the stage of developing program elements that the actual adaptation or modification of curriculum, instructional materials and methods also has to be carried out.

"Seed grants" to keen and committed school jurisdictions, who might already have a history of successful concern for the educational needs of the academically exceptional, have a high probability of yielding dividends. Appropriate publicity about the success of funded programs is likely to generate interest in other school districts by osmosis or cross-fertilization of ideas. An overall state policy statement should be conceived in terms which establish the constraints and philosophical guidelines within which programs may be developed, but there should be freedom and flexibility within this general framework for schools and school districts to develop their own program elements according to their own particular circumstances.

Program policies

A state policy should be augmented at the school district level by a local policy statement which delineates the roles and interrelationships between the different personnel involved. There needs to be a clear understanding of the relationship of the gifted education component to the total educational program, especially where some individuals' professional responsibilities will be partly to the "gifted program" and partly to the general educational program. It is particularly important at this stage to consider the duties of the person who has overall responsibility for the establishment or implementation of a special educational program for the academically exceptional.

Allocation of resources

"Resources" refers to the human, administrative and financial resources which the local education agency may employ in delivering

special services to academically exceptional children. The necessary
financial outlay can be far less than many detractors — and even some
advocates — imagine. Stanley (1984) wisely counsels educators to use
what they "already have, rather than build up expensive, politically
vulnerable special programs," for example curricular flexibility and
appropriate articulation. If special classes are congregated in a single
school or in schools that are in the same neighborhood there will be
transportation costs and, if opportunity to participate in the program is
to be equally available to all, those costs — which can be expensive —
should be borne by the public purse. Transportation costs are also
involved if itinerant teachers are employed, but they disappear if a
resource teacher model is used. Some of the necessary program services
can be carried out by personnel already employed, for instance resource
teachers and teachers who can be released part time to act as
coordinators, and the utilization of voluntary community resources
should not be discounted. Identification can be unnecessarily expensive
if undue reliance is placed on the individual testing of large numbers of
children. Routinely administered group tests however, as has already
been pointed out in Chapter 3, can provide excellent screening data,
and a program which emphasizes cumulative observation and
assessment by teachers will provide superior identification data over
time, at far less cost than one which relies on a single battery of
individually administered tests. One of the most expensive pieces of
equipment likely to be associated with programs for academically
exceptional students is the computer, but microcomputers are rapidly
becoming standard school equipment.

The *per capita* cost of financing a program for academically
exceptional students is no greater than that of programs for the mildly
mentally retarded or the learning disabled, and is far less than the cost of
programs for the visually or hearing impaired. Some educational
jurisdictions (e.g., Saskatchewan, Department of Education, 1981, p.
16) automatically allocate monies to school districts, and thence to
schools, over and above the regular grant, recognizing that a proportion
of the school population, say three percent, have mild handicaps that
require special educational treatment. It would be compatible with the
philosophy of encouraging local autonomy, innovation and flexibility
(Renzulli, 1984) to apply a similar policy — with safeguards of
accountability — to finance special programming for those students
with special needs on account of their superior abilities.

Program evaluation

The implementation of a special program for academically exceptional students requires that there be an evaluation plan which will

enable data to be systematically collected, analyzed and reported. It will be appreciated that evaluation, by definition, involves answers which call for value judgements — answers which are difficult and sometimes impossible to obtain from objective data. The sort of questions to be answered are: "Did the program do any good?", "Was it worth the time and effort?", "Is it working as well as expected?" (Hawaii Department of Education, 1972, p. 30). To answer such questions, particularly the last question, Stake (1967) has provided a model of evaluation which has proved useful in a somewhat similar situation, namely that of evaluating a program which sought to implement the "full-service school" concept in a rural community (McLeod, 1979b). In essence, Stake's model analyzes the evaluation process into three sequential stages — "antecedents," "transactions" and "outcomes." Two parallel sequences are considered, one relating to intentions and the other relating to observations; the congruence, or agreement, between observations and intentions forms the basis of evaluation.

Complete evaluation encompasses not only evaluation of student products, in terms of the extent to which behavioral objectives are achieved, but also evaluation of administrative and instructional processes, such as the effectiveness of staff utilization and student appraisal procedures. Indeed, evaluation of the program through assessment of student performance should be done with a degree of caution. A number of technical factors, e.g., the unreliability of standardized test scores at the extremes of performance and the ever present "regression toward the mean" phenomenon, militate against students achieving spectacular gains over their earlier (exceptionally high) performance at the time when they were identified. Similarly, predictions that special programming will lead to the quick eradication of educational underachievement can prove overoptimistic if underachievement is equated simply with the quantified difference between measured potential and measured achievement. Full diagnosis of a truly underachieving student will invariably reveal associated neurological, social or emotional problems and, while the special educational programming can have beneficial therapeutic effects, instant rehabilitation is the exception rather than the rule.

Reference has already been made in a number of places to the scarcity of convincing evidence about the fostering of excellence. Where evidence is available, it is frequently of anecdotal rather than experimental nature. In addition, lack of clear definition of terms and inconsistencies of methods have not infrequently led to results which seem at first to contradict each other. Sometimes, the best that can be said is that certain approaches cannot be shown to have actually done any harm! The fact is that serious methodological difficulties arise when attempts are made to assess the benefits to the children in question of special educational provision (not necessarily provision for the academically able). Some of these have been discussed by Stanley (1977, p. 87). In essence, the main difficulty is to estimate what the specially treated students would have achieved if they had *not* received the treatment in question. There are, for instance, numerous studies (e.g., Gelmon and MacLean, 1974) which report significantly more academic scholarships, higher achievement in later life, greater evidence of leadership behavior, etc. by persons who had been accelerated, but the question whether such superior performance would have been demonstrated if acceleration had not taken place remains unanswered. Did these people succeed to the extent which they did, because of being accelerated, in spite of being accelerated, or was acceleration irrelevant to their subsequent successful achievement? Would they have succeeded better, less well or about the same, if they had not been accelerated?

In order to answer such questions definitively, it would be necessary to design an experiment along the following lines. First a group of unusually able children (by definition, a comparatively rare breed) would have to be identified, then allocated in an unbiased way to either an "experimental" group to receive special treatment or to a "control," i.e., untreated group. After several years, both groups would then be assessed on appropriate criterion measures (achievement, personal or social development, motivation, etc.), and results of the two groups compared. Since some of the benefits of special treatment might not become apparent until adulthood, it would be necessary to follow both groups into middle or later life, as Terman did. It would be difficult in practice, and in our view ethically questionable, to withhold special educational treatment from the control group (although this is precisely what is done to the majority of unusually able children!), although it is just as questionable to subject children to ineffective treatments. There are also enormous logistical problems associated with locating individuals over a span of years.

Stanley and Benbow (1986) analyzed the issues in some detail. They listed, among others, the following reasons for not carrying out rigorous experiments for the evaluation of special procedures:

1. Ethical reasons (the morality of deliberately withholding appropriate treatment from able youngsters is questionable; it is necessary to deceive the members of the control group or else to obtain measures of their unusual ability by stealth);
2. Technical reasons (it is difficult to construct a large control group in an area where the proportion of qualified subjects is low, since exceptionally able people are rare, anyway; widespread publicity for special measures and programs means that the members of the control group would be "contaminated" by information in the media).

Much earlier, Renzulli (1975) developed a set of guidelines for evaluating special measures. However, he too drew attention to the serious difficulties in the area. One of the goals of the measures is to promote individual development along possibly idiosyncratic lines in people with unusual ability, special patterns of interests and motives, and even the capacity to make intellectual leaps which are not immediately obvious to observers. How is it possible to carry out highly standardized studies under these circumstances?

Nonetheless, most writers who present overviews and offer future perspectives (see for instance several chapters in Horowitz and O'Brien, 1985) call for research on, among other things, the effectiveness of educational measures. Indeed, it would be absurd to argue that such research should not be carried out. Among the questions which should be asked are:

1. What age is optimal for the commencement of special measures? Are there different ages for different measures?
2. Are there key content areas which should take precedence in fostering exceptional ability?
3. Are there special teacher qualifications which are necessary for certain kinds of promotion of excellence?
4. What are the advantages and disadvantages (in terms of the development of excellence) of the various kinds of measure outlined here and in Chapter 12?
5. What special dangers are associated with participation in special measures? What dangers are associated with non-participation?
6. How can special provision foster the growth of a sense of humility and social responsibility, without at the same time inhibiting individual drive, willingness to go out on a limb or acceptance of the risk of failure and ridicule?

The question that arises is thus not that of whether or not to evaluate special educational measures, but of how to do it.

Among the approaches which offer themselves as alternatives to "classical," experimental designs are case studies, clinically oriented approaches (in-depth interviews, etc.), and essentially phenomenological studies (possibly of a single person), in which the psychological significance of being treated as exceptionally able is explored through self-reports of subjective states and processes. As has already been mentioned, elements of these approaches can be seen in the longitudinal study of Hendrickson (1986). In view of what has just been said, it becomes apparent that the research questions just posed have not been formulated in the most appropriate form. What is needed are questions such as: "What is the nature of the interaction between age and reaction to special treatment?", "What factors (for instance psychological) modify, steer, accelerate or slow down development in the framework of this interaction?'' These questions should be attacked in a quantitative, process oriented (rather than qualitative, outcome oriented) way: for instance by asking "how strong is the relationship between variables X and Y and how do they act upon each other?" rather than "are groups A and B different from each other? What different treatments caused this?" Data gathering approaches of an appropriate kind have already been mentioned (case studies, etc.). In addition, where suitable data exist, analytical procedures of a multivariate kind are called for, in order to tease out interactions, moderating factors and the like; path analysis, for instance, suggests itself.

Personnel

The program coordinator

One of the characteristic differences between successful and less successful programs in a study by Ornestein (1984) was that the successful programs more typically placed responsibility for the program at a level below that of an assistant superintendent, usually with a program coordinator or consultant. The skills and duties of the program coordinator are vital for the successful implementation and healthy continuance of a quality program. Newland (1976, p. 190) suggests that there should be one consultant for every 5000 schoolchildren, or one for every three to five hundred gifted youngsters. However, the scope of duties — with implications for the number and nature of supportive staff requirements — will depend on the particular educational service delivery model that is adopted. For example, if children are merely being given enrichment activities within their regular classrooms, much of the coordinator's time and energies, which will be thinly spread, will be taken up with consultation with class teachers about individual children. On the other hand, if students are congregated within special classes, or if every school has a competent resource teacher providing activities on a pull out basis, the coordinator will be free to concentrate on more strategic issues, such as arranging inservice programs (including seminars for the teachers directly involved in the program), providing a leadership role in identification arrangements, and acting as a higher level resource person by keeping others in the program up to date with current materials and developments.

Several of the respondents to Gallagher, Weiss, Oglesby and Thomas's (1983) survey of State Directors of Gifted Education suggested that the number of program directors and coordinators should not be geared to the number of children in the program, but rather that there should be one, or two, directors for each *program*, and that the number of coordinators should be determined by the number of regions to be served. In the same survey, a part-time director was perceived as an *essential* element of a successful program, but a full-time director was rated only as "desirable." To expect one person to have the expertise and perspective which can encompass kindergarten through Grade 12, and which extends from the fine arts and humanities to mathematics and physics, is a tall order. Two half-time coordinators, one with a strong background in the sciences and experience in either the elementary or secondary grades, the other with complementary experience and expertise, might be preferable to a single full-time coordinator.

The duties of the director, consultant, coordinator or whatever combination of administrative resource people carry responsibility for a planned program, can be classified into two categories: (1) duties which are associated with the preparatory stage of program development; and (2) ongoing duties once the program is in place. At the preparatory stage, the coordinator needs to become familiar, not only with the extent and nature of all existing school and community services which are already available, but also with potential local resources that are ready and willing but which have not yet been tapped. Teachers need to be given guidance in methods of assessing students and in recognizing symptoms of special abilities and innovative thinking skills, but also need to be warned that the quick, infallible test which will provide instant identification is an impossible dream.

Part of the coordinator's job will be in the nature of a public relations operation, i.e., "selling" the program, preferably by educating consumer opinion rather than by preaching. Consumers, who include teachers, parents and the community at large, need to be educated into fully accepting the proposed program, or at least sympathetically tolerating it. In order to achieve this goal, some professional misconceptions will probably have to be modified. For example, because individual differences are more pronounced, and acting out behavior by insufficiently challenged students is more obvious and unmanageable at higher grade levels, some educators take for granted that special educational provision should begin at around Grade 12 and work downwards through the system, rather than beginning in the lowest grades and working upwards. At all times during the preparatory and ongoing phases of program implementation, the coordinator should ponder the impact of her/his own activities on teachers' reactions. Prospects for progress will be brighter if regular teachers perceive the activities of resource personnel as part of a team effort in the discharge of a task which they themselves recognize as necessary, and not as an authoritarian, unilateral imposition.

Specialist teachers

In the present text, "teacher preparation" will be generally used in preference to "teacher training." As Newland (1976, p. 208) observes, "the term *training* connotes establishing of rather specific habits . . .. Preparation, on the other hand, means the establishment of the underlying general principles on the basis of which certain habits may be formed." The element rated most important in Renzulli's (1968) early study of special provision for the unusually able was the teacher. Later reviews such as Gallagher, Weiss, Oglesby and Thomas (1983) and Ornestein (1984) have emphasized the importance of specialist teachers of academically exceptional students. We have also laid great weight upon the role of the teacher, in earlier chapters. It is important to ask now what such teachers should be like and how they should be educated.

Personal properties of teachers

One question which occurs immediately is whether certain attributes must be present prior to the beginning of teacher preparation, as a necessary foundation which facilitates the growth of the necessary characteristics during teacher education. In fact, several studies have enumerated the qualities desirable in such teachers. According to Maker's (1975) summary, these include high intelligence, flexibility, creativity, self-confidence, wide variety of interests, sense of humor, fairness, firmness, patience, sympathy with the problems of academically exceptional children and enjoyment in working with such children, self-understanding, willingness to put in extra time and effort, enthusiasm for both learning and teaching, and willingness to be a facilitator rather than a director of learning. Later, Maker reduced these to two absolutely basic characteristics — ability to relate to gifted students and openness to change. Subsequently, she rephrased this somewhat to (a) an accepting or nonjudgemental attitude and (b) flexibility (Maker, 1982).

Feldhusen (1984) reviewed a number of relevant publications and distilled a summary of 13 studies in the area carried out by Hultgren and Seeley (1982) into the following list of personal characteristics of the ideal teacher of the gifted. Such a person should

1. Be intelligent and knowledgeable;
2. Have broad interests;
3. Be hardworking and achievement oriented;
4. Be well organized;
5. Be highly enthusiastic about the work;
6. Possess a good sense of humor;

7. Be flexible;
8. Understand and accept gifted students.

It is worth noting in passing, that these characteristics would be highly desirable in *all* teachers. There is a danger that such lists simply encompass "all the virtues of mankind" (Gallagher, 1960, p. 115).

In view of the emphasis in earlier chapters on creativity as an element in true outstanding ability, it is interesting to compare the list of personal characteristics in the preceding paragraph with Cropley's (1982a) list of teaching characteristics of "creativity fostering" teachers, who;

1. Encourage their students to learn independently;
2. Have a cooperative, socially integrative style of teaching;
3. Motivate their students to master factual knowledge, so that they are thus free to think divergently;
4. Delay judging students' ideas until they have been thoroughly worked out and formulated;
5. Encourage flexible thinking in students;
6. Promote self-evaluation in students;
7. Take students' questions and suggestions very seriously;
8. Offer students opportunities to work with a wide variety of materials and under many different conditions;
9. Help students to learn to cope with frustration and failure, so that they have the courage to try the new and unusual, and avoid quick and easy success.

It is apparent that tolerance, flexibility, broadness of interests, knowledgeability, willingness to work hard and acceptance of students' special needs and characteristics all play an important role in this list too.

A picture thus begins to emerge of the characteristics of teachers who encourage dedicated, divergent work in students. Furthermore, a study by Bishop (1975) suggests that such traits are not simply a "motherhood" list. He took the relatively unusual step of carrying out an empirical study of successful teachers of the gifted, and comparing them with teachers in general, using questionnaires and interviews. His results showed that traits such as those just listed discriminated significantly between "successful" teachers of the gifted and a random sample of "ordinary" teachers.

Knowledge and skills

As with personal characteristics, there also seem to be a number of skills and attitudes, as well as areas of special knowledge, which are particularly important for teachers of the exceptionally able. Both Sisk (1975) and Seeley (1979) listed "knowledge," "skills" and/or "competencies" needed by teachers of the exceptionally able. These include (Sisk, 1975):

1. Knowledge of the nature and needs of gifted students;
2. Knowledge of new developments in education;
3. Knowledge of relevant current research.

To these can be added:

4. Knowledge of the subject being taught;
5. Knowledge of the course of psychological development;
6. Knowledge about special teaching methods.

Sisk also listed a number of *skills*, adapted to some degree in the present context, which include:

1. Skill in educational diagnosis;
2. Skill in counseling and guidance;
3. Skill in devising learning experiences involving all levels of cognitive functioning;
4. Skill in arousing the necessary affective conditions (e.g., motivation, self-confidence, etc.).

Once again, however, the question of "motherhood" statements arises. Do experts simply list the knowledge and skills of an idealized teacher when asked to describe the kind of teacher needed for unusually able students, possibly on the principle that idealized students require idealized teachers? A study by Hultgren and Seeley (1982) certainly provides support for this suspicion, as they found that a group of several hundred experts and practitioners agreed with every one of 24 obviously desirable traits, when asked which ones were important for teachers of the gifted! An empirical study by Silverman (1982) is more helpful. She observed experienced and successful teachers of the gifted ("master teachers") during actual lessons, and compared their behavior with that of student teachers who were also observed in action. Her results showed that the master teachers promoted self-directed learning; they avoided spoon feeding information and encouraged students to think things out for themselves; they asked provocative or divergent questions, the answers to which required a reasoned argument; they encouraged students to form their own judgements and to evaluate themselves. A final characteristic of the master teachers was that they developed a much closer personal relationship with the students, not only listening to them and joining in the process of learning and solving problems, but also spending time with them before and after class.

Preparing teachers of the academically able

Even if it is possible to avoid simply listing all desirable properties of an idealized teacher, and establish a list of traits which are truly necessary in teachers of gifted students, the question still remains whether such characteristics can be acquired by a deliberate effort, through teacher preparation, or whether their level of development is already immutably established by the time such preparation begins. Gold (1974) has made an important distinction in this respect, differentiating between ''entering'' characteristics (necessary or advantageous attributes), and ''exiting'' characteristics. The former must be present before training begins, whereas the latter are acquired during teacher preparation.

It seems clear that not everybody is capable of possessing the personal characteristics, knowledge and skills needed by those who accept primary responsibility for teaching academically exceptional students. For at least 25 years (e.g., Gallagher, 1960) it has been accepted that prospective teachers of academically able children ought to be required to meet certain minimum entrance requirements before being accepted for specialized preparation, and this view has recently been echoed by Feldhusen (1984). In other words, something special must be present before preparation begins. Unfortunately, such conditions have rarely been enforced (Maker, 1975). Nonetheless, there is a high level of agreement that teachers of the gifted require special training; Hultgren and Seeley (1982), for instance, report that 75 percent of teacher educators and practitioners in the area of the gifted were of the opinion that specialized preparation is necessary.

Mulhern and Ward (1983) have suggested a ''profile of the gifted teacher'' which involves a distinction between ''personal characteristics'' (which must be present at the beginning of preparation) and ''professional characteristics,'' which can be developed during training. This profile, which provides a useful framework for planning a program of professional development, is summarized in Table 13.1. It has been used by Mulhern and Ward in an actual teacher training program, both for the selection of persons to be included in the program, and also as a set of goals and criteria for the program itself.

In Canada, Shore (1983) has proposed two main focuses for programs aimed at preparing teachers to work with academically exceptional students (to whom Shore referred as ''gifted and talented youth''). These are (1) emphasis on mastery of subject matter and development of teaching competence and (2) development of positive

TABLE 13.1. *The profile of a gifted teacher*

Personal characteristics (on entry to program)	Professional characteristics (on completion of program)
(a) Intellectual achievement	(a) Subject matter knowledge
(b) Interpersonal skills	(b) Information-handling skills
(c) Personal success	(c) Classroom teaching skills
(d) Secure personality	(d) Diagnostic skills
(e) Intellectual curiosity	(e) Prescriptive teaching skills
(f) Personally organized	(f) Program development skills
(g) Leadership ability	(g) Program leadership skills

attitudes to the exceptionally able and to the provision of special services for them. He also poses three important questions, which we have paraphrased as follows:

1. Should there be special university degrees in Education of Academically Exceptional Students?
2. Should any such training be confined to the postgraduate level?
3. Do specially trained teachers provide better teaching for exceptionally able students?

In general, Shore could be interpreted as answering the first and third questions with a tentative ''Yes''.

As far as the second question is concerned, however, it seems that there is no single answer about how educators who are to be associated with special programs for academically exceptional children should receive their professional preparation. The US National Association for Gifted Children (NAGC, 1983) presented a comprehensive report on teacher preparation for academically exceptional children, in which they proposed standards for assessing the quality of programs, perceived as essentially graduate in nature. The authors of that report also made proposals for inservice education as a major form of teacher preparation. They see such training as relevant not only for teachers, but also for college personnel, school administrators, school support staff and even parents and community groups. The United Kingdom National Assocation for Gifted Children (NAGC, 1982) also delivered a report on teacher preparation in which inservice education was emphasized. The purpose of inservice training would include development of an awareness of the needs of exceptionally able students, promotion of favorable attitudes to them, providing information about exceptional ability and available programs, and increasing skills in all those who have contact with academically exceptional children.

Inservice education has a role to play in the total picture of professional education preparation, but a number of factors, stemming from philosophical considerations, from the lessons of experience and from sheer logistical issues, combine to suggest that professional preparation must be thought of as a multistage process. For instance:

1. Curricula in Teachers' Colleges and University Education Departments are crowded to the extent that they can, at most, provide only a single course on the special needs of all exceptional children, together with one, possibly two, additional senior undergraduate electives (Maker, 1975; NAGC, 1982);
2. There is a general consensus that teachers of the academically exceptional should be experienced, and have demonstrated ability to teach in a regular program, which means that in-depth specialized preparation has to be delayed until a few years after preservice preparation;
3. A significant trend has therefore developed, whereby degree programs in Education of the Gifted are increasingly offered at the graduate, rather than at the undergraduate level (Maker, 1975, p. 22), which means that they are not available to all teachers;
4. It is impossible to expect one teacher to meet the wide variety of subject matter demands corresponding to each gifted student's abilities and interests (Gallagher, 1960, p. 124; Maker, 1975, p. 17, Stanley, 1980).

The preparation of professional educators for work with academically exceptional students — and with other highly talented children — can be conceptualized as calling for programs at three distinctive levels, along the lines proposed by Hardy, McLeod, Minto, Perkins and Quance (1971).

1. A basic survey class for all teachers on children with special educational needs, developing an orientation toward diagnostic teaching and a sensitization to the need to amend goals and teaching methods with academically exceptional students. This is the type of class which lends itself admirably to the inservice mode.
2. A graduate program for teachers who are planning to become resource teachers, local coordinators or facilitators of special educational provision for academically exceptional students. The content of this program would include elements designed to develop competencies relating to knowledge of the needs and characteristics of academically exceptional children, identification, diagnosis and prescriptive teaching, expertise in subject matter, and curriculum development skills.
3. A higher level graduate program for potential directors of gifted education programs, which would include higher research, administrative and leadership skills.

Educators who graduate from the second of the three stages of professional preparation could expect to possess competencies which would equip them to carry out the duties of the resource teacher; i.e., activities ranging from occasional professional advice to the classroom teacher to scheduled work directly with academically exceptional students over an extened period. The professional characteristics listed by Mulhern and Ward provide useful first guidelines for the sort of curriculum for this important stage of teacher preparation.

Closing remarks

The implementation of teaching and learning methods for fostering academic excellence in the classroom can only occur within a favorable organizational and administrative framework. This means one which is open to change but, over and above that, is well planned and capable of being evaluated. The first key step in planning is that of developing commitment; although this is often triggered off by pressure "from below" — especially from parents — it must also come down "from above," i.e., from policy makers, senior administrators and the like. Careful informing of teachers, for instance through inservice training, is also of great importance. Other major steps in the introduction of special educational provision at the system level include formulation of a philosophy or policy, assessment of needs in the area, establishment of priorities and definition of program objectives. These steps permit goal directed allocation of resources and eventual evaluation of the degree to which the measures introduced have been successful.

As is the case with any educational innovation, the personnel who actually implement it are of vital importance. Experience suggests that programs for fostering academic excellence need close coordination from people with special responsibility for this area (program directors or coordinators). In addition, the actual classroom teachers play a vital role. Not all are necessarily suited for work with the unusually able; they may be opposed to special provision, may feel themselves threatened or may have an unrealistic image of the clever child. Those teachers who have received special training seem, as a group, to be more confident about their own effectiveness, more interested in and supportive of the needs of able youngsters and more open to suggestions for change. This supports the importance of special preparation of teachers. While it seems probable that the *basic elements* of this training should be offered within the framework of bachelor, master's and postgraduate diploma courses in colleges and universities, there is obviously an important place for inservice training. The goals of such teacher preparation are not confined to teaching and learning techniques, however, but also include personal properties — attitudes, values and the like. Some of these seem to be necessary prerequisites which must be present before commencement of training, but others can be fostered during professional preparation.

Epilogue

Simple fairness, or "justice" as it might be put, demands that any society which prides itself on adopting educational measures aimed at enhancing the development of individual children according to their special individual needs and potentials should also seek to foster the realization of intellectual gifts and talents. Indeed, most countries — regardless of degree of technological development or political orientation — stress the importance of such a differentiated, individually based approach. Naturally, academic excellence is only one aspect of human potential, but it is no less important than other aspects, even if it demands more discipline, effort and acceptance of criticism than some. Indeed, there are strong voices being raised, not only in North America but also in other countries, which call for more and better scholarship (in the traditional sense of the term) in schools.

Although our call for the fostering of academic excellence is part of our conviction that all children and all ethically acceptable patterns of interest and ability should be recognized and fostered in schools, emphasis on academic excellence can also be justified by less idealistic arguments: some countries see it as an important element in national development, as an aid in the integration of national minorities, or as an instrument for the modernization of society. In many countries the existence of able individuals offers hope of developing leaders who will do all of these things while helping to preserve national culture and identity. Thus, it cannot be denied that there is a utilitarian aspect to our interest in fostering academic excellence, although this does not seem to us to be something of which we should be ashamed.

Traditionally, intellectual ability has been equated with high IQ scores. This approach is not to be rejected totally and out of hand. However, what seems to us to be more important is the *way* in which people (in the present context, schoolchildren) go about attacking intellectual tasks; i.e., the *processes* of excellent thinking, and we hope to see a continuation and strengthening of emerging research, both basic and applied, in this area. Academic excellence requires a combination of detailed knowledge, logical thinking, accuracy and the like (the processes which tend to be emphasized in schools) with branching out, seeking the unexpected, seeing the relevance of the "illogical," noticing defects in received wisdom, spotting problems and difficulties and so on (processes which tend to be underemphasized in the conventional classroom). Such a combination of thinking processes offers interesting prospects for working in the classroom, since we are talking more about *styles* or *tactics* for thinking and less about *levels*. One of the practical consequences of this is that much of what we suggest for classroom work with able youngsters is also desirable for children of all ability levels. Acceptance of our practical proposals would lead to better achievement for all pupils — once again, hardly a principle of which schools should be ashamed, even if it is an idea that has recently taken a back seat to goals such as fostering social integration. These latter goals are worthy ones, but should not, to put it mildy, totally overshadow the school's function in fostering achievement.

Getting children to work hard on a special topic, acquire plentiful basic knowledge, seek the novel or elegant solution, criticize their own efforts, try new lines of attack and so on, is not merely a matter of ways of thinking. It also depends upon willingness to concentrate effort, openness to new ideas, the courage to deviate from the norm, and similar personal properties, many of which are influenced by inability to resist pressure to conform to social norms, fear of seeming odd or being made into an outsider, rejection of the risk of being misunderstood or of receiving low marks and so on. Thus, the promotion of academic excellence involves not only the cognitive, but also the personal, motivational and social domains. Once again, it seems to us that concentrated research on the theoretical and practical implications of this view is needed.

The really challenging work for the researcher and the teacher lies, in all probability, not with children whose personal, financial and social background already offers many opportunities for the realization of intellectual potentials, but with the "outsider." We do not underestimate the challenges even with the "privileged" child and do not mean to suggest that such children should be left to fend for themselves; however, we see a special challenge in the case of children from social outgroups and underprivileged groups of various kinds. Not only do these youngsters have most of the problems of able children from relatively favorable backgrounds, but they must also struggle with special problems such as lack of appropriate models at home, pressure from peers to conform to negative attitudes to schools and schooling, lack of reinforcement for success or of opportunities to develop a positive self-image and the like. Furthermore, the factors just listed, and others like them, mean that such children may behave in ways which are, in terms of their horizons, obviously gifted, but go unappreciated by teachers, for whom academic potential manifests itself in reading skills, articulacy in the dominant language, respect for traditional school values, etc. Thus, the culturally different, the disadvantaged, the emotionally disturbed, the chronically ill, and similar groups, pose a special problem for the definition of indicators of potential excellence, and for the whole area of diagnosis and selection. This probably means that "rotating" or "open door" admission policies to special programs, allied to expanded definitions of how to recognize gifts and talents and alternative, close-to-real-life identification procedures are called for. These latter might well include not only fairly obvious extensions such as rating scales and personality inventories, but also nominations, biographical analyses, biographical questionnaires, life event inventories, or even diaries.

An important trend in the provision of special measures aimed at promoting academic excellence is to be seen in the proliferation of out-of-school measures. In some countries such as the Federal Republic of Germany or France, this is practically the only source of such provision. These measures include clubs and special interest groups, Saturday Clubs and Workshops, Vacation Camps, practica in commercial laboratories or those of universities, etc. Where the school atmosphere is unfavorable, as is the case in many West European countries, such activities are frequently run by community groups or special interest groups, by industry, or by universities. If anything, this seems to be the most promising line of development in a number of countries, where questions concerning "the gifted program," the relationship between acceleration and enrichment, the need for specialist teachers and the like are purely academic.

A number of issues remain to be clarified still further. The first group involves what might be called "conceptual issues". Among these is the question of *defining intellectual giftedness*. Even within the cognitive domain, new approaches have raised questions about, for instance, the nature of intelligence; it is increasingly being seen as more a matter of judging the appropriateness of different approaches, recognizing blind alleys quickly, combining solution strategies, etc., rather than of possession of skills such as numerical facility or spatial orientation. A second conceptual issue concerns working out *developmental models of the emergence of excellence*. Although global models of the relationship between intellectual potential and environment exist, what is needed now are analyses of the developmental phenomenology of academic excellence: what does it "feel like" to be unusually able, what tactics are developed for coping with this situation, what factors and forces alter, facilitate or hinder the emergence of excellence, etc.? Methodologically, longitudinal case studies offer interesting prospects for the conduct of appropriate research.

At the practical level, definitional issues again take on special prominence. *How does potential for academic excellence signal its presence?* This question is especially interesting in regard to disadvantaged and deprived groups, the physically handicapped, or the chronically ill. What are the signs of excellence in members of social outgroups? Other practical questions center on *the part played by parents in the emergence and nurture of academic excellence.* Practical work with parents shows that many of them are unsure of how to act, are afraid of making a mistake, or even of being laughed at by family and friends if they do not force their children to behave "normally." This means that appropriate *counseling procedures* need to be worked out and made available. In the case of the children themselves, approaches are needed which help them cope with social isolation, ambivalence about themselves, perfectionism and fear of failure, or the feeling of being denied a childhood.

Turning to practical issues directly related to the school curriculum, we will borrow to some extent from Passow (1987). What is needed is a *comprehensive or total curriculum response.* Such a curriculum would not only be highly differentiated, but it would involve a *climate for excellence.* We are thinking here of considerably more than plentiful and better resource rooms or special forms of acceleration, etc. What we are referring to is a curriculum which is infused throughout with the desire to promote the realization of abilities. In this sense, our suggestions have implications for the instruction of all children. The curriculum we envisage would go beyond conventional achievement to emphasize creative production, socially valuable work and the like. It is also important to emphasize the achieving of a balance between the cognitive and noncognitive elements of intellectual functioning, as well as to call for more concern about moral and ethical issues. These principles — totality of response; acknowledgement of the importance of creativity and social worth; recognition of the contribution of noncognitive factors in the emergence of excellence; concern about morality and ethics — seem to us to be important guidelines for the further development of the school curriculum with the intention of fostering academic excellence.

References

Altshuller, G. S. (1984). *Creativity as an exact science*. New York: Gordon & Breach.

Amabile, T. M. (1983). *The social psychology of creativity*. New York: Springer.

Anderson, C. C. & Cropley, A. J. (1966). Some correlates of originality. *Australian Journal of Psychology*, **18**, 218–227.

Andreasen, N. C. (1987). Creativity and mental illness. *American Journal of Psychiatry*, **144**, 1288–1292.

Andrews, E. G. (1930). The development of imagination in the preschool child. *University of Iowa Studies in Character*, 3.

Armstrong, H. G. (1967). Wastage of ability amongst the intellectually gifted. *British Journal of Educational Psychology*, **37**, 257–259.

Armstrong, J. M. (1980). *Achievement and participation of women in mathematics: An overview*. Denver, Colorado: Education Commission of the States.

Australian Schools Commission (1980). *The education of gifted students*. Canberra: Australian Schools Commission.

Bailes, L. (1985). Using new computer technology in a gifted program. Paper presented at the Sixth World Conference on Gifted and Talented Children, Hamburg, August 1985.

Baldwin, A. Y. (1985). Programs for the gifted and talented: Issues concerning minority populations. In: F. D. Horowitz and M. O'Brien (eds), *The gifted and talented: Developmental perspectives*. Washington, DC: American Psychological Association.

Barron, F. X. (1955). The disposition towards originality. *Journal of Abnormal and Social Psychology*, **51**, 478–485.

Barron, F. X. (1963). *Creativity and psychological health*. New York: Van Nostrand.

Barron, F. X. (1969). *Creative person and creative process*. New York: Holt, Rinehart & Winston.

Barron, F. & Harrington, D. M. (1981). Creativity, intelligence and personality. *Annual Review of Psychology*, **32**, 439–476.

Bayley, N. (1949). Consistency and variability in growth from birth to 18 years. *Journal of Genetic Psychology*, **75**, 165–196.

Belcher, T. L. (1975). Modeling original divergent responses: An initial investigation. *Journal of Educational Psychology*, **67**, 351–358.

Benbow, C. P. & Benbow, R. M. (1984). Biological correlates of high mathematical reasoning ability. In: G. J. DeVries, J. P. C. DeBruin, H. B. M. Uylings & M. A. Corner (eds), *Sex differences in the brain — the relation between structure and function. Progress in Brain Research*. Vol. 61.

Benbow, C. P. & Stanley, J. R. (1983). Sex differences in mathematical reasoning ability: More facts. *Science*, **222**, 1029–1031.

Bereiter, C. A. & Engelmann, S. (1966). *Teaching disadvantaged children in the preschool*. Englewood Cliffs, NJ: Prentice-Hall.

Bereiter, C. A. (1976). SMPY in social perspective. In: D. P. Keating (ed), *Intellectual talent: Research and development*. Baltimore: Johns Hopkins University Press.

Bernstein, B. (1961). Social class and linguistic development. A theory of social learning. In: A. H. Halsey, J. Floud & C. A. Anderson(eds), *Education, economy and society*. New York: The Free Press.

Berse, P. (1977). *A study of the transition from the "Sunday Club" to the "Saturday Club."* London: Tavistock Institute of Human Relations.

Besemer, S. B. & Treffinger, D. J. (1981). Analysis of creative products: Review and synthesis. *Journal of Creative Behavior*, **15**, 68–73.

Binet, A. (1912). *Die neuen Gedanken über das Schulkind*. Leipzig: Wunderlich.

Binet, A. & Simon, Th. (1905). Application des methodes nouveaux au diagnostic du niveau intellectuel chez des enfants normaux et anormaux d'hospice et d'école primaire. *L'Année Psychologique*, 245.

Birch, J. W. (1984). Is any identification procedure necessary? *Gifted Child Quarterly*, **28**, 157–161.

Bishop, W. E. (1975). Successful teachers of the gifted. *Exceptional Children*, **34**, 317–325.

Bloom, B. S. (ed), (1956). *Taxonomy of educational objectives*. New York: David McKay.

Bloom, B. S. (1985). *Developing talent in young people*. New York: Ballantine.

Bongartz, K., Kaißer, U. & Kluge, K. J. (1985). *Die verborgene Kraft*. Munich, Minerva.

Boyd, R. (1986). Academically talented high school girls. In: A. J. Cropley, K. K. Urban, H. Wagner & W. H. Wieczerkowski (eds), *Giftedness: A continuing worldwide challenge*. New York: Trillium.

Braggett, E. J. (1985). *Education of gifted and talented children*. Canberra: Australian Schools Commission.

Broomand, I. (1986). Gifted leadership for peace. In: A. J. Cropley, K. K. Urban, H. Wagner & W. H. Wieczerkowski (eds), *Giftedness: A continuing worldwide challenge*. New York: Trillium.

Brown, R. A. (1977). Creativity, discovery and science. *Journal of Chemical Education*, **5**, 720–724.

Bruner, J. S. (1967). *On knowing: Essays for the left hand*. New York: Athaneum.

Bryden, M. P. (1982). *Laterality: Functional asymmetry in the intact brain*. New York: Academic Press.

Burke, R. L. (1982). *CAI sourcebook*. Englewood Cliffs, NJ: Prentice-Hall.

Burks, B. B., Jensen, D. W. and Terman, L. M. (1930). *The promise of youth: Follow-up studies of a thousand gifted children*. Stanford: Stanford University Press.

Burt, C. (1937). *The backward child*. London: University of London Press.

Burt, C. (1962). General introduction: The gifted child. In: G. Z. F. Bereday & J. A. Lauwerys (eds), *The gifted child: The Yearbook of Education*. London: Evans.

Burt, C. (1975). *The gifted child*. London: Hodder & Stoughton.

Carter, R. (1981). Logo and the great debate. *Microcomputing*, **5**, 48–51.

Case, R. (1978). Intellectual development from birth to adult-hood: A neo-Piagetian interpretation. In: R. S. Siegler (ed), *Children's thinking. What develops?* Hillsdale, NJ: Lawrence Erlbaum.

Clark, B. (1979). *Growing up gifted*. Columbus, Oh: Merrill.

Clarke, G. (1983). *Guidelines for the reception of gifted pupils*. London: Longmans for Schools Council.

Cleary, A., Moyes, T. & Packham, D. (1976). *Educational technology: Implications for early and special education*. London: John Wiley.

Clements, D. H. (1986). Effects of Logo and CAI environments on cognition and creativity. *Journal of Educational Psychology*, **78**, 309–318.

Cline, V. B., Richards, J. M. & Abe, C. (1962). The validity of creativity tests in a high school sample. *Educational and Psychological Measurement*, **22**, 781–784.

Colangelo, N. & Dettman, D. F. (1983). A review of research on parents and families of gifted children. *Exceptional Children.* **50**, 20–27.

Conant, J. B. (1946). *General education in a free society.* Cambridge, Ma: Harvard University Press.

Congdon, P. J. (1985). Disabilities depressing potential giftedness. Workshop conducted at the Sixth World Conference on Gifted and Talented Children, Hamburg, August 1985.

Coopersmith, S. (1967). *The antecedents of self-esteem.* San Francisco: Freeman.

Coutant, M. F. (1985). The computer in creative mathematics — Part I. Paper represented at the Sixth World Conference on Gifted and Talented Children, Hamburg, August 1985.

Covington, M. V. & Crutchfield, R. S. (1965). Facilitation of creative problem solving. *Programmed Instruction*, **4**, 3–5, 10.

Cox, C. M. (1926). *Genetic studies of genius: The early mental traits of three hundred geniuses.* Stanford: Stanford University Press.

Cox, J. (1983). Continuous progress and nongraded schools. *Gifted Education International*, **2**, 1, 61–65.

Cox, J., Daniel, N. & Boston, B. (1986). *Educating early learners: Programs and promising practices.* Austin: University of Texas Press.

Cronbach, L. J. (1968). Intelligence? Creativity? A parsimonious reinterpretation of the Wallach Kogan data. *American Educational Research Journal*, **5**, 491–511.

Cropley, A. J. (1967a). *Creativity.* London: Longmans.

Cropley, A. J. (1967b). Divergent thinking and science specialists. *Nature*, **215**, 671–672.

Cropley, A. J. (1969). Creativity, intelligence and intellectual style. *Australian Journal of Education*, **13**, 3–7.

Cropley, A. J. (1972a). Originality scores under timed and untimed conditions. *Australian Journal of Psychology*, **24**, 31–36.

Cropley, A. J. (1972b). A five-year longitudinal study of the validity of creativity tests. *Developmental Psychology*, **6**, 119–124.

Cropley, A. J. (1973). Creativity and culture. *Educational Trends*, **8**, 19–27.

Cropley, A. J. (1978). *Unterricht ohne Schablone.* Ravensburg: Maier.

Cropley, A. J. (1982a). *Kreativität und Erziehung.* Munich: Reinhardt.

Cropley, A. J. (1982b). Educational technology and educational practice: The case of lifelong education. In: C. K. Knapper (ed), *New directions for teaching and learning: Expanding learning through new communications technologies.* San Francisco: Jossey-Bass.

Cropley, A. J. (1983). *Educating immigrant children.* London: Croom Helm.

Cropley, A. J. (1988). Education of the gifted and talented. In: T. Husen & T. N. Postlethwaite (eds), *International Encyclopedia of Education*, Supplement 1. Oxford: Pergamon.

Cropley, A. J. & Ahlers, K. H. (1975). Development of verbal skills in first-born and only boys. *Journal of Biosocial Science*, **7**, 297–306.

Cropley, A. J. & Clapson, L. G. (1971). Long term test–retest reliability of creativity tests. *British Journal of Educational Psychology.* **41**, 206–208.

Cropley, A. J. & Feuring, E. (1971). Training creativity in young children. *Developmental Psychology*, **4**, 105.

Cropley, A. J. & Maslany, G. W. (1969). Reliability and factorial validity of the Wallach–Kogan creativity tests. *British Journal of Psychology*, **60**, 395–398.

Cropley, A. J. & McLeod, J. (1986). Preparing teachers of the gifted. *International Review of Education*, **32**, 125–136.

Cropley, A. J. & Sikand, J. S. (1973). Creativity and schizophrenia. *Journal of Consulting* and Clinical Psychology, **40**, 462–468.

Cruickshank, W. M. (1986). *Disputable decisions in special education*. Ann Arbor: University of Michigan Press.

Crutchfield, R. S. (1955). Conformity and character. *American Psychologist*, **10**, 191–198.

Cunningham, C. H., Thompson, B. & Alston, H. A. (1978). The use of SOI abilities for prediction. *Gifted Child Quarterly*, **22**, (4), 506–512.

Dannenberg, H. (1975). Kreativität und mehrperspektivischer Unterricht. In: G. Neff (ed), *Kreativität in Schule und Gesellschaft*, Ravensburg, Maier.

Dansky, J. L. (1980). Make-believe: A mediator of the relationship between play and associative fluency. *Child Development*, **51**, 576–579.

Davis, G. A. & Scott, J. A. (1971). *Training creative thinking*. New York: Holt, Rinehart & Winston.

Dellas, M. & Gaier, E. L. (1970). Identification of creativity: The individual, *Psychological Bulletin*, **73**, 55–73.

Denton, F. C. J. (1985). Children with high ability: The search for an appropriate means of identification and provision. Paper presented at Conference on Gifted Children, Hamburg, 30 May 1985.

Deutsch, M. (1964). Facilitating development in the preschool child. Social and psychological perspectives. *Merrill-Palmer Quarterly*, **10**, 240–263.

Dewey, J. (1910). *How we think*. Boston: Heath.

Dewing, E. (1970). The reliability and validity of selected tests of creative thinking in a sample of seventh grade West Australian children. *British Journal of Educational Psychology*, **40**, 35–42.

Dickson, P. J. (1975). Teacher preparation of educationally handicapped children as a function of contact with them in the regular school. Unpublished M.Ed. Thesis, University of Saskatchewan.

Dipasquale, G. W., Moule, A. D. & Flewelling, R. W. (1980). The birthdate effect. *Journal of Learning Disabilities*, **13**, 234–238.

Doman, G. (1964). *How to teach your baby to read*. New York: Random House.

Doorly, A. (1980). Microcomputers for gifted children. *G/C/T*, **3**, 62–64.

Douglas, J. W. B. (1964). *The home and the school*. London: University of London Press.

Dover, A. (1983). Computers and the gifted. Past, present and future. *Gifted Child Quarterly*, **27**, 81–85.

Drevdahl, J. E. & Cattell, R. B. (1958). Personality and creativity in artists and writers. *Journal of Clinical Psychology*, **14**, 107–111.

Eccles, J. S. (1985). Why doesn't Jane run? Sex differences in educational and occupational patterns. In F. E. Horowitz & M. O'Brien (eds), *The gifted and talented: Developmental perspectives*. Washington, DC: American Psychological Association.

Educational Research Services (ERS) (1975). *Gifted students: Identification techniques and program organization*. Arlington, Virginia: Educational Research Services.

Emmett, W. G. (1942). *An inquiry into the prediction of secondary school success*. London: University of London Press.

Endriss, L. (1982). Entwicklung und Auswirkung eines Kreativitätstrainings — Förderung des spielerischen Denkens bei jungen Erwachsenen. Unpublished Master's Thesis, University of Hamburg.

Engelmann, T. & Engelmann, S. (1966). *Give your child a superior mind*. New York: Simon & Schuster.

Eysenck, H. J. (1953). *Uses and abuses of psychology*. Harmondsworth: Penguin.

Eysenck, H. J. (1967). Intelligence assessment: A theoretical and experimental approach. *British Journal of Educational Psychology*, **37**, 81–98.

Eysenck, H. J. (1973). *The inequality of man*. London: Temple Smith.

Eysenck, H. J. (1986). The biological basis of intelligence. In: A. J. Cropley, K. K. Urban, H. Wagner & W. H. Wieczerkowski (eds), *Giftedness: A continuing worldwide challenge*. New York: Trillium.

Facaoaru, C. (1985). *Kreativität in Wissenschaft und Technik*. Bern: Huber.

Facaoaru, C. & Bittner, R. (1986). Skalen zur Erfassung divergent-konvergenter Problemlöseprozesse bei Hochbegabten. Paper presented at the 35th Annual Conference of the German Psychological Society, Heidelberg.

Farisha, B. (1978). Mental imagery and creativity. Review and speculation. *Journal of Mental Imagery*. **2**, 209–238.

Favero, J., Dombrower, J., Michael, W. B. & Richards, L. (1975). Interrelationships among 76 individually-administered tests intended to represent 76 different Structure-of-Intellect abilities and a standardized general intelligence test in a sample of 34 nine-year-old-children. *Educational and Psychological Measurement*, **35**, 993–1004.

Feger, B. & Prado, T. (1986). The first Information and Counselling Center for the Gifted in West Germany. In K. A. Heller & J. F. Feldhusen (eds), *Identifying and nurturing the Gifted*. Bern: Huber.

Feger, B., Wieczerkowski, W. H. & Prado, T. (1987). Special age-related problems of giftedness in children. Paper presented at the Seventh World Conference on Gifted and Talented Children, Salt Lake City, August 1987.

Feldhusen, J. F. (1984). The teacher of gifted students. Paper presented at the Symposium on Gifted Children, Hamburg, 30 May 1984.

Feldhusen, J. F. & Treffinger, D. J. (1980). *Creative thinking and problem solving in gifted education*. Dubuque, Ia: Kendall/Hunt.

Feldman, D. H. (1979). The mysterious case of extreme giftedness. In: A. H. Passow (ed), *The gifted and the talented: Their education and development*. Chicago: NSSE Yearbook.

Feldman, D. H. (1980a). Faulty construct-ion. *Contemporary Psychology*, **15**, 3–4.

Feldman, D. H. (1980b). *Beyond universals in cognitive development*. Norwood, NJ: Ablex.

Feldman, D. H. (1984). A follow-up study of subjects scoring above 180 IQ in Terman's "Genetic Studies of Genius." *Exceptional Children*, **50**, 518–523.

Ferguson, M. (1979). Foreword. In B. Clark, *Growing up gifted*. Columbus, OH:Merrill.

Ferrara, J. M., Parry, J. D. & Lubke, M. M. (1985). Expert systems authoring tools for the microcomputer: Two examples. *Educational Technology*, April, 39–41.

Fiday, D. (1983). Programming from second grade on . . . and the Laraway Logo experience. *G/C/T*, **6**, 16–19.

Findley, W. G. & Bryan, M. M. (1971). *Ability grouping: 1970 status, import and alternatives*. Athens, Ga:Center for Educational Improvement, University of Georgia.

Fiske, E. B. (1983). Wide differences noted in schools of U.S., Japan. *Toronto Globe & Mail*, 11 July.

Flanagan, J. C., Dailey, J. T., Shaycoft, M. F., Gorham, W. A., Orr, D. B. & Golberg, I. (1962). *Design for a study of American youth*. Boston: Houghton Mifflin.

Foster, J. (1971). *Creativity and the teacher*. London: Macmillan.

Fox, L. H. (1974). Facilitating the development of mathematical talent in young women. Unpublished doctoral dissertation, Johns Hopkins University. *Dissertation Abstracts International*, **35**, 3553B, University Microfilms No. 74–29027.

Fox, L. H. (1976). Sex differences in mathematical and scientific precocity. Bridging the gap. In: D. P. Keating (ed), *Intellectual talent: Research and development*. Baltimore: Johns Hopkins University Press.

Fox, L. H. (1978). Sex differences. Implications for program planning for the academically gifted. In: J. C. Stanley, W. C. George & C. H. Solano, *Educational programs and intellectual prodigies*. Baltimore: Johns Hopkins University Press.

Fox, L. H. (1979). Programs for the gifted and talented: An overview. In: A. H. Passow (ed), *The gifted and talented: Their education and development*. Chicago: NSSE Yearbook.

Fox, L. H. (1981). Identification of the academically gifted. *American Psychologist*, **36**, 1103–1111.

Frank, R. (1985). School, business and industry — forming partnerships to educate the gifted and talented. Paper presented at the Sixth World Conference on Gifted and Talented Children, Hamburg, August 1985.

Franklin, B. S. & Richards, P. N. (1977). Effects on children's divergent thinking abilities of a period of direct teaching for divergent production. *British Journal of Educational Psychology*, **47**, 66–70.

Freehill, M. F. (1961). *Gifted children*. New York: Macmillan.

Freeman, J. (1979). *Gifted children*. Lancaster: MTP.

Freeman, J. (1983). Emotional problems of the gifted child. *Journal of Child Psychology and Psychiatry*, **24**, 481–485.

Freeman, J. (1985). Gifted children 10 years on. Paper presented at the Sixth World Conference on Gifted and Talented Children, Hamburg, August 1985.

Freud, S. (1910). *Leonardo da Vinci: A study in psychosexuality*. New York: Random House.

Gabriel, J. (1976). Creativity and play. In W. R. Lett (ed), *Creativity and education*. Melbourne: Australian International Press and Publications.

Gallagher, J. J. (1960). *Analysis of research on the education of gifted children*. State of Illinois: Office of the Superintendent of Public Instruction.

Gallagher, J. J. (1975). *Teaching the gifted child*, 2nd Ed. Boston: Allyn & Bacon.

Gallagher, J. J. (1986a). Hochleistungsförderung und Chancengleichheit — ein weltweiter Konflikt. In: W. H. Wieczerkowski, H. Wagner, K. K. Urban & A. J. Cropley (eds), *Hochbegabung, Gesellschaft, Schule*. Bonn: Federal Ministry of Education and Science.

Gallagher, J. J. (1986b). The conservation of intellectual resources. In A. J. Cropley, K. K. Urban, H. Wagner & W. H. Wieczerkowski (eds), *Giftedness: A continuing worldwide challenge*. New York: Trillium.

Gallagher, J. J. & Moss, J. W. (1963). New concepts of intelligence. *Exceptional Children*, **29**, 1–5.

Gallagher, J. J., Weiss, P., Oglesby, K. & Thomas, T. (1983). *The status of gifted/talented education*. Ventura, CA: Superintendent of Ventura County Schools.

Galton, F. (1869). *Hereditary genius*. London: Macmillan.

Gardner, H. (1983). *Frames of mind: The theory of multiple intelligences*. New York: Basic Books.

Garwood, D. S. (1964). Personality factors related to creativity in young scientists. *Journal of Abnormal and Social Psychology*, **68**, 413–419.

Gelcer, E. & Dick, S. (1986). Families of gifted children: Achievers and under-achievers. In: A. J. Cropley, K. K. Urban, H. Wagner & W. H. Wieczerkowski (eds), *Giftedness: A continuing worldwide challenge*. New York: Trillium.

Gelmon, P. & MacLean, M. (1974). *A followup study of two groups of gifted children in the Saskatoon Public School system*. Saskatoon, Saskatchewan: Public Board of Education.

George, K. R. & George, T. D. (1986). Native American Indians: Gifted leadership. In: A. J. Cropley, K. K. Urban, H. Wagner & W. H. Wieczerkowski (eds), *Giftedness: A continuing worldwide challenge*. New York: Trillium.

Gergen, K. J. & Berger, I. (1965). Two forms of inference and problems in the assessment of creativity. *Proceedings of the 73rd Annual Convention of the American*

Psychological Association. Washington, DC: American Psychological Association.

Getzels, J. W. & Dillon, J. T. (1973). The nature of giftedness and the education of the gifted child. In: R. W. M. Travers (ed), *Second handbook of research on teaching.* Chicago: Rand McNally.

Getzels, J. W. & Jackson, P. W. (1962). *Creativity and intelligence.* New York: John Wiley.

Geuβ, H. & Urban, K. K. (1982). Hochbegabte Kinder. In W. Wieczerkowski & H. zur Oeveste (eds), *Lehrbuch der Entwicklungspsychologie.* Düsseldorf: Schwann.

Gibson, J. & Light, P. (1967). Intelligence among university scientists. *Nature,* **213,** 441–443.

Gifted Children Task Force. (1982). *Cluster groups.* Melbourne: Education Department of Victoria.

Ginsberg, G. & Harrison, C. H. (1977). *How to help your gifted child.* New York: Monarch Press.

Gittings, J. (1978). Why the children of China are on their marks. *Manchester Guardian Weekly,* 10 December, 9.

Glover, J. & Gary, A. L. (1976). Procedures to increase some aspects of creativity. *Journal of Applied Behavior Analysis,* **9,** 79–84.

Goertzel, M. C., Goertzel, V. & Goertzel, T. C. (1978). *300 eminent personalities.* San Francisco: Jossey-Bass.

Gold, M. (1974). Preparation of teachers for gifted and talented youngsters. Unpublished manuscript cited in C. J. Maker, (1975). *Training teachers for the gifted and talented: A comparison of models.* Reston, VA: Council for Exceptional Children.

Goldstein, H., Moss, J. W., & Jordan, L. J. (1965). *The efficacy of special class training on the development of mentally retarded children.* Urbana: University of Illinois Institute for Research on Exceptional Children.

Goleman, D. (1980). 1528 little genuises and how they grew. *Psychology Today,* February, 28–43.

Gordon, W. J. (1961). *Synectics.* New York: Harper.

Gowan, J. C. (1955). The underachieving gifted child — a problem for everyone. *Exceptional Children,* **21,** 247–249.

Gray, W. A. & Gray, M. M. (1986). Parents as mentors of their own children: Returning to the basics. In: A. J. Cropley, K. K. Urban, H. Wagner & W. H. Wieczerkowski (eds), *Giftedness: A continuing worldwide challenge.* New York: Trillium.

Green, D. A. (1962). A study of talented high school dropouts. *Vocational Guidance Quarterly.* **10,** 171–172.

Griggs, S. A. (1984). Counselling for the gifted and talented based on learning styles. *Exceptional Children.* **50,** 429–432.

Gross, M. (1986). Radical acceleration in Australia. *G/C/T,* **9** (4), 2–9.

Grote, J. et. al. (1969). Untersuchungen zur Kreativität. *Zeitschrift für Pädagogik,* **15,** 135–171.

Gruber, E. H. (1982). On the hypothesized relation between giftedness and creativity. In: D. H. Freeman (ed), *Developmental approaches to giftedness and creativity.* San Francisco: Jossey-Bass.

Guilford, J. P. (1950). Creativity. *American Psychologist,* **5,** 444–454.

Guilford, J. P. (1977). *Way beyond the IQ.* Buffalo, NY: Creative Education Foundation.

Guilford, J. P. (1981). A map for an intelligent education. *Education,* **101,** 310–314.

Guilford, J. P. & Christensen, P. R. (1973). The one-way relation between creative potential and IQ. *Journal of Creative Behavior,* **7,** 247–252.

Hagen, (1980). *Identification of the gifted.* New York: Teachers College, Columbia University.

Hallahan, D. P. & Kauffman, J. M. (1978). *Exceptional children*. Englewood Cliffs, NJ: Prentice-Hall.

Hammill, D. D. & Wiederholdt, J. L. (1972). *The non-categorical resource room*. Philadelphia: Buttonwood Farms.

Hardy, M., McLeod, J., Minto, H., Perkins, S. A. & Quance, W. R. (1971). *Standards for educators of exceptional children in Canada. The SEECC Report*. Toronto: National Institute on Mental Retardation.

Hare, A. P. (1982). *Creativity in small groups*. Beverly Hills, CA: Sage.

Harrington, D. M., Block, J. & Block, J. H. (1983). Predicting creativity in preadolescence from divergent thinking in early childhood. *Journal of Personality and Social Psychology*, **45**, 609–623.

Hasan, P. & Butcher, H. J. (1966). Creativity and intelligence. A partial replication with Scottish children of Getzels and Jackson's study. *British Journal of Psychology*, **57**, 129–135.

Hattie, J. A. (1977). Conditions for administering creativity tests. *Psychological Bulletin*, **84**, 1249–1260.

Hattie, J. A. (1980). Should creativity tests be administered under testlike conditions? An empirical study of three alternative conditions. *Journal of Educational Psychology*, **72**, 87–98.

Hauck, B. B. (1972). Dick — a gifted delinquent. In: B. B. Hauck & M. F. Freehill (eds), *The gifted — case studies*. Dubuque, Ia: Brown.

Havighurst, R. J. (1958). The importance of education for the gifted. In: N. B. Henry (ed), *Fifty-seventh Yearbook of the National Society for the Study of Education*. Chicago: University of Chicago Press.

Hawaii Department of Education (1977). *A state plan for providing appropriate educational opportunities for the gifted and talented*. Honolulu: Department of Education, State of Hawaii.

Hayes-Roth, F., Waterman, D. A. & Lenat, D. B. (eds), (1983). *Building expert systems*. Reading, MA: Addison-Wesley.

Hebb, D. O. (1949). *Organization of behavior*. New York: John Wiley.

Heinelt, G. (1974). *Kreative Lehrer — kreative Schüler*. Freiburg: Herder.

Heinze, J. (1982). Begabtenförderung im Bildungswesen der Volksrepublik China: das System der "Schwerpunktschulen." *Deutsche Zeitschrift für Politik, Wirtschaft und Kultur*, **4**, 29–58.

Helson, R. (1966). Personality of women with imagination and artistic interests: The role of masculinity, originality, and other characteristics in their creativity. *Journal of Personality*, **34**, 1–25.

Helson, R. (1983). Creative mathematicians. In: R. S. Albert (ed), *Genius and eminence: The social psychology of creativity and exceptional achievement*. Elmsford, NY: Pergamon Press.

Hendrickson, L. (1986). A longitudinal study of precocity in music. In: A. J. Cropley, K. K. Urgan, H. Wagner & W. H. Wieczerkowski (eds), *Giftedness: A continuing worldwide challenge*. New York: Trillium.

Henry, N. B. (1958. (ed). *Fifty-seventh Yearbook of the National Society for the Study of Education*. Chicago: University of Chicago Press.

Henslowe, S. A. (1986). *Handbook of instructional materials for education of the gifted and talented*. Edmonton, Alberta: Alberta Education Planning Services.

Hildreth, G. H. (1966). *Introduction to the gifted*. New York: McGraw-Hill.

Hilgendorf, E. (1984). *Informationen zur schulischen Hochbegabtenförderung. 1. Die Förderung besonders befähigter Schüler in der Deutschen Demokratischen Republik*. Berlin: Pädagogisches Zentrum.

Hitchfield, E. (1973). *In search of promise*. London: Longman.

HMI (1977). *Gifted children in middle and comprehensive schools.* London: Her Majesty's Stationery Office.

Hocevar, D. (1980). Intelligence, divergent thinking and creativity. *Intelligence,* **4**, 25-40.

Hocevar, D. (1981). Measurement of creativity: Review and critique. *Journal of Personality Assessment,* **45**, 450-464.

Hofmeister, A. M. (1985). *A model for the development and validation of expert systems in education.* Logan, UT: Artificial Intelligence Research and Development Unit, Utah State University.

Hoge, R. D. & Cudmore, L. (1986). The use of teacher judgement measures in the identification of gifted pupils. In: A. J. Cropley, K. K. Urban, H. Wagner & W. Wieczerkowski (eds), *Giftedness: A continuing worldwide challenge.* New York: Trillium.

Holden, C. (1987). Creativity and the troubled mind. *Psychology Today,* **21**(4), 9-10.

Hollingworth, L. S. (1926). *Gifted children: Their nature and nurture.* New York: Macmillan.

Hollingworth, L. S. (1938). An enrichment curriculum for rapid learners at Public School 500: Speyer School. *Teachers College Record,* **39**, 296-306.

Hollingworth, L. S. (1942). *Children above 180 IQ Stanford Binet: Origin and development.* New York: World Books.

Hoomes, E. W. (1984). Future problem solving. *G/T/C,* **7**, 15-18.

Horn, W. (1962). *Das Leistungsprüfsystem2.* Göttingen: Hogrefe.

Horowitz, F. D. & O'Brien, M. (1986). Gifted and talent children: State of knowledge and direction for research. *American Psychologist,* **41**, 1147-1152.

Howieson, N. (1981). A longitudinal study of creativity — 1965-1975. *Journal of Creative Behavior,* **15**, 117-134.

Howieson, N. (1984). Is Western Australia neglecting the creative potential of its youth? Paper presented at the 1984 Annual Conference of the Australian Psychological Society, Perth, 12-17 August 1984.

Hoyle, E. & Wilks, J. (1974). *Education today: Gifted children and their education.* London: HMSO.

Hudson, L. (1963). Personality and scientific aptitude. *Nature,* **196**, 913-914.

Hudson, L. (1966). *Contrary imaginations.* London: Methuen.

Hudson, L. (1968). *Frames of mind.* London: Methuen.

Huffman, R. (1985). The Community Laboratory Research program: A mentor program. Paper presented at the Sixth World Conference on Gifted and Talented Children, Hamburg, August 1985.

Hultgren, H. W. & Seeley, K. R. (1982). *Training teachers of the gifted: A research monograph on teacher competencies.* Denver: School of Education, University of Denver.

Humes, C. W. (1985). Counselling the gifted handicapped. Paper presented at the Sixth World Conference on Gifted and Talented Children, Hamburg, August 1985.

Humphreys, L. G. (1985). A conceptualization of intellectual giftedness. In F. D. Horowitz & M. O'Brien (eds), *The gifted and talented: Developmental perspectives.* Washington, DC: American Psychological Association.

Hunt, J. McV. (1961). *Intelligence and experience.* New York: Ronald Press.

Jacobs, J. C. (1971). Effectiveness of teacher and parent identification of gifted children as a function of school level. *Psychology in the Schools,* **8**, 140-142.

Jäger, A. O. (1967). *Dimensionen der Intelligenz.* Göttingen: Hogrefe.

Janos, P. M. & Robinson, N. M. (1985). Psychosocial development in intellectually gifted children. In: F. E. Horowitz & M. O'Brien (eds), *The gifted and talented: Developmental perspectives.* Washington, DC: American Psychological Association.

Jenkins, J. J. & Paterson, D. G. (1961). *Studies in individual difference.* New York: Appleton-Century Crofts.

Jensen, A. R. (1981). *Straight talk about mental tests.* New York: The Free Press.

Jensen, A. R. & Wedman, J. (1983). The computer's role in gifted education. *G/C/T,* **6**, 10–11.

Jordan, I. & Smith, S. (1985). Word processing and gifted children's writing. Paper presented at the Sixth World Conference on Gifted and Talented Children, Hamburg, August 1985.

Jorm, A. F. (1983). Determinants of individual differences in reading achievement. *Australian Journal of Psychology,* **35**, 163–174.

Kaplan, S. (1974). *Providing programs for the gifted and talented: A handbook.* Ventura, CA: Superintendent of Ventura County Schools.

Karnes, M. B., Schwedel, A. M. & Lewis, G. F. (1983). Short term effects of early programming for the young gifted handicapped child. *Exceptional Children,* **50**, 103–109.

Keating, D. P. (1976). *Intellectual talent: Research and development.* Baltimore, MD: Johns Hopkins University Press.

Keating, D. P. (1983). The creative potential of mathematically precocious boys. In: R. S. Albert (ed), *Genius and eminence: The social psychology of creativity and exceptional achievement.* Elmsford, NY: Pergamon.

Kerlinger, F. N. (1964) *Foundations of behavioral research.* New York: Holt, Rinehart & Winston.

Kerry, T. (1981). *Teaching bright pupils in mixed ability classes.* London: Macmillan.

Khatena, J. & Morse, D. T. (1987). Preliminary study of the Khatena–Morse Multitalent Perception Inventory. *Perceptual and Motor Skills,* **64**, 1187–1190.

Khatena, J. & Torrance, E. P. (1976). *Khatena–Torrance Perception Inventory.* Chicago: The Stoelting Company.

Kirk, S. A. (1960). Are special classes beneficial? *Slow Learning Child,* **7**, 11–14.

Kirk, S. A. & Gallagher, J. J. (1983). *Educating exceptional children.* Boston: Houghton Mifflin.

Kirk, S. A. & Kirk, W. D. (1975). *Psycholinguistic learning disabilities: Diagnosis and remediation.* Urbana, Il: University of Illinois Press.

Kirk, S. A. & McCarthy, J. J. (1961). The Illinois Test of Psycholinguistic Abilities — an approach to differential diagnosis. *American Journal of Mental Deficiency,* **66**, 399–412.

Kirk, S. A., McCarthy, J. J. & Kirk, W. D. (1968). *The Illinois Test of Psycholinguistic Abilities.* Urbana, IL: University of Illinois Press.

Kirst, W. & Diekmeyer, U. (1973). *Kreativitätstraining.* Reinbek bei Hamburg: Rowohlt.

Klein, H. (1986). Situation, problems and development trends in provision for especially gifted children and youth in the German Democratic Republic. In: A. J. Cropley, K. K. Urban, H. Wagner and W. H. Wieczerkowski (eds), *Giftedness: A continuing worldwide challenge.* New York: Trillium.

Kline, B. E. & Meckstroth, E. A. (1986). Meeting the emotional needs of the gifted. In: A. J. Cropley, K. K. Urban, H. Wagner & W. H. Wieczerkowski (eds), *Giftedness: A continuing worldwide challenge.* New York: Trillium.

Klix, F. & van der Meer, E. (1986). Mathematical giftedness: Its nature and possible early identification. In: A. J. Cropley, K. K. Urban, H. Wagner & W. H. Wieczerkowski (eds), *Giftedness: A continuing worldwide challenge.* New York: Trillium.

Kneller, G. F. (1965). *The art and science of creativity.* New York: Holt, Rinehart & Winston.

Knapper, C. K. & Cropley, A. J. (1985). *Lifelong learning and higher education*. London: Croom Helm.

Kogan, N. (1983). Stylistic variation in childhood and adolescence: Creativity, metaphor, and cognitive styles. In: J. H. Flavell & E. M. Markman (eds), *Handbook of child psychology: Vol. 3. Cognitive development*. New York: John Wiley.

Kogan, N. & Pankove, E. (1972). Creative ability over a five year span. *Child Development*, **43**, 427–442.

Kolmogorov, A. N., Valilov, V. V. & Tropin, I. T. (1985). *Die mathematisch-physikalische Schule an der staatlichen Moskauer Lomonossov-Universität*. Bielefeld: Institut für Didaktik der Mathematik der Universität Bielefeld.

Krapp, A. (1986). Begabung. In: W. Sarges & R. Fricke (eds), *Psychologie für die Erwachsenenbildung*. Göttingen: Hogrefe.

Krause, R. (1972). *Kreativität*. Munich: Goldmann.

Krause, R. (1977). *Produktives Denken bei Kindern*. Weinheim: Beltz.

Lacattiva, C. (1985). Caution: Intellectually gifted ahead! Paper presented at the Sixth World Conference on Gifted and Talented Children, Hamburg, August 1985.

Landau, E. (1986). "Needs" and "wants" in gifted leadership. In: A. J. Cropley, K. K. Urban, H. Wagner & W. H. Wieczerkowski (eds), *Giftedness: A continuing worldwide challenge*. New York: Trillium.

Lane-Smith, D. R. (1986). The Shad Valley Program: How industry in Canada supports gifted education. In: A. J. Cropley, K. K. Urban, H. Wagner & W. H. Wieczerkowski (eds), *Giftedness: A continuing worldwide challenge*. New York: Trillium.

Laycock, F. (1979). *Gifted children*. Glenview, IL: Scott Foresman.

Lehwald, G. (1985). *Zur Diagnostik des Erkenntnisstrebens bei Schülern*. Berlin: Volk & Wissen.

Lewis, D. (1979). *How to be a gifted parent*. London: Souvenir.

Lindenau, S. E. (1984). Lights and wires in a box. The computer orientated information age in support of higher education. *Educational Technology*, February, 18–23.

Lombroso, C. (1891). *The man of genius*. London: Scott.

Lowndes, G. A. V. (1938). *The expansion of public education in England and Wales, 1895–1935*. Oxford: Oxford University Press.

Lucito, L. J. (1964). Gifted children. In: L. M. Dunn (ed), *Exceptional children in the schools*. New York: John Wiley.

Luidgren, H. C. (1967). Brainstorming and the facilitation of creativity expressed in drawing. *Perceptual and Motor Skills*, **24**, 350.

Luria, A. R. (1961). *The role of speech in the regulation of normal and abnormal behavior*. New York: Pergamon Press.

Luria, A. R. (1963). *The mentally retarded child*. Oxford: Pergamon Press.

Luria, A. R. (1966). *Higher cortical functions in man*. London: Tavistock.

Lutz, S. B. & Lutz, F. B. (1980). Gifted pupils in the elementary school setting. An ethnographic approach. Paper presented at the AERA Conference, Boston (ERIC Document Ed 191 190).

MacKinnon, D. W. (1962). The nature and nurture of creative talent. *American Psychologist*, **17**, 484–495.

MacKinnon, D. W. (1983). Creative architects. In: R. S. Albert (ed), *Genius and eminence: The social psychology of creativity and exceptional achievement*. Elmsford, NY: Pergamon Press.

Mackler, B. (1962). Creativity and life styles. Unpublished doctoral dissertation. Lawrence, Kansas: University of Kansas.

Mairie, P. & Foix, C. (1917). Les aphastes de guerre. *Revue Neurologie*, **1**, 53–87.

Maker, C. J. (1975). *Training teachers for the gifted and talented: A comparison of models.* Reston, VA: Council for Exceptional Children.

Maker, C. J. (1982). *Curriculum development for the gifted.* Rockville, MD: Aspen Publications.

Maltby, F. (1984). *Gifted children and teachers in the primary school.* London: Falmer Press.

Maltzmann, I., Simon, S., Raskin, D. & Licht, I. (1960). Experimental studies in the training of originality. *Psychological Monographs,* **6**.

Mansfield, R. S., Busse, T. V. & Krepelka, E. J. (1978). The effectiveness of creativity training. *Review of Educational Research,* **48**, 517–536.

March, R. (1977). Too bright for their own comfort. *Guardian,* 11 October.

Martinson, R. A. (1972). An analysis of problems and priorities: Advocate survey and statistics sources. Appendix B in: S. P. Marland (ed), *Education of the gifted and talented.* Washington, DC: US Government Printing Office.

Martinson, R. A. (1975). *The identification of the gifted and talented.* Reston, VA: Council for Exceptional Children.

Maslany, G. W. (1973). Predictive validity of intellectual tests. Unpublished doctoral dissertation, Calgary, Alberta: University of Calgary.

Masuda, Y. (1981). *The information society as post-industrial society.* Washington, DC: World Future Society.

McClelland, W. (1949). *Selection for secondary education.* London: University of London Press.

McCloy, W. & Meier, N. C. (1931). Re-creative imagination. *Psychological Monographs,* **51**, 108–116.

McGrath, E. (1983). Schooling for the common good. *Time,* **122**, (5), 64–65.

McGreevy, J. (1982). *My book of things and stuff. An interest questionnaire for young children.* Mansfield, CT: Creative Learning Press.

McIntosh, D. M., Walker, D. A. & MacKay, D. (1962). *The scaling of teachers' marks and estimates.* Edinburgh: Oliver & Boyd.

McLeod, J. (1959). After the White Paper: An inquiry into the relationship between 11 + and I.Q. and subsequent performance in G.C.E. *Bulletin of British Psychological Society,* **38**, 30A.

McLeod, J. (1972). *The use of tests, ratings and sociometric techniques for the identification of more able students in Grades 5 and 6.* Saskatoon: University of Saskatchewan, Institute of Child Guidance.

McLeod, J. (1979a). *The Saskatoon Saturday Club: An evaluative report.* Saskatoon: Institute of Child Guidance and Development.

McLeod, J. (1979b). *The Saskatoon region project: Provision of educational services to children with special needs in rural and sparsely populated regions.* Saskatoon: University of Saskatchewan Institute of Child Guidance and Development.

McLeod, J. (1983). La non-fiabilité psychométrique et ses implications dans une politique pour les enfants doués. *Revue Canadienne de Psycho-éducation,* **12**, 118–131.

McLeod, J. (1986). Initial identification of academically gifted students: An operationalization of Renzulli's definition of giftedness. In: A. J. Cropley, K. K. Urban, H. Wagner & W. H. Wieczerkowski (eds), *Giftedness: A continuing worldwide challenge.* New York: Trillium.

McLeod, J. & Kluckmann, I. (1985). *A Trans-Canada survey of programming for gifted children. A preliminary report.* Saskatoon, Canada: University of Saskatchewan, Institute of Child Guidance and Development.

McLeod, J., Colbourn, M. & Robertson, G. (1984). Computer guided expert system. *SIG Bulletin, International Council for Computers in Education,* **1** (5), 48–51.

McLeod, J., Markowsky, M. D. & Leong, C. K. (1972). A followup study of early entrants to elementary schools. *Elementary School Journal,* **73**, 10–19.

McNemar, Q. (1964). Lost: Our intelligence? Why? *American Psychologist*, **19**, 871–882.
Mednick, S. A. (1962). The associative basis of creativity. *Psychological Review*, **69**, 220–232.
Meeker, M. N. (1978). *SOI Newsletter*, September. El Segundo: SOI Institute.
Meili, R. (1964). Die faktorenanalytische Interpretation der Intelligenz. *Schweizerische Zeitschrift für Psychologie*, **23**, 135–155.
Messer, D. J., Jackson, A. & Mohamedali, M. (1987). Influences on computer-based problem solving: Help facilities, intrinsic orientation, gender and home computing. *Educational Psychology*, **7**, 33–46.
Miles, C. C. (1954). Gifted children. In: L. Carmichael (ed), *Manual of child psychology*. New York: John Wiley.
Milgram, R. M. (1983). Validation of ideational fluency measures of original thinking in children. *Journal of Educational Psychology*, **75**, 619–624.
Miller, G. W. (1970). Factors in school achievement and social class. *Journal of Educational Psychology*, **61**, 260–269.
Milner, S. D. & Wildberger, A. M. (1977). Determining appropriate uses of computers in education. *Computers and Education*, **1**, 117–123.
Mistry, J. & Rogoff, B. (1985). A cultural perspective on the development of talent. In: F. E. Horowitz & M. O'Brien (eds), *The gifted and talented: Developmental perspectives*. Washington, DC: American Psychological Association.
Mönks, F. J., van Boxtal, H. W., Roelofs, J. J. W. & Sanders, M. P. M. (1986). The identification of gifted children in secondary education and a description of their situation in Holland. In: K. A. Heller & J. F. Feldhusen (eds), *Identifying and nurturing the gifted*. Bern: Huber.
Mordock, J. B. (1975). *The other children*. New York: Harper.
Motamedi, K. (1982). Extending the concept of creativity. *Journal of Creative Behavior*, **16**, 75–88.
Mulhern, J. D. & Ward, M. (1983). A collaborative program for developing teachers of gifted and talented students. *Gifted Child Quarterly*, **27**, 152–156.
NAGC/ILEA (1978). *The Saturday Club for gifted children*. London: National Association for the Gifted Children/Inner London Education Authority.
Naisbitt, J. (1984). *Megatrends*. New York: Warner Books.
Nathan, C. N. (1979). Parental involvement. In: A. H. Passow (ed), *The gifted and the talented: Their education and development*. Chicago: NSSE Yearbook.
National Association for Gifted Children (NAGC) (1982). *Teaching able and gifted children: A study of initial and in-service teacher training in England, Scotland and Wales, 1981/82*. London: National Association for Gifted Children.
National Association for Gifted Children (NAGC) (1983). *Report of the committee on graduate programs, course content, inservice training and teacher certification*. St. Paul, Minnesota: National Association for Gifted Children.
Nay, F. (1981). Computer challenge. The Henry Taitt story. *G/C/T*, **4**, 48–50.
Necka, E. (1986). On the nature of creative talent. In: A. J. Cropley, K. K. Urban, H. Wagner & W. H. Wieczerkowski (eds), *Giftedness: A continuing worldwide challenge*. New York: Trillium.
Neff, G. (1975). *Kreativität in Schule und Gesellschaft*. Ravensburg: Maier.
Newland, T. E. (1976). *The gifted in socioeducational perspective*. Englewood Cliffs, NJ: Prentice Hall.
Obuche, N. M. (1986). The ideal pupil as perceived by Nigerian (Igbo) teachers and Torrance's creative personality. *International Review of Education*, **32**, 191–196.
Ogilvie, E. (1980). The Schools Council Curriculum Enrichment Project. In: R. Povey (ed), *Educating the gifted child*. London: Harper & Row.
Ornestein, A. J. (1984). What organizational characteristics are important in planning,

implementing and maintaining programs for the gifted? *Gifted Child Quarterly*, **28**, 99–105.

Osborn, A. F. (1960). *Applied imagination*. New York: Scribner.

O'Tuel, F. S., Ward, M. & Rawl, R. K. (1983). The SOI as as identification tool for the gifted: Windfall or washout? *Gifted Child Quarterly*, **27**, 126–134.

Overall, T., Howley, J. & Leventhal, S. (1981). Learning with Logo at the Lamplighter School. *Microcomputing*, **5**, 36–40, 43.

Papert, S. (1980). *Mindstorms, children and powerful ideas*. Brighton: Harvester Press.

Paraskevopoulos, J. & Kirk, S. A. (1969). *The development and psychometric characteristics of the revised Illinois Test of Psycholinguistic Abilities*. Urbana: University of Illinois Press.

Parker, J. A. & Parker, C. J. (1986). Use of the microcomputer to enhance higher order thinking skills. In: A. J. Cropley, K. K. Urban, H. Wagner & W. H. Wieczerkowski (eds), *Giftedness: A continuing worldwide challenge*. New York: Trillium.

Parnes, S. J. (1967). *Creative behaviour guidebook*. New York: Scribner.

Parloff, M. D. & Handlon, J. H. (1964). The influence of criticalness on creative problem-solving. *Psychiatry*, **27**, 17–27.

Parsons, D. L. (1985). The computer in creative mathematics — Part II. Paper presented at the Sixth World Conference on Gifted and Talented Children, Hamburg, August 1985.

Passow, A. H. (1977). The gifted and the disadvantaged. In: J. Miley, I. Sato, W. Luckhe, P. Weaver, J. Curry & I. Ponce (eds), *Promising practices: Teaching the gifted and talented*. Ventura, CA: Office of the Superintendent of Ventura Country Schools.

Passow, A. H. (1985). Education of the gifted and talented. In: T. Husen & T. N. Postlethwaite (eds), *International Encyclopedia of Education*, Oxford: Pergamon Press.

Passow, A. H. (1987). Issues and trends in curriculum for the gifted. *Gifted International*. **4**, 3–6.

Paulsen, W. J. (1985). Guidance for the gifted. Paper presented at the Sixth World Conference on Gifted and Talented Children, Hamburg, August 1985.

Pedulla, J. J., Airasian, P. W. & Madaus, G. F. (1980). Do teacher ratings and standardized test results of students yield the same information? *American Educational Research Journal*, **17**, 291–302.

Pegnato, C. W. & Birch, J. W. (1959). Locating gifted children in junior high schools: A comparison of methods. *Exceptional Children*, **25**, 300–304.

Piechowski, M. M. (1979). Developmental potential. In: N. Colangelo & R. T. Zaffrann (eds), *New voices in counselling the gifted*. Dubuque: Kendal/Hunt.

Perino, S. C. & Perino, J. (1981). *Parenting the gifted*. New York: Bowker.

Perkins, D. N. (1981). *The mind's best work*. Cambridge, MA: Harvard University Press.

Prasisto, A. J. (1978). The Saturday workshop of the Gifted Child Society of New Jersey. In: J. C. Stanley, W. C. George & C. H. Solano (eds), *Educational programs and intelligence prodigies*. Baltimore: Johns Hopkins University Press.

Prat, G. (1979). Vingt ans de psychopathologie de l'enfant doué et surdoué en intervat psychopathologique. *Neuropsychiatrie de l'enfance et de l'adolescence*. **27**, 467–474.

Pregler, H. (1954). The Colfax Plan. *Exceptional Children*, **20**, 198–201.

Pressey, S. L. (1949). *Educational acceleration: Appraisal and basic problems*. Columbus: Ohio State University Bureau of Educational Research Monographs.

Preston, D., Greenwood, C. R., Hughes, V., Yuen, P., Thibadeau, S., Critchlow, W. & N Harris, J. (1984). Minority issues in special education: A principal-mediated inservice program for teachers. *Exceptional Children*, **51**, 112–121.

Pringle, M. L. (1970). *Able misfits. The educational and behavioural difficulties of intelligent children*. London: Longman.

Rabinowitz, M. & Glaser, R. (1985). Cognitive structure and process in highly competent performance. In: F. D. Horowitz & M. O'Brien (eds), *The gifted and talented: Development perspectives*. Washington, DC: American Psychological Association.

Rader, J. R. (1976). The development and evaluation of a simulation on the identification of the gifted and talented. *Viewpoints*, **52**, 33–52.

Rathje, H. & Dahme, G. (1985). Achievement motivation, self-concept and giftedness — An empirical study. Paper presented at the Sixth World Conference on Gifted and Talented Children, Hamburg, August 1985.

Rawson, M. (1968). *Developmental language disability: Adult accomplishments of dyslexic boys*. Baltimore: Johns Hopkins University Press.

Renzulli, J. S. (1968). Identifying key features in programs for the gifted. *Exceptional Children*, **35**, 217–221.

Renzulli, J. S. (1975). *A guidebook for evaluating programs for the gifted and talented*. Ventura, CA: Office of the Superintendent of Ventura County Schools.

Renzulli, J. S. (1977). *The enrichment triad model: A guide for developing defensible programs for the gifted and talented*. Wethersfield, CT: Creative Learning Press.

Renzulli, J. S. (1978). What makes giftedness? Reexamining a definition. *Phi Delta Kappa*, November, 180–194.

Renzulli, J. S. (1980). Will the gifted child movement be alive and well in 1990? *Gifted Child Quarterly*, **24**, (1), 3–9.

Renzulli, J. S. (1982). What makes a problem real: Stalking the illusive meaning of qualitative differences in gifted education. *Gifted Child Quarterly*. **26**, 147–156.

Renzulli, J. S. (1984). The triad/revolving door system. A research-based approach to identification and programming for the gifted and talented. *Gifted Child Quarterly*, **28**, 163–171.

Renzulli, J. S. (1986). The three-ring conception of giftedness: a developmental model for creative productivity. In: R. J. Sternberg & J. E. Davidson (eds), *Conceptions of giftedness*. Cambridge: Cambridge University Press.

Renzulli, J. S. & Smith, L. H. (1977). Two approaches to identification of gifted students. *Exceptional Children*, **38**, 211–214.

Renzulli, J. S. & Smith, L. H. (1983). Curriculum compacting. An essential strategy for working with gifted students. *Gifted Education International*, **1**, 97–102.

Renzulli, J. S., Hartmann, R. K. & Callahan, C. M. (1971). Teacher identification of superior students. *Exceptional Children*, **38**, 243–248.

Renzulli, J. S., Reis, S. M. & Smith, L. H. (1981). The revolving door model: A new way of identifying the gifted. *Phi Delta Kappan*, May, 648–649.

Renzulli, J. S., Smith, L. H., White, A. J., Callahan, C. M. & Hartman, R. K. (1976). *Scales for rating the behavioral characteristics of superior students*. Mansfield Center, CT: Creative Learning Press.

Rimland, B. *Infantile autism*. New York: Appleton-Century-Crofts, 1964.

Rimm, S. & Davis, G. A. (1980). Five years of international research with GIFT: An instrument for the identification of creativity. *Journal of Creative Behavior*, **14**, 35–46.

Roe, A. (1952). *The making of a scientist*. New York: Dodd, Mead.

Roe, A. (1963). Psychological approaches to creativity in science. In: M. A. Coler (ed), *Essays on creativity in the sciences*. New York: New York University Press.

Roldan, A. (1986). Report on a survey of gifted education based on the Fifth World Conference in Manila. In: A. J. Cropley, K. K. Urban, H. Wagner & W. H. Wieczerkowski (eds), *Giftedness: A continuing worldwide challenge*. New York: Trillium.

Rossman, J. (1931). *The psychology of the inventor: A study of the patentee*. Washington DC:

Inventors' Publishing Co.

Rump, E. E. (1979). Divergent thinking, aesthetic preferences and orientation towards Arts and Sciences. Unpublished Ph.D. dissertation, University of Adelaide.

Salend, S. J., Michael, R. J. & Taylor, M. (1984). Competencies necessary for instructing migrant handicapped children. *Exceptional Children*. **51**, 50–55.

Sanche, R. P., Chapman, D. & Dineen, T. (1976). Attitude change during preservice teacher education. *Saskatchewan Journal of Educational Research and Development*, **7**, 25–28.

Sappington, A. A. & Farrar, W. E. (1982). Brainstorming v. critical judgement in the generation of solutions which conform to certain reality constraints. *Journal of Creative Behavior*, **16**, 68–73.

Saskatchewan Department of Education (1981). *Special education: A manual of legislation, regulations, policies and guidelines*. Regina: Saskatchewan Provincial Department of Education.

Sato, I. S. (1985). Strategies to improve productive thinking for the gifted/talented. Paper presented at the Sixth World Conference on Gifted and Talented Children, Hamburg, August 1985.

Schmidt, M. H. (1977). *Verhaltensstörungen bei sehr hoher Intelligenz*. Bern: Huber.

Schubert, J. (1967). Effects of training on the performance of the WISC Block Design subtests. *British Journal of Social and Clinical Psychology*, **6**, 144–149.

Schubert, J. (1973). *The VRB Apparatus*. Regina, Saskatchewan: Department of Psychology, University of Regina.

Seeley, K. R. (1979). Competencies for teachers of gifted and talented children. *Journal for the Education of the Gifted*, **3**, 7–13.

Shore, B. M. (1983). The training of teachers for gifted pupils. *Apprentissage et Socialisation*, September.

Shore, B. M. & Tsiamis, A. (1986). Identification by provision: Limited field test of a radical alternative for identifying gifted students. In: K. A. Heller & J. F. Feldhusen (eds), *Identifying and nurturing the gifted*. Bern: Huber.

Silverman, L. K. (1982). The gifted and talented. In: E. L. Meyen (ed), *Exceptional children and youth*. Denver: Love.

Simmons, M. M. (1962). Intelligent delinquents. *Times Educational Supplement*, 26 January, 129.

Simpson, R. M. (1922). Creative imagination. *American Journal of Psychology*, **33**, 234–235.

Singer, D. L. & Whiton, M. B. (1971). Ideational creativity and expressive aspects of human figure drawing in kindergarten-age children. *Developmental Psychology*, **4**, 366–369.

Sisk, D. (1978). Computers in the classroom: An invitation and challenge for the gifted. *G/C/T*, **1**, 18–21.

Skager, R. W. (1978). *Lifelong education and evaluation practice*. Oxford: Pergamon Press.

Skager, R. W., Schultz, C. B. & Klein, S. P. (1965). Quality and quantity of accomplishment as measures of creativity. *Journal of Educational Psychology*, **56**, 31–39.

Skeels, H. M. & Dye, H. B. (1939). A study of the effects of differential stimulation on mentally retarded children. *Proceedings of the American Association of Mental Deficiency*, **44**, 114–136.

Stake, R. E. (1967). The countenance of educational evaluation. *Teachers College Record*, **68**, 523–540.

Stanley, J. C. (1976). Use of tests to discover talent. In: D. P. Keating (ed), *Intellectual talent: Research and development*. Baltimore: Johns Hopkins University Press.

Stanley, J. C. (1977). Rationale of the study of mathematically precocious youth

(SMPY) during its first five years of promoting educational acceleration. In: J. C. Stanley, W. C. George & C. H. Solano (eds), *The gifted and the creative: A fifty-year perspective*. Baltimore: Johns Hopkins University Press.

Stanley, J. C. (1978). Finding the ablest mathematical reasoners in a specifically designated group. In: A. Y. Baldwin, G. H. Gear & L. J. Lucito (eds), *Educational planning for the gifted*. Reston, VA: Council for Exceptional Children.

Stanley, J. C. (1979). Educational non-acceleration: An international tragedy. In: J. J. Gallagher (ed), *Gifted children: reaching their potential*. Jerusalem: Kollek.

Stanley, J. C. (1980). On educating the gifted. *Educational Researcher*, **9**, 8–12.

Stanley, J. C. (1984). Use of general and specific aptitude measures in identification: Some principles and certain cautions. *Gifted Child Quarterly*, **28**, 177–180.

Stanley, J. & Benbow, C. P. (1986). Youth who reason exceptionally well mathematically. In: R. J. Sternberg & J. E. Davidson (eds), *Conceptions of giftedness*. Cambridge: Cambridge University Press.

Stedtnitz, U. (1985). Influence of educational enrichment on self-efficacy in young children. Paper presented at the Sixth World Conference on Gifted and Talented Children, Hamburg, August 1985.

Stern, W. (1918). Methode der Auslese Befähigter Volksschüler in Hamburg. *Zeitzchrift für Pädagogische Psychologie, experimentelle Pädagogik und jugendliche Forschung*, **26**, 289–307.

Stern, A. & Stern, H. (1984). *Kreativität — psychoanalytische und philosophische Aspekte.*, Munich: Johannes Bermanns.

Sternberg, R. J. (1985). *Beyond IQ: A triarchic theory of human intelligence*. New York: Cambridge University Press.

Sternberg, R. J. & Davidson, J. E. (eds), (1986). *Conceptions of giftedness*. Cambridge: Cambridge University Press.

Swan, D. (1982). Memorandum to Principals, 23 March 1981. Sydney: New South Wales Department of Education.

Taft, R. & Gilchrist, M. B. (1970). Creative attitudes and creativity among students. *Journal of Educational Psychology*, **61**, 136–143.

Tannenbaum, A. J. (1979). Pre-sputnik to Post-Watergate concern about the gifted. In: A. H. Passow (ed), *The gifted and the talented: Their education and development*. Chicago: NSSE Yearbook.

Taylor, I. A. (1975). An emerging view of creative actions. In: I. A. Taylor & J. W. Getzels (eds), *Perspectives in creativity*. Chicago: Aldine.

Taylor, C. W. & Ellison, R. L. (1978). *Manual for alpha biographical inventory — Form U*. Salt Lake City: Institute for Behavioral Research in Creativity.

Terman, L. M. (1916). *The measurement of intelligence*. Boston: Houghton Mifflin.

Terman, L. M. (1925). *Genetic studies of genius*. Stanford: Stanford University Press.

Terman, L. M. (1954). The discovery and encouragement of exceptional talent. *American Psychologist*, **9**, 221–230.

Terman, L. M. & Merrill, M. A. (1937). *Measuring intelligence*. Boston: Houghton Mifflin.

Terman, L. M. & Merrill, M. A. (1960). *Stanford–Binet Intelligence Scale*. Boston: Houghton Mifflin.

Terman, L. M. & Oden, M. H. (1947). *Genetic studies of genius*, Vol.4. Stanford: Stanford University Press.

Terman, L. M. & Oden, M. H. (1959). *Genetic studies of genius*, Vol.5. Stanford: Stanford University Press.

Thorndike, R. L. (1966). *Some methodological issues in the study of creativity. Testing problems in perspective*. Washington: American Council on Education.

Thurstone, L. L. (1938). *Primary mental abilities*. Chicago: University of Chicago Press.

Thurstone, L. L. (1948). Psychological implications of factor analysis. *American Psychologist*, **3**, 402–408.

Torrance, E. P. (1959). *Explorations in creative thinking in the early school years: VIII. IQ and creativity in school achievement.* Minneapolis: University of Minnesota Bureau of Educational Research.

Torrance, E. P. (1963). *Education and the creative potential.* Minneapolis: University of Minnesota Press.

Torrance, E. P. (1966). *Torrance Test of Creative Thinking.* Columbus, OH: Personnel Press/Testing.

Torrance, E. P. (1969). Prediction of adult creative achievement among high school seniors. *Gifted Child Quarterly*, **13**, 223–229.

Torrance, E. P. (1972). Predictive validity of the Torrance Test of Creative Thinking. *Journal of Creative Behavior*, **6**, 401–405.

Torrance, E. P. (1976). Examples and rationales of test tasks for assessing creative abilities. In: A. M. Biondi & S. J. Parnes (eds), *Assessing creative growth: Measured changes — Book two.* Great Neck, New York: Creative Education Foundation.

Torrance, E. P. (1980a). Lessons about giftedness from a nation of 115 million overachievers. *Gifted Child Quarterly*, **24**, 10–14.

Torrance, E. P. (1980b). Growing up creatively gifted: A 22-year longitudinal study. The creative child and adult. *Creative Child and Adult Quarterly*, **5**, 148–158, 170.

Torrance, E. P. & Hall, L. K (1980). Assessing the further reaches of creative potential. *Journal of Creative Behavior.* **14**, 1–19.

Torrance, E. P., Tan, C. & Allman, T. (1970). Verbal originality and teacher behaviour: A predictive validity study. *Journal of Teacher Education*, **21**, 335–341.

Torrance, E. P., Torrance, J. P., Williams, S. J., Ruey-yun Horng (1978). *Handbook for training future problem solving teams.* Athens, GA: Programs for Gifted and Talented Children, Department of Educational Psychology, University of Georgia.

Trefffinger, D. (1975), Teaching for self-directed learning: A priority for the gifted and talented. *Gifted Child Quarterly*, **19**, (1), 46–59.

Treffinger, D. C. (1978). Guidelines for encouraging independence and self-direction among gifted students. *Journal of Creative Behavior.* **12**, 14–19.

Treffinger D. J. & Gowan, I. C. (1971). An update representative list of methods and educational materials for stimulating creativity. *Journal of Creative Behavior*, **5**, 236–252.

Treffinger, D. J., Isaksen, S. G. & Firestien, R. L. (1983). Theoretical perspective on creative learning and its facilitation. *Journal of Creative Behavior*, **17**, 9–17.

Tyerman, M. J. (1985). Identification: Learning ability not intelligence. Paper presented at the Sixth World Conference on Gifted and Talented Children. Hamburg, August 1985.

Tyson, M. (1966). Creativity. In: B. M. Foss (ed), *New horizons in psychology.* London: Pelican.

Undheim, J. O. & Horn, J. L. (1977). Critical evaluation of Guilford's Structure-of-Intellect theory. *Intelligence*, **1**, 65–81.

Urban, K. K. (1983). A comparison of attitudes towards the education of "normal" handicapped and gifted children. *First Yearbook of Gifted and Talented Children.* New York: Trillium Press.

Urban, K. K. & Jellen, H. (1986). Assessing creative potential via drawing production: The Test for Creative Thinking–Drawing Production (TCT-DP). In: A. J. Cropley, K. K. Urban, H. Wagner & W. H. Wieczerkowski (eds), *Giftedness: A continuing worldwide challenge.* New York: Trillium.

Vaughan, M. M. (1971). Music as model and metaphor in the cultivation and measurement of creative behavior in children. Unpublished doctoral dissertation, University of Georgia, Athens, Georgia.

Vernon, P. E. (1955). The assessment of children. *Studies in Education*, **7**, 189–215.

Vernon, P. E. (ed) (1957). *Secondary school selection*. London: Methuen.

Vernon, P. E. (1964a), The psychology of intelligence and creativity. In: J. Cohen (ed), *Readings in psychology*. London: Allen & Unwin.

Vernon, P. E. (1964b). Creativity and intelligence. *Educational Research*, **6**, 163–169.

Vernon, P. E. (1971). *The structure of human abilities*. London: Methuen.

Vernon, P. E. (1979). *Intelligence: Heredity and environment*. San Francisco: W. H. Freeman.

Vernon, P. E. & Parry, J. B. (1949). *Personnel selection in the British forces*. London: Univerity of London Press.

Vernon, P. E., Adamson, G. & Vernon, D. F. (1977). *The psychology and education of gifted children*. London: Methuen.

Wagner, H. & Zimmermann, B. (1986). Identification and fostering of mathematically gifted students. In: A. J. Cropley, K. K. Urban, H. Wagner & W. H. Wieczerkowski (eds), *Giftedness: A continuing worldwide challenge*. New York: Trillium.

Wagner, H., Zimmermann, B. & Stüven, N. (1986). Identifizierung und Förderung von mathematisch besonders befähigten Schülern. In: W. H. Wieczerkowski, H. Wagner, K. K. Urban & A. J. Cropley (eds), *Hochbegabung, Gesellschaft, Schule*. Bonn: Federal Ministry for Education and Science.

Wall, W. D. (1976). *Constructive education for children*. London: Harrap.

Wallace, D. B. (1985). Giftedness and the construction of a meaningful life. In: F. D. Horowitz & M. O'Brien (eds), *The gifted and the talented: Developmental perspectives*. Washington, DC: American Psychological Association.

Wallach, M. A. (1970). Creativity. In: P. H. Mussen (ed), *Carmichael's manual of child psychology*. New York: John Wiley.

Wallach, M. A. (1985). Creativity testing and giftedness. In: F. D. Horowitz & M. O'Brien (eds), *The gifted and the talented: Developmental perspectives*. Washington, DC: American Psychological Association.

Wallach, M. A. & Kogan, N. (1965). *Modes of thinking in young children*. New York: Holt, Rinehart & Winston.

Wallach, M. A. & Wing, C. W. (1969). *The talented student*. New York: Holt, Rinehart & Winston.

Wallbrown, F. H. & Huelsman, C. B. (1975). The validity of the Wallach–Kogan creativity operations for inner-city children in two areas of visual art. *Journal of Personality*, **43**, 109–126.

Watson, J. B. (1930). *Behaviorism*. New York: Norton.

Wavrik, J. J. (1980). Mathematics education for the gifted elementary school student. *Gifted Child Quarterly*, **24**, 169–173.

Wechsler, D. (1944). *Measurement of adult intelligence*. Baltimore: Williams & Wilkins.

Wechsler, D. (1974). *WISC-R manual*. New York: Psychological Corporation.

Weiler, D. (1978). The Alpha children: California's brave new world for the gifted. *Phi Delta Kappan*, November, 185–187.

Weinert, F. E. & Waldmann, M. R. (1986). How do the gifted think: Intellectual abilities and cognitive processes. In: A. J. Cropley, K. K. Urban, H. Wagner & W. H. Wieczerkowski (eds), *Giftedness: A continuing worldwide challenge*. New York: Trillium.

Weir, S. (1981). LOGO and the exceptional child. *Microcomputing*, **5**, 76–84.

Weisberg, P. S. & Springer, K. J. (1961). Environmental factors in creative function. *Archives of General Psychiatry*, **5**, 554–564.

Welch, L. (1946). Recombination of ideas in creative thinking. *Journal of Applied Psychology* **30**, 638–643.

Whipple, G. M. (1924). *Twenty-third Yearbook of the National Society for the Study of Education*. Chicago: University of Chicago Press.

Whitehead, A. N. (1946). *The aims of education*. London: Williams & Norgate.

Whitmore, A. N. (1980). *Gifted, conflict and underachievement*. Boston: Allyn & Bacon.

Wiens, B. J. (1977). Higher education's commitment to inservice education. ERIC Document ED 141 528.

Williams, F. E. (1976a). Intellectual creativity and the teacher. In: W. R. Lett (ed), *Creativity and education*. Melbourne: Australian International Press and Publications.

Williams, F. E. (1976b). Encouraging your child's creative potential. In: W. R. Lett (ed), *Creativity and education*. Melbourne: Australian International Press and Publications.

Williams, F. E. (1976c). Is creativity an innovation in education? In: W. R. Lett (ed), *Creativity and education*. Melbourne: Australian International Press and Publications.

Willings, D. (1985). The gifted at university. Paper presented at the Sixth World Conference on Gifted and Talented Children, Hamburg, August 1985.

Witty, P. (ed) (1951). *The gifted child*. Lexington: Heath.

Wodtke, K. H. (1964). Some data on the reliability and validity of creativity tests at the elementary school level. *Educational and Psychological Measurement*, **24**, 399–408.

Wolfensberger, W. (1972). *Normalization*. Toronto: National Institute on Mental Retardation.

Woodcliffe, H. M. (1977). *Teaching gifted learners: A handbook for teachers*. Toronto: Ontario Institute for Studies in Education.

Wresch, W. (ed) (1984). *The computer in composition instruction: A writer's tool*. Chicago, Ilinois: National Council of Teachers of English.

Yamamoto, K. (1965). Effects of restriction of range and test unreliability on correlation between measures of intelligence and creative thinking. *British Journal of Educational Psychology*, **35**, 300–305.

Yarborough, M. D. & Johnson, L. W. (1983). Identifying the gifted: A theory–practice gap. *Gifted Child Quarterly*, **27**, 135–138.

Yewchuk, C. R. (1986). Gifted learning of disabled children: Problems of assessment. In: A. J. Cropley, K. K. Urban, H. Wagner & W. H. Wieczerkowski (eds), *Giftedness: A continuing worldwide challenge*. New York: Trillium.

Zillman, C. (1981). *Begabte Schulversager*. Munich: Reinhardt.

Ziv, A. (1976). Procedures to increase some aspects of creativity. *Journal of Educational Psychology*, **68**, 318–322.

Author Index

Subject Index